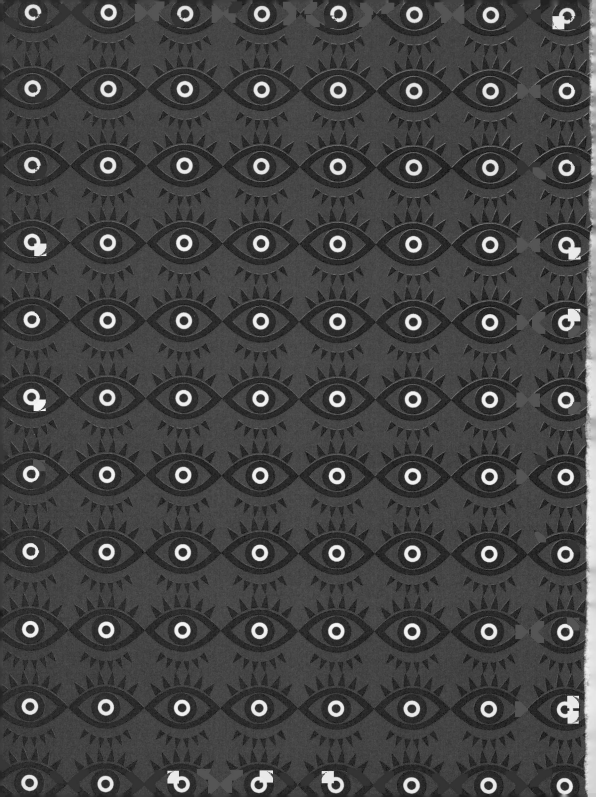

THE WORLD OF

Italian Folk Magic

THE WORLD OF

Italian Folk Magic

Magic and herbal cures from the wise women of Italy

ROSE INSERRA

ROCKPOOL

A Rockpool book
PO Box 252
Summer Hill
NSW 2130
Australia

rockpoolpublishing.com
Follow us! **f** 🄾 rockpoolpublishing
Tag your images with #rockpoolpublishing

ISBN: 9781922785978

Published in 2024 by Rockpool Publishing
Copyright text © Rose Inserra 2024
Copyright design © Rockpool Publishing 2024

Design and typesetting by Sara Lindberg, Rockpool Publishing
Edited by Jess Cox
Images from Shutterstock

 A catalogue record for this book is available from the National Library of Australia

Printed and bound in China
10 9 8 7 6 5 4 3 2 1

INGREDIENTS AND MEASUREMENTS

Please note that the recipes in this book have been tested using Australian measurements and ingredients.

1 cup = 250 ml (8½ fl oz) | 1 tablespoon = 20 ml (½ fl oz) | 1 teaspoon = 5 ml

For Penelope and Lily
With love

Contents

Part 3: Spiritual practices 243

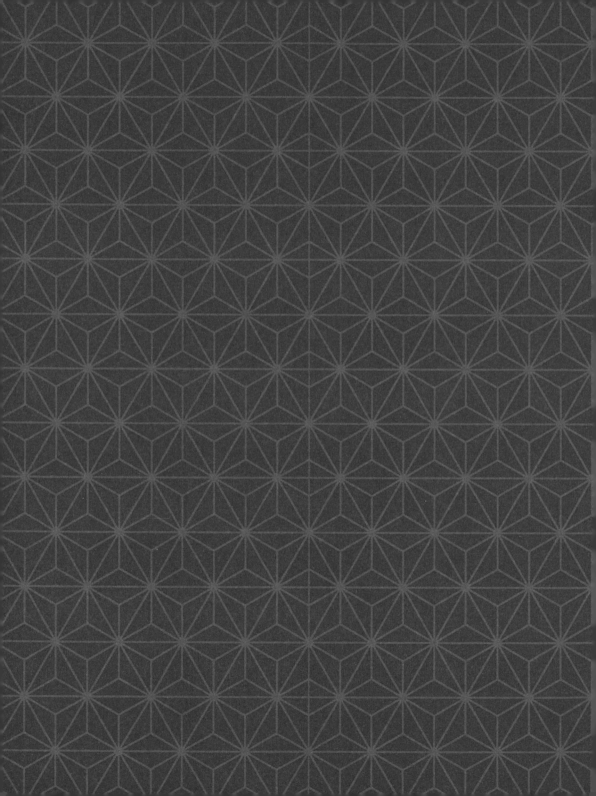

Introduction

When I was just 12 months old, I had a life-threatening respiratory illness. Back then, in the Italian village of Spinete in the hills of Molise in central Italy, the illness didn't have a medical name. The doctor had no known cure for this condition and prepared my parents for the worst. Despite being devout Catholics, they weren't so easily convinced of this terrible prognosis. They knew one thing they could do. Ask the *magara*, the healer, who lived higher up in the mountains, close to where Our Lady of Sorrows first appeared in 1888.

That was where my parents left me.

'What do you mean left me there? Alone?' I asked my parents when they told me this story.

'Sì.' It was always the same answer with no explanation.

Imagine a parent doing this today! Unable to make sense of how they had trusted a stranger, who lived in an isolated place with no means of communication should things go wrong, I had a barrage of questions.

'How long was I there for?'

'Three days and three nights.'

While I have no memories of my time with the *magara*, I came away with my health restored and a coin-shaped scar just below my throat, which wasn't there before. What did she do to help me breathe? Was it a form of tracheotomy?

My parents don't recall the events exactly, only that I was healed. They had total faith in the *magara*, who we would call a medicine woman, healer/herbalist or shaman. Today, I still have a deep and unquestioning gratitude to this magical healer, who followed her tradition of healing from previous generations.

I lived in Molise, in the province of Campobasso, until I was nine years old. Molise is the youngest Italian region, established in 1963 when 'Abruzzi e Molise' was split into two regions. I grew up with superstitions, fear of the *malocchio* (evil eye) and its curse, the *strega* (witch) entering the house through the keyhole, and the *mazzamauriello* (imp) who caused havoc and plaited our horse's mane, then broke things in the house.

I grew up in a world surrounded by fear of this mysterious phenomena. In my village, there were superstitions – especially the *malocchio* that followed my parents to their new country. This was the belief that a jealous look or feeling – whether done on purpose or not – could curse a person. Babies were particularly susceptible to the *malocchio*. You'd avoid saying a baby was beautiful, unless following it with 'God bless them.' If the curse went unnoticed, consequences included illness, headaches, rash, fatigue, stomach upset and more. People experiencing *malocchio* could suffer from health problems, emotional issues and even spiritual sickness.

Growing up Italian in Australia meant these 'old superstitions' were no longer relevant in a new country that had no connection to the old ways. The stories of the *malocchio*, the *mazzamauriello* or herbal cures no longer factored in this productive new life, which was not part of the rural and *contadino* (peasant) experience. Even the term 'Italian folk magic' elicits a confused response from people of Italian heritage in Australia. What is that? Do you mean *le streghe* (the witches)? This is followed by an awkward scoff as if to say, 'What, that old stuff?' But underneath the cynicism lies a genuine interest in these fascinating cultural phenomena.

My zia taught me how to remove the *malocchio*, which I've adapted to suit a modern pagan practice. This practice has opened my eyes, literally, to how negative energies work and how powerful we can be when we learn how to manipulate any kind of energy. Ultimately, the *malocchio* teaches us that thoughts are entities and everything we do influences the world around us (both our inner and outer worlds). The more intentional we are, the more we see evidence of the world around us responding to our thoughts – either negatively or positively. It's easy to project a sense of 'lack' onto another person, for instance, when we feel like we don't have enough.

We can all cast the *malocchio* without being aware of it. You can call this a magical power without requiring a spell. Even if you don't mean that envious glance, it reflects something about you and your wants. The truth is that we're all casting a *malocchio* 'spell' when we have jealous or envious thoughts or actions. Social media creates FOMO (fear of missing out) and highlights our sense of having less than someone else – whether it's body image, holidays, romance or fun activities.

I've helped people who never believed this was possible. And yet, the proof is there – removing the *malocchio* has given them hope and lifted the dark energy from their lives. One person cut ties with toxic friends and colleagues, enabling her to open doors to new business opportunities that had been evading her.

The lure of folk magic is returning and many, including young people, are eager to rediscover these ancient magical practices with a deep connection to nature and the environment. Some have lost their parents and grandparents, and long to rediscover the magic behind these practices and belief systems that were part of living in Italy for countless generations. Writing *The World of Italian Folk Magic* comes after years of disregarding its cultural importance and relevance in my own life. You don't need to have Italian heritage to practise folk magic. All readers are invited to learn more about the world of Italian folk magic, but should have respect for its origins and people in the form it was originally practised. While you may learn to integrate or adapt practices from another culture, you should first honour its original beginnings.

This is the energy I want to capture in this book – a rediscovered treasure trove of magical cures, spells and stories that will help to simplify our lives, declutter our minds and hearts, and return to fulfilling our lives' most basic needs – namely warmth, nourishment and connection to the magical and the spiritual.

In recent years, with the renewed interest in Italian folk magic, many people are seeking to learn more about these ancient practices and integrate them into their modern lives.

This book will give you a guided tour of my life of Italian magic filled with knowledge from ancient healers and wise women, who have passed on their wisdom so you can create your own magical practices.

Stregoneria, as Italian folk magic is often translated, is not a religion but a set of principles. Anyone can incorporate them into their own spiritual practices, regardless of their beliefs. I've included a section on saint worship because this is an essential part of Italian tradition. There is also a strong theme on earth-based spirituality because folk magic derived from rural Italian regions. I have sourced information from firsthand interviews with those in the Italian diaspora (countries where Italians have migrated) who are keeping the magic alive through their practices. I have focused mainly on central and southern Italy because of my Molisano heritage and my friends, who are mostly from southern regions in Italy and whose parents and grandparents settled in Australia, along with the United States of America, Canada, Argentina and Brazil. Thanks to them, I could access their stories, recipes, spells and folklore.

I hope these practices will fill you with passion and a strong desire to learn or reacquaint yourself with Italian ancestral knowledge, which was mostly passed down from mother to daughter.

Benedizioni,

Rose

PART I

History of Italian folk magic

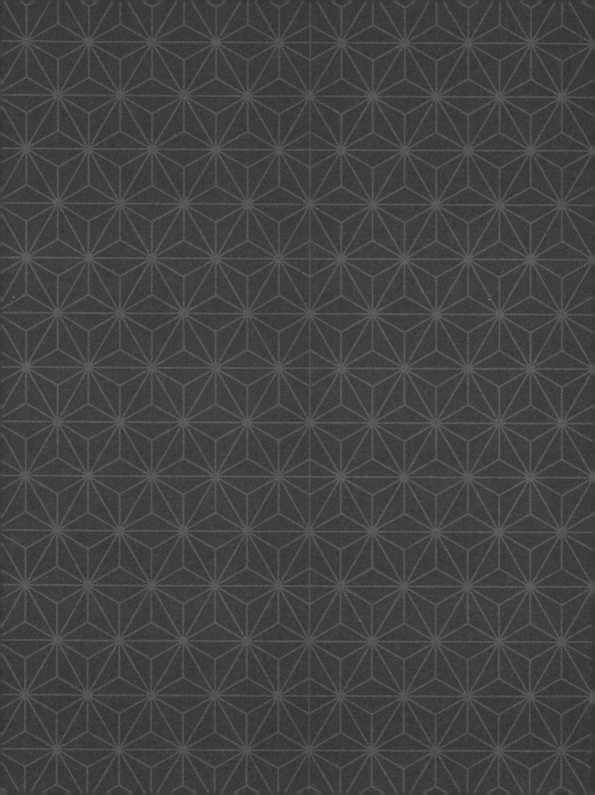

Chapter 1

What is Italian folk magic?

You've got the *malocchio*!' my zia said, watching the oil drops disperse to the bowl's edge.

'But I haven't got a headache or anything,' I said, knowing that a persistent headache was a sure sign someone had given me the *malocchio*.

'Well, you've been feeling low for no reason. Now we know.'

Looking at the odd kidney-shaped blobs of oil in the bowl, spreading to the sides, I had to agree it was odd – water and oil shouldn't mix.

In Italian folk magic tradition, all it takes is a glance or seemingly innocent compliment from someone for them to 'give' you the evil eye. The symptoms are varied and hard to pinpoint, but older Italians assure me that headaches, fever, stomach aches, dizziness, things going wrong, depression, financial problems and more are all signs you've been cursed.

Italian folk magic is much more than believing in the *malocchio* – it encompasses a range of magical practices and beliefs passed down through generations of Italian families. Today, many people practise Italian folk magic to connect with their heritage and access the power of the unseen world.

The word 'magic' can be defined as using unseen forces (energy) to influence or manipulate the world around us through various tools and practices. 'Folk' magic describes the magic practised by common 'folk', who may have been known traditionally as the shaman, herbalist or village witch, or the wise old woman who knew spells and incantations, and most likely acted as the local midwife and death doula.

Once considered primitive and simple, these practices and beliefs have been revived due to our longing for reconnection with nature, our ancestors and the world around us. Folk magic has survived because it is a practical, functional and everyday 'common folk' way of life. It is not 'magical' in sense of fairy-tales, but is grounded in deep natural wisdom that ensures our survival and protection from the elements and from those around us who wish us harm.

Folk magic and witchcraft (*stregoneria*)

The Italian word for 'witchcraft' is *stregoneria*. Because of its negative connotations, most native Italian speakers don't use this term when describing their folk magic traditions. In this book, I won't refer to *stregoneria* unless in a historical context such as the witches of Benevento and when describing dark magic practices.

Stregoneria was used in the past to describe a harmful practice involving magical interference to create harm or illness. Traditionally, being called a *strega* (witch) was considered an insult and offensive. Traditional folk magic practitioners would have been called folk 'healers', 'helpers' or 'fixers'. They could cure various illnesses and ranged from those who healed with herbs, magic incantations and Catholic prayers, to sorcerers who were only called in when someone experienced a serious psychic attack.

Their roles often overlapped, so their names depended on their roles. Each region has its own name, but generally included the following: *fattucchiere* (fixers), *guaritrici* (healers) and *magare* (magic workers). Italian folk magic practitioners are predominantly female. My mother used to talk about one local *stregone* (male witch) in our town; the rest were female *streghe*. Once called gypsies (*zingari*), the Roma people were also known to cast the *malocchio* and create hexes and spells.

Each region within Italy has a distinct culture with different languages, food and religious practices. Most Italian immigrants to Australia and other countries come from central and southern regions of Italy with their own folk magic traditions in their dialects and heritage.

In this book, the term 'Italian' describes the folkloric healing practices of people who mostly originated in rural central and southern Italy: Naples (Campania), Molise, Abruzzo, Rome (Lazio), Le Marche, Calabria, Puglia, Basilicata, Sicily, Aeolian Islands and Sardinia.

Knowing which region and even which village you are descended from is vitally important because of its individual identity.

One thing was common – they each held onto their regional traditions and shared the best of life in the old country. Each time I visited an Italian friend, from anywhere in Italy, I would be greeted by these iconic things – the lemon tree, *fichi d'India* (prickly pears), persimmon tree and bay laurel in the front yard, which was surrounded by hedges of rosemary, roses and a flash of red from the ubiquitous geraniums in terracotta pots by the front door, entering the hearth and home. The backyard was an oasis of shady ancestral trees, such as walnut, fig, oak, plum and citrus; herbs like basil, oregano, sage, parsley, chamomile; and seasonal vegetables that provided year-round sustenance as part of the healthy Mediterranean diet.

Italy only became a unified country in 1861 – before then, it consisted of multiple city states occupied by foreign rulers. These foreign occupiers brought with them a huge array of cultural histories, environmental and socio-political differences, customs, dialects and cuisines. Each region is its own mini-country.

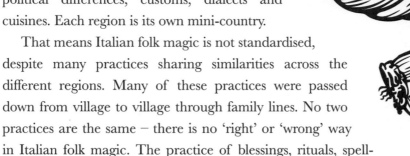

That means Italian folk magic is not standardised, despite many practices sharing similarities across the different regions. Many of these practices were passed down from village to village through family lines. No two practices are the same – there is no 'right' or 'wrong' way in Italian folk magic. The practice of blessings, rituals, spell-casting and cooking are woven into the tapestry of Italian culture.

Living in the Italian diaspora was different from the motherland – people from different regions mingled and shared their techniques, so original practices evolved and morphed over time. Those who followed the family's practices remained loyal to their family's region of origin; it is to their credit that third- and fourth-generation descendants have a connection to their ancestral region and are openly proud of their heritage. Over the years, I've adapted my traditional practice of removing the *malocchio* to my new understanding of how to use energy and included other modalities of spell craft and herbal remedies.

If you want to practise folk magic and are of Italian ancestry, I'd recommend first learning about your family's region of Italy and town, including its patron saint, festivals, legends and special cuisine, before making any adaptations.

A short history of Italian folk magic

Italian folk magic has a long and diverse history, dating back to ancient times and pagan religions. Over time, it evolved and merged with other belief systems such as Christianity, known as syncretism. This resulted in a unique blend of magical practices.

For those who want to follow the traditional Italian folk Catholicism practices, you'll note I use Catholic symbols and rituals in the spells and blessings. This is not the Catholicism of church dogma, but the type of veneration the common folk were interested in and so created their own rituals of prayers and votive offerings. I also provide the original alternative deriving from pagan and pre-pagan or animistic beliefs. The practical magical methods are unique to the Italian experience; their origins are unknown due to the influence of ancient peoples who form part of today's Italian identity.

There were ancient Italic peoples who lived in a time before the Italy of Rome, such as the Samnites. I am proud of my Samnite heritage. These people were formidable warriors (even the women) who fought bravely against the Romans for centuries. I come from this bloodline; its tradition is ancient and rich, and contains magical and religious rituals to express something intensely spiritual.

Why is the word *strega* not a friendly term?

The word *strega* (*streghe* in plural) has had several derogatory connotations throughout history, and those accused of these 'evil' practices were jailed and often killed during the Inquisition. It was essential for secrecy; the tradition was only passed down to those who could be trusted, mostly family. Being a witch or practising witchcraft thus became associated with being anti-Catholic and devil worship. This label has stuck and some stigma remains. Even today it's not appropriate to call yourself a witch. Older family members still warn me not to mess with *le cose contra la chiesa* (things against the church). So tarot card or psychic readings, palm or coffee cup readings, or anything that contradicts the church's teachings were and still are frowned on and feared. This is the legacy of the church's dogma.

It's very unlikely to hear someone describe themselves as a *strega* or *stregone* (male witch or sorcerer) in my Italian community, despite whether they practise the rituals. *Strega* is associated with those who practise black magic, whereas the *'maga'* or similar words describes those who practise white magic and healing. In the general community, however, the word 'witch' has extended to mean 'a healer' and herbalist.

In Italian, words in various dialects and regions encompass all these meanings and overlapping roles. It does seem ironic, however, that the *Befana*, who brings gifts to children on 6 January, the Epiphany (*Epifania),* is the stereotypical witch – an old woman with wrinkled skin, long nose and black shawl flying on a broomstick. Other than the flying broomstick, the *Befana* is just your average nonna wearing her black clothes, headscarf, apron and shawl.

Terms used for healer/magic worker

People who practise healing and protective magic have several names, which are a blend of healer, medicine person and magician. Healers would break witches' spells and restore health using curative and natural magic, so life could return to a positive balance in uncertain and unsettling times for their community.

The following regional terms describe the many roles of the healer/magic worker. Spelling may vary within the region.

NAME	REGION
Janara ('j' has a 'y' sound)	Campania
Majara	Sicily
Magara	Calabria, Abruzzo, Molise
Majarza	Sardinia
Segnatore (healing with signs)	Emilia Romagna
Guaritrice/guaritore (healer)	Generic
Fattucchiera (fixer of spells)	Generic
Commare/cumare (godmother, also a term for wise woman)	Generic

Why were women healers so essential?

Where did these traditional folk healers go? Do they still exist today? Are they even needed when we have science, technology and medical advances?

Italian folk magical practice developed in rural communities – life was harsh and survival was the main priority. Until World War II, most Italians lived in small rural towns and villages, in conditions well below modern standards. Education was not encouraged, especially for women, so there was a high level of illiteracy. This meant people had to rely on oral tradition to maintain their folk history. My paternal nonna was illiterate because she had to work as a shepherd – *a guardare le pecore* (to look after sheep) – when she was just five years old. She eventually learned to read as an adult through sheer determination, but no-one encouraged her. I became the first woman in my family to get a university degree. This has been a huge leap for the women in my family.

Guaritrici (healers) had extensive knowledge of herbs and their use and could treat less serious ailments in their community. But life was still perilous and fraught with poor health and education, and high death rates. A lack of local medical doctors meant that ordinary people relied on their folk healers to take care of them, especially in delivering babies. I was one of these home-birth babies. Many babies did not survive beyond their second year.

People in rural communities relied on the land for their livelihoods. They were intimately connected to the cycles of nature, such as planting and harvesting seasons, and observed agricultural and seasonal rituals. This encouraged their belief in nature spirits and using natural elements in folk magic practices. Invoking or appeasing saints, angels, spirits or demons was not *stregoneria* (witchcraft) – it was a practical way to ensure survival.

People performed rituals to ensure bountiful harvests, protect their crops from pests and diseases, and promote their livestock's well-being. These often involved charms, amulets, and prayers for good fortune and protection. Folk beliefs and magical practices were passed down orally, creating a strong continuity of traditions and giving rise to the term 'lineage healer'.

Life in rural and agricultural pre-war Italy provided a fertile ground for developing and continuing folk magic practices. The intertwined relationship among people, nature and community, coupled with rich folklore and traditions, nurtured a diverse and vibrant folk magic tradition that is still alive today. Italian folk magic is a complex and diverse system of ancestral, cultural, and magical beliefs and practices. Some of the points I make in this book will hopefully provide the reader with context and a basic checklist of what this broad term encompasses.

Although the terms Italian folk magic and *stregoneria* are seen as describing the same tradition, they have different elements. A revivalist movement, especially in the Italian diaspora, aims to reclaim these ancestral traditions, spiritual beliefs and practices, and the wisdom passed down through the generations. Chapters 2–4 will give the historical context to help understand and hopefully reclaim these wonderful practices.

Chapter 2

The *strega* folklore

The stereotype of what an evil 'witch' looks like from old fairy-tales and folktales is an old, unattractive woman referred to by the unflattering term 'hag'. In Italian folk magic she is much more complex because she can heal and hex at the same time. The crone stereotype is still common, including the *Befana*. The witch has many names, but is often known as the derogatory *strega*. *Streghe* were feared for giving the *malocchio* (evil eye) and more harmful magical attacks – known as *attaccatura* (attachment), or *fascino* or *legatura* (binding) – which used the victim's body for harm. In some regions, witches were known as *la maga* (sorceress). Not much is known about male witches – the terms *mago* or *stregone* could mean sorcerer.

Not all *streghe* practised black magic. Some *streghe* were healers or cunning folk, using herbs, divination and spells. This is why other names were used to differentiate between the 'good' and 'bad' *streghe*, such as *is praticas* (wise people or cunning folk), *magare* (magic healers), *guraritori* (healers), *fattucchiere* (fixers), and *donne che aiutano* (women who help). Many of these practitioners inherited their gifts from their ancestors. At times, they were collectively referred to as *streghe* (witches), but you would never call them that to their face.

Good and bad witches

In the past, ordinary people relied on folk healers to cure their ailments and local midwives to deliver their babies. These women often had considerable knowledge of herbs and their uses, and could help with alleviating minor illnesses. But their expertise only went so far – their knowledge was patchy in places, because information was passed down orally and became mixed with popular magic and folk Catholicism. Life was seen as dangerous – and it was! Using magic was one protective strategy that could help families survive.

This idea of good and bad witches and folk magic created tension in small rural communities, because the witch was simultaneously a real person and supernatural figure. Witchcraft was feared but also needed for protection. The *strega* came long before the Inquisition when many innocent women were burned and killed as witches. In ancient Roman times, people believed that *striges* (witches) transformed into birds of prey at night, looking to kill babies in their cradles.

The bad witch of folktales is usually female; performs supernatural feats like transforming into animals such as a hare, cat, wolf or raven; flies through the night on the back of animals; tangles people's hair while they sleep; steals milk from nursing mothers and farm animals; sucks blood from living beings; and paralyses dreamers in their sleep.

She can easily make herself small enough to fit through a keyhole and appear in your room while you sleep. The only way to keep her out is having a twig broom upside down outside your room. She must count each twig before sunrise.

In the witch's headquarters at Benevento, the witches meet and dance under the walnut tree and circle dance in the church square.

All the southern and central Italian rural regions describe this folkloric witch the same way. She represented their worst fears. When speaking to older Italians about the *streghe*, I was met with a nervous glance and replied to in hushed tones. A *strega* could be a healer, a *benedetta* (one who practised *benedicaria)* on the side of good and God, or she could be a dangerous *strega* who could give you the evil eye, causing distress, illness and harm.

This is what I learned from my *paesani* (people from my town): the upside-down broom left outside the front door and scattered grains are the major weapons to combat the *strega*. She cannot enter until she counts each individual grain or twig from the broom before sunrise. The *strega's* mortal enemy is sunlight – it will render her powerless. The lesson is to buy a big, thick broom! If that doesn't work, you could toss buckets of grains and extra salt on your front doorstep for protection.

If you find a witches' ladder, you'll know for sure that you and your family have been cursed. The witches' ladder is a three-strand rope into which black feathers are inserted and twisted like a garland. Some are made with black hens' feathers tied into the knots. The witches were said to recite a malediction or hex when tying each knot.

Candles, onions or lemons with pins in them also indicate a black-magic hex. The conjuration of lemons and pins aims to make someone ill; the caster removes some peel and pierces the lemon with pins, reciting a spell each time. This type of dark magic is dangerous because it is conjured to cause harm. The healer-type witch causes no harm with their rituals.

Pandafeche (succubi witches)

In regions of Marche, Abruzzo and Molise, succubi are called *pandafeche*. In Sardinia, they are called *ammuntadore* – creatures that mount sleeping people's chests to give them nightmares. They are also known in places as *streghe*. These terrifying ghostlike creatures were regarded as vampiric witches or succubi, and were associated with sleep paralysis.

Sleep paralysis is a state of being awake in your sleep but unable to move. In technical terms, you're still in a dream-like state when you are in sleep paralysis – you're not awake enough to be alert, but enough to be aware you can't move. Dream experts explain that it's our brain and muscles being out of synch when waking up, therefore communication between them is delayed. When you're in this dream-like state, your fears instantly surface, with your brain creating an evil entity that is holding you down. I've had this myself and it took a huge mental effort to shake myself fully awake from the fearful experience. In many other cultures, the incubi, succubi and old hag apparitions are blamed for the same phenomena; people share similar emotions of being paralysed with terror and feeling like they cannot breathe.

In some regional Italian areas, it is a nocturnal entity believed to be the ghost of an evil woman who is cursed to wander the town at night. She lies on the sleeper's body, pushing on their chest, 'stealing' their breath and making it impossible for them to move. I've heard about this traumatic experience from *paesani* from my region, and they swear it's true. They said they then slept with a bag of beans or legumes on one side of them and rock salt on the other. As we know, a *strega* has to count each grain or bean before sunrise to reach her victim. The salt provides extra protection.

If the victim could manage to move and make the sign of the cross, they could wake up from the sleep paralysis and push off the creature. Or if they grabbed the shadow creature's hair and recited short phrases mentioning the word *ferro* (iron, considered a protection amulet), the witch was forced to respond, which broke the sleep paralysis.

I used to ask my nonna questions like: 'How did the witch get in when everything was locked and nobody saw her?' The answer was always the same: 'Because she has no body. She's invisible like a ghost.' That was it. No more explanation was given. My young life was haunted, imagining invisible *streghe* coming to attack me.

One explanation for this supernatural phenomenon is shape-shifting and astral travel. The vampiric *strega*, for instance, is both a shape-shifter and disembodied spirit. The *strega* could shape-shift into a small animal and psychically spy on her victim by projecting her double. If you could manage to grab the tail of the shape-shifted cat, the *strega* would have to reveal her identity.

Vampiric *strega* and *sugatura*

Whenever bruises appeared on a child's body or neck, it was taken as a serious indication that it was *sugatura* and the *strega* was held responsible. The word *sugatura* means 'sucked dry'; it refers to a type of childhood anaemia. Physical marks, called *sugature*, appeared as bruises and symptoms included weight loss, lethargy, loss of appetite, slow movements, and being pale and sickly looking.

This anaemia was blamed on blood being drawn by witches who astral-travelled during the night. They would enter the house through keyholes or chimneys – not in their physical forms, but as disembodied spirits (who would have to return to their bodies by sunrise). These disembodied spirits could use their lips like a suction cup over their victims without breaking the skin.

Sugatura was therefore considered to be a psychic illness affecting the blood, resulting in anaemia especially in young children. While adults were also afflicted with the *sugature* marks, their stronger constitutions meant they could heal with herbal remedies more readily.

For protection against *sugatura*, people wore amulets, did smoke cleansing with leaves such as juniper, and used filter items. Apotropaic (protective) plants were regarded as having curative and magical properties. These plants were used to make brooms or hung in bundles with special powers to filter out negativity. These brooms or bundles were placed at each point of entry to a house – the front door, windows and balconies – to prevent the disembodied *strega* from entering in the first place. Prevention was the only effective method. The vampiric *strega* would have to stop and count the individual broom fibres or grains of salt, getting lost in the counting and having to flee before sunrise.

Common filters used were millet, straw, twig brooms, salt, pulses, sand or grains, seeds, skeins of hemp, wool fibres or similar hanging on the door, horseshoe (iron), branches of holly or juniper, and twigs/branches of lightning wood (wood that was protective against lightning).

In the worst-case scenario, when the disembodied witch was successful in entering and sucking the victim (especially if it was a child), a family member had to keep watch 24 hours a day for the next nine days. My mother tells me this vigil was used on me as a baby, because I'd been given the *malocchio* from the local *strega* – a dangerous spell indeed.

● ● ●

A *paesano* who grew up in our town told me about his experience with witches when he was a child. He would tell his parents, '*M'e pigliann' l' streg' e m' sugann'* *(Mi pigliano le streghe e mi sugano)*, which translates as 'The witches take me and suck me.'

In the morning, he would see bruises on his body. Because the skin wasn't broken, he wasn't sucked like in vampire movies with punctures in the neck.

He told me the *stregone* (male head witch) and other *streghe* would take him to participate in their ritual. At their gathering, they'd toss him to one another over the open fire, saying, *'Te' cumma' (prendi, commare), te' cumpa' (prendi, compare)*, which translates as 'Take him, godmother, take him, godfather.' The words *commare* and *compare* can have different meanings – *commare* can mean a godmother, companion, neighbour or gossip, while *compare* can mean a godfather, friend or comrade.

Over a short space of time, my *paesano* became thin and sickly. To help him get well, a millet broom was turned upside down behind a door with grains of wheat scattered on the floor. Before the witch could get the boy, she had to count all the millet and wheat, but had to leave at sunup so never finished counting. The next night, she had to start again. For nine nights, two people sat to watch over him. This preventative protection against the *strega* eventually saved my *paesano*. He began to thrive.

Like the *janare*, my aunt told me, the *strega* in our town has to be stopped before entering the house and becoming invisible. You do this by putting an upside-down *saggina* (straw or millet) broom at the front door. The more fibres the better – the *strega* has to count each strand before entering. You also place a bowl of salt by the window, and anything made of iron should be at the front and back doors and windows. Known as *tocca ferro* (touch iron), this is another effective protection item against the *malocchio* or *streghe*.

Benandanti

Where evil lurked, 'light' would keep the balance. Such was the case with the *benandanti*, a folk tradition from the Friuli region of north-eastern Italy during the 16th and 17th centuries. The term *benandanti* translates to 'good walkers' or 'do-gooders'. This group of folk healers and spiritual practitioners believed they were gifted with special abilities to combat malevolent forces and ensure their communities' prosperity. They would carry large fennel stalks, which were believed to have psychic powers, into their 'night battles' against the *streghe*.

The story tells that *benandanti* were born with a 'caul' on their head. This gave them the ability to take part in night-time visions that occurred on specific days of the year. Caul is a piece of membrane that covers a newborn's head and face. It was regarded as a sign of having the potential for scrying, divination and seeing the future.

The beliefs and practices of the *benandanti* (both men and women) were closely tied to agricultural cycles; they battled against forces they perceived as harmful to crops and the community's well-being. They believed their spirits left their bodies during their dreams (astral travel), taking the form of animals such as mice, cats, rabbits or butterflies, or supernatural creatures. In this form, they travelled to a mystical realm known as the 'battlefield' where they engaged in spiritual battles with witches and evil spirits, fighting to protect their community's crops, livestock and the overall prosperity.

When not taking part in visionary journeys, the *benandanti* could use their magical powers for healing. They would perform rituals and blessings to ensure the well-being of their community members and livestock.

The beliefs and practices of the *benandanti* faded over time, and today their traditions are largely lost. But some modern *benandanti* groups have revived this cultural tradition. Their purpose is to enter astral realms and battle to protect the world from negative and harmful energies.

Dual roles of *streghe*

Italian folk magic is referred to as *stregoneria* because it comes from the belief that those with supernatural powers could heal or harm. The *strega* held both these roles – she was seen as a necessity – a healer and midwife – and as a counter-hexer, using black magic to restore balance or redress a grievance. In a society lacking access to formal medical knowledge and doctors, that also distrusted science-based treatments, the witchy-wise woman was essential to the local community.

Le streghe were thus both real individuals living in communities who practised as healers, and also frightening supernatural figures. These two roles overlapped in people's minds, leading to accusations of witchcraft. Today, the term *strega* still carries the stigma of the pagan, dangerous, devil-worshipping character from the Inquisition.

The *strega* is remembered as part of Italian celebrations. Italians celebrate the night between 23 and 24 June as the 'night of the witches', a popular festivity dedicated to Saint John the Baptist around the time of the summer solstice. (For more information, see pages 270–71.)

This feast day is celebrated in many ways in regional areas, with the syncretic blending of a saint's day, the solstice and the witches' night. This distinct blend of folk magic makes this living cultural tradition something that continues to evolve.

THE WITCHES AND THE INQUISITION

In many parts of Italy, witches were believed to be responsible for devil worship and harming others in the community. The Witch Museum in Triora, Liguria, is one of several witch museums that offers insight into the horrific witch trials and murders that occurred in the late 16th century, which resulted in women accused of witchcraft being executed. In this dark period, fear and superstition led to persecution of and violence against innocent women.

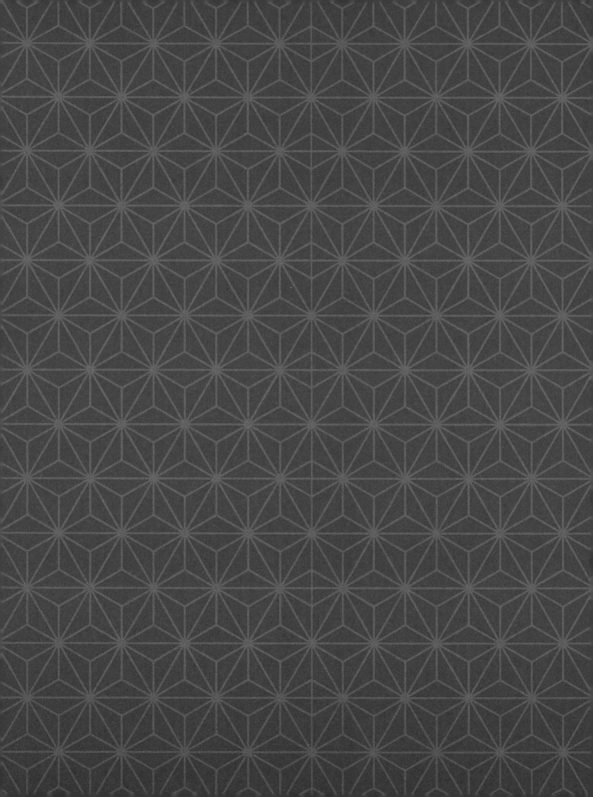

Chapter 3

The witches of Benevento

L ong ago, on the night of San Giovanni, now known as the 'night of the witches', it was said that thousands of witches from all parts of Europe, flew to the Great Sabbath held at the walnut tree in Benevento (*la noce di Benevento*). They gathered to engage in magical and ritualistic activities. In Benevento, traditionally this gathering falls on the night of 30 April (May eve), also known as as 'Walpurgis Night' or 'Witches' Sabbath' in other parts of Europe. Today, the witches' night is celebrated in many parts of Italy on different dates – but with the same level of connection to witchcraft and magic.

Benevento is in the Campania region. Our town is only 65 kilometres away from Benevento, and our family is descended from the ancient Italic Samnite tribe of this region. Growing up, the stories I heard about the *streghe* were based on the *janare* of Benevento.

WITCHES' BREW

In my drinks cabinet sits a bottle of Strega liqueur. The label shows naked women dancing under Benevento's walnut tree on the Witches' Sabbath. In 1860, the story of the witches of Benevento inspired Giuseppe Alberti to make a love potion, inducing women to connect to nature, the moon and uninhibited love. Included in Strega are Apennine juniper, Samnite mint from Benevento, fennel, cloves, star anise, cinnamon, white pepper, nutmeg and saffron. Its heady effects make me realise how well Alberti captured the intoxicating rituals of the Witches' Sabbath. It's my personal version of the witches' flying ointment. (For more information, see page 33.)

Benevento's walnut tree was a famous meeting place for witches. These gatherings were attended by witches from all over Italy and Europe as part of the Witches' Sabbath. The walnut tree was sacred to the Lombards (a Germanic tribe), who ruled and settled in this area. The Lombards were devotees of the god Odin and worshipped the tree, which held special magical powers. Later, the Lombards converted to Catholicism.

The folklore began with the *janare*, who were seen chanting, dancing naked around trees, riding backwards on horses, making animal sacrifices, anointing parts of their bodies and calling on Lucifer (supposedly in goat form) to participate in evil rituals. Over centuries, the legend grew, telling that witches from all over the world would gather under the walnut tree to hold their Witches' Sabbaths, including feasts, orgies, spell-casting and devil worship.

What made the walnut tree so iconic was its location near the river Sabato, or Sabbath. It was considered to be a dangerous tree – to sleep in its shade would give you a fever, and cattle would get sick after eating its tree roots. Eventually, a church was built over it, but the legend remains. If you are ever in Benevento, check out the Witches' Museum there.

Ancient Benevento and the goddess cult

Benevento was once the sanctuary of the followers of the holy witch Aradia, who was believed to have lived in the 14th century. Aradia is associated with the book *Aradia, or the Gospel of the Witches* published in 1899 by folklorist Charles Godfrey Leland. According to Leland, he was given the text by a woman named Maddalena, who claimed to be a hereditary witch and priestess of a group practising Italian *stregoneria* (witchcraft).

In the book, Aradia is depicted as a powerful figure, the daughter of the moon goddess Diana (Artemis) and the god Lucifer (often interpreted as a representation of the horned god or a divine masculine figure, not the devil). She was a wise and compassionate teacher, imparting her magical knowledge to the downtrodden and oppressed, empowering the poor to defend themselves against their oppressors.

Like Aradia, the deity Diana is not generally venerated as part of folk magic tradition in southern Italian regions. In ancient Rome, Diana was the protector of the lower class (plebeians) and slaves, and many slaves received sanctuary in her temples. Because Diana was the goddess of fertility and childbirth, many women visited her sanctuary at Lake Nemi (south of Rome) to ask for help in conceiving or with childbirth.

We don't really know how the *janare*, or the witches of Benevento, originated. Some scholars believe the *janare* were followers of the goddess Diana, with their name stemming from the word '*Dianara*'. Diana, the goddess of the moon, who represented women's cycles, fertility, childbirth and animals, appealed to female healers, midwives and herbalists, as well as women who lived in rural areas and had to survive during challenging times.

Others think the name stems from *ianua*, the local term for 'door' (the *janare* have to count the broom's fibres or scattered grains before entering a house). And some say they are women of San Gennaro (pronounced *Yennaro*, also known as *Janarius*), the patron saint of Naples and Bishop of Benevento, who died a martyr in 305 CE. Nobody knows for sure, except that the *janare* were both feared and needed as healers.

The *janare* had the power to harm in many ways – cause miscarriages, create deformed babies, cast the *malocchio*, ruin crops, cast deadly spells, cause supernatural occurrences, manipulate people's minds, and even make livestock sick and die. Despite being labelled as witches in these negative roles, they were also traditional healers with the knowledge of herbal remedies used to cure illness.

The witches' trials and the Inquisition

In several Inquisition trials, the city of Benevento was mentioned as a destination for Witches' Sabbaths. Matteuccia de Francesco, an alleged witch and nun from the village of Ripabianca, Umbria, was put on trial in Todi and burned at the stake for witchcraft in 1428. She was accused of being a prostitute, committing desecration with other women, selling love potions, having 'flown' to a tree, and shape-shifting as a fly on a demon's back after using an ointment (*unguento*) made of the blood of newborn children. She admitted to attending the Benevento Sabbaths.

One of the spells attributed to Matteuccia is this famous one, which my nonna and zia could recite off by heart:

Unguento unguento
portami al noce di Benevento
sopra l'acqua e sopra il vento
sopra ogni altro maltempo.

Ointment, ointment
take me to the walnut tree of Benevento,
over rain and over wind
and over every other bad weather.

There are other versions, but this one means flying to Benevento in any weather.

Flying ointments

Witches' ointments or flying salves are probably the most famous *unguenti*. These herbal preparations were made from psychedelic plants that could shift consciousness and also relieve pain. Flying ointments are usually infused oils made from olive oil or lard/fat. The remedy is applied directly onto the skin and the herbal ingredients soak into the bloodstream. These ointments can relax the body and mind, lowering resistance and opening up the practitioner to a trance-like state.

But how are they 'flying' ointments? These ointments contain hallucinogenic herbs that are placed in a salve or oil, rubbed on the body, and absorbed through the skin. Flying does not refer to the physical activity of flying, but the mentally altered state of 'being high' from the ointment.

During the witch trials, some people believed that Witches' Sabbaths were real and their flying ointment, which contained noxious ingredients, helped them fly unseen to these gatherings, which were attended by the devil. Others (more sensible ones) believed that the Witches' Sabbath was a delusion induced by the hallucinogenic ingredients in these ointments – the women on trial were experiencing visions brought on by these dangerous plants.

The *janare* used plants with psychotropic and visionary qualities such as poppy of Troy (*Papever setigerum*) and plants of the nightshade family (*Solanaceae*) such as thorn apple (*Datura stramonium),* deadly nightshade (*Atropa belladonna*), mandrake (*Mandragora autumnalis*) and henbane (*Hyoscyamus niger*).

The 'deliriums' described in the witch trials of flying in spirals, shape-shifting and meeting up with monstrous creatures can be attributed to the mind-altering effects of hallucinogenic plants. As skilled herbalists, the *janare* prepared ointments with these plants to take their spirits into 'ecstasy'. There, they would meet nature and ancestral spirits, and gain knowledge of healing and future events. The trance-like state brought on by the hallucinogenic ointments would allow the *janare* to descend into the underworld – like the powerful goddess Ecate (Hecate) – and meet with spirits of the dead.

So, why are brooms so often part of witch lore? Brooms were often made of birch but some used the plant called broom (*Cytisus scoparius*), which was a psychoactive plant.

Many of the herbs used both for hexing and in *unguenti* (flying ointments) come from the Solanaceae or nightshade family and are associated with spirits of the underworld, the darkness and dark magic. Known for their poisons and witchcraft, the three dark goddesses – Ecate (Hecate), Circe (her daughter) and Proserpina (Persephone) are connected with these herbs. Some of these plants are connected to the nocturnal world of spirits. The *unguenti* have psychedelic powers that allow trance, astral travel and summoning spirits. These are dangerous and mostly toxic plants. Most plants used in the past for flying ointment were the more dangerous ones from the Solanaceae family. I have listed the more common herbs for flying ointment for information and historical interest only.

> **Important note:** Flying ointments containing these plants are dangerous due to their toxic and potentially lethal nature. Do not attempt to induce altered states of consciousness using these substances. There are more reliable methods and well-established therapeutic practices for doing so.

Belladonna (*Atropa belladonna*)

Although belladonna means 'beautiful lady', it is also known as deadly nightshade and the devil's berry. The Italian term comes from the women who would drip the juice of the plant into their eyes to dilate their pupils so they would appear more attractive.

The queen of poisonous herbs, witches and sorcerers have traditionally used belladonna to gain spiritual visions and spirit flight (altered state or trance). They also used it as an effective sedative and for pain relief – but only in very small doses. A wrong dose could mean death.

It's only right that the queen of poisonous herbs should be sacred to Ecate, the goddess of black magic and the underworld, who ruled over the sea and sky. Belladonna is a gatekeeper, much like Ecate, and was widely used by the *janare*. But beware, she is not called 'deadly' nightshade for nothing. Other than rituals, the belladonna is dangerous and should never be ingested.

Black henbane (*Hyoscyamus niger*)

Henbane was used in black magic rituals and ceremonies and in shamanism. Another sacred herb to the dark goddesses, Ecate and Proserpina (Persephone), the *janare* burned and smoked (smoke cleansed) henbane's leaves. Mostly, henbane was used for scrying, seeing demons and spirits in its smoke patterns, and inducing trance-like states.

Mugwort and wormwood (*Artemisia* spp.)

Artemisia is named after Artemis, ancient Greek goddess of the hunt. The *janare* used mugwort and wormwood to enhance their psychic abilities, help with divination, communicate with spirits and the dead, induce lucid dreams, and encourage prophetic dreams. Mugwort is especially useful for promoting lucid dreams when drunk in tea before bedtime. Like henbane, both mugwort and wormwood were used for inducing a trance when burning their leaves and for scrying when prepared as an infusion. Once used to improve blood circulation and reduce pain in joints and muscles, midwives also used it as an abortifacient (to induce abortion). These herbs can be dangerous if used incorrectly.

Mandrake (*Mandragora officinarum*)

The mandrake is a favourite witchy plant. The bifurcated root's resemblance to a human is bizarre. Over time, it's become known as a symbol of sorcery and enchantment. Witches were said to know the secret knowledge of how to bring the 'mannikin' to life and do their bidding. Legend says that, when the mandrake was torn from the earth, it gave forth such a fearful cry that whoever heard it would either go mad or fall dead on the spot.

Because it looked like a human body, people believed the mandrake could control the body: it could induce love or conception, or bring good fortune, wealth and power.

A member of the nightshade plant family, mandrake contains hallucinogenic and narcotic alkaloids. If these alkaloids are ingested (sometimes added to wine) or transmitted through the skin, they induce hallucinations, sleepiness, and sometimes comas or death. This herb of bewitchment was dug up before sunrise when it was its most active and could be willing to act as a familiar spirit.

Mandrake became known as a demonic herb because its root was the most powerful part of the plant (where the narcotic and hallucinogenic alkaloids are found), which was found underground. Like belladonna, mandrake is associated with Ecate (Hecate) and her daughter, Circe.

Although the root is the most potent part, burning or ingesting mandrake leaves can also be dangerous.

Opium poppy (*Papaver somniferum*)

Due to its soporific (sleep-inducing) effect, this poppy was the most common plant for witches' flying ointments. The flower is associated with the goddesses Ceres (Demeter) and her daughter Proserpina (Persephone), goddess of spring and the underworld. In one version of the myth, Ceres grew the flower after Proserpina was kidnapped by Pluto (Hades), god of the underworld. In another, Proserpina was in the fields picking poppies when she was abducted and taken to the underworld.

Perhaps the gods gave Ceres poppy to help her sleep after Proserpina was abducted. All these versions point to it as a symbol of sleep and pain relief. It is the plant of the underworld – the realm between life, death and sleep. As the plant of the realm of the dead, the ancient Romans used it in offerings to appease the spirits of the dead.

Opium poppy was used in flying ointment recipes not only for its pain-relieving and sedative properties, but also for its

hallucinatory effects. The opium poppy contains the alkaloids morphine, codeine and noscapine – all dangerous and potentially toxic substances.

Vervain (*Verbena officinalis*)

Known as the divine weed or *herba sacra* (sacred herb) to the Romans, vervain was said to cure bites and the plague, and avert sorcery. During the Middle Ages, vervain was often used in magicians' and witches' potions. In folk medicine, vervain was used for protection, but also as an aphrodisiac, which is why it was named *herba veneris*, or 'herb of love.' It was prized for its properties of clarifying the mind and enhancing psychic ability. When added to water as a wash, it increased one's scrying abilities and cleansed magical tools.

Vervain was a good all-rounder herb to treat abdominal issues because it was anti-spasmodic, anti-inflammatory, good for the lungs and helped to ease headaches. Vervain is a uterine stimulant and can help induce labour, so it should not be used in pregnancy.

Today, flying ointments and ritual entheogens are becoming better known and more used in witchcraft. The mind-altering experiences they induce can help with divination, travelling to other worlds to retrieve knowledge (such as a shamanic trance or soul retrieval), and communicating with the spirits (deceased, ancestor and nature spirits). You can find information online and in books with recipes for non-toxic flying ointments.

The *janare* today

Despite centuries of persecution and vilification, the *janare* still exist today and have managed to pass on their knowledge in secret and through family lineages. As rural healers, herbalists and midwives, their skills were called on to help save people's lives, especially those of babies. In times of high infant mortality before the world wars, the death of a child in childbirth was often blamed on the *janara*. Equally, she was thanked for her help in bringing life and ending it early if necessary.

As healers, *janare* treated bone fractures using casts made from flour and egg whites. They practised pranotherapy – healing by placing their hands on the bodies of sick people. They also cured illness caused by the *malocchio* and removed worms in children with the same method. While you don't have to be a *janara* to be a healer, it does help if you're born on Christmas Eve (the winter solstice), at the bedside of a dying *janara* or touched by an old *janara*.

Over time, the *janare* have been many things – skilled herbalists, healers, midwives, animistic priestesses, astral travellers and shamans – but what they have in common is a special connection with the natural world passed down through generations of women healers. Plant spirits are their allies with properties to heal body and soul. Today, natural medicine offers a vast pharmacopoeia of remedies that medical science has only just begun to discover, and that old folk magic *nonne* knew all along.

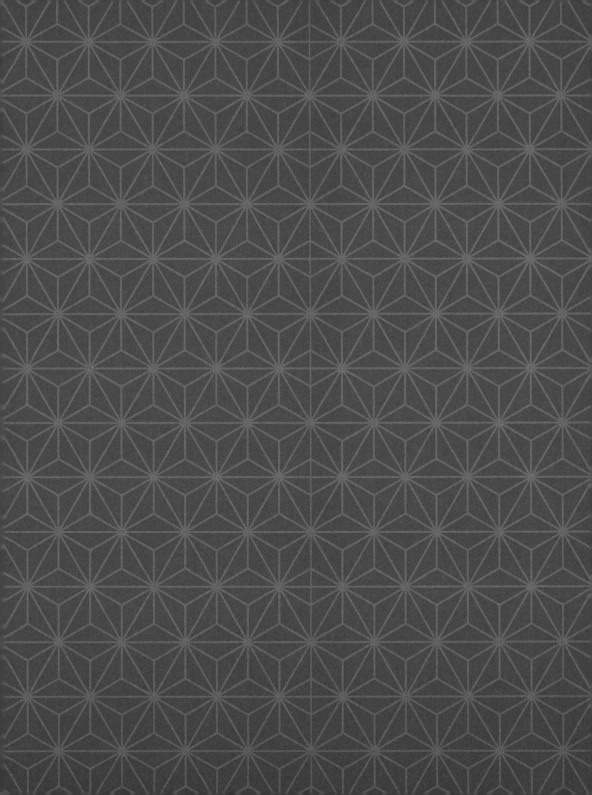

Chapter 4

Lineage healers, herbalists and wise women of Italy

The Italian word for 'healer' is *guaritrice/guaritore*. Healers are generally lineage healers whose knowledge and methods have passed down through the family line. They use prayers, incantations, rituals such as the *malocchio*, protection spells and special hand actions to cure illness and remove negative energy. However, the names and roles of healers vary with the regions, and even within each province, city, town or village. In Italian folk magic, all information has been transferred as oral tradition and little written material is recorded. Many practitioners inherited their gifts from their ancestors. A complicating factor is that sometimes the *streghe* and *guaritrici* were one and the same.

NAMES OF HEALERS AND WITCHES

While the names used for healing practitioners vary, most would understand these self-explanatory roles: *guaritori* (male healers), *guaritrici* (female healers) *fattucchiere* (fixers), *commari* (godmothers) and *donne che aiutano* (women who help). At times, healers were referred to as *streghe* (witches), although not to their faces, by those who were sceptical of their powers or believed they dealt in black magic only.

In Sicily, the *majare/maiare* are lineage healers with special knowledge of plants and herbs. They are also called *magare* in Abruzzo, Molise and Calabria.

In Sardinia, *is praticas* are seers, similar to 'cunning folk' in English, who can remove the evil eye and hexes. *Is bruxa* is more of an oracle teller, psychic and someone who does black magic with hexes (*fattucchiera*).

The *janare* from Campania are experts in magic spells and lineage cures.

I segnatori from Le Marche perform signs or gestures on the body to heal illnesses with special words only the practitioner knows. An example is marking the forehead with oil after the *malocchio* ritual.

It's impossible to include all the ways in which healers worked, but their healing and spell craft practices – both white and black magic – give a sense of the village healer's power. They could heal and curse; give life or bring death.

Most healers in rural Italy were *fattucchiere,* or 'fattura-breakers' or 'fixers' – they would undo and break spells (*fatture*). They knew how to *sfascinare* (undo spells).

Love spells and hexes

Healers were consulted for matters of fertility and love, providing remedies and charms to enhance fertility, attract love and maintain harmonious relationships. Many a love match was made possible thanks to the local *fattucchiere*, but the flip side was forcing someone to fall in love with you or not stray from the marriage through magic. Love magic included courtship rituals, invocations, prayers, *ligature* bindings and *fatture* poppets.

Because there was no divorce in Italy, marriage was for life; it was serious business where parents arranged marriages. My grandparents' marriage was arranged, and my aunt was a proxy bride – her marriage was arranged before she even met the man, who was in Australia. My grandfather was the local matchmaker, so it was up to him to carry the *'mbasciate* or the message of the potential bride's or groom's parents to their prospective in-laws. Traditionally, he was given a white handkerchief for his effort, and if the marriage deal was sealed, he was gifted with a *gallo* (rooster) or *gallina* (hen).

When curative spells, prayers and invocations to Madonnas and saints didn't work, and you needed urgent action, you called in the *fattucchiera*. They knew ways to ensure a successful marriage that resulted in attraction and fertility, namely spells, bindings and *fatture* using a poppet, known as *la puppia*.

Love spells often involved creating potions, called *filtri* (philters), using a few drops of menstrual blood or semen in coffee or food, without the desired one's knowledge.

In our village, there was a young woman who fancied a young man, and asked her aunt to find a *magara* who would make him fall in love with her. His parents weren't pleased with her affections, but it was to no avail. The wedding went ahead. But the wedding night didn't go as planned – the young man was unable to perform his marital duty.

Shortly after the wedding, outside the church after Sunday mass, a stranger cried out – a woman whose dialect indicated she came from another town. 'You who promised me the coin. I'm now here to collect it,' she shouted for all to hear.

In front of all the villagers, the aunt approached the woman and gave her money from her purse. This was the money intended for the love spell. Without payment, the spell had the reverse effect. The object of the young woman's love had failed to give her what she wanted.

This was the power of the healer in rural communities.

Today, we can honour the *fattura* breaker by using poppets for healing, protection and manifesting a better life for ourselves, rather than for negative purposes.

Legature

Binding spells, or *legature*, are used to bind someone to you or break up a personal or business relationship. The *legature* ritual is based on the knots the *magare* would use to cure sprains, twisted muscles, torn ligaments, or anything needing to be held or tied together for it to heal and prevent the illness from spreading or getting worse.

Italian folk magic healers prepared remedies such as herbal based teas, poultices, ointments, tonics and of course, some protection herbs. Some common conditions they were believed to cure or alleviate include:

- ▶ physical illnesses such as colds, flu and respiratory problems
- ▶ digestive issues and stomach ailments
- ▶ headaches and migraines
- ▶ skin conditions and wounds
- ▶ muscular and joint pain

- conjunctivitis
- eczema
- herpes
- sprains
- mysterious ailments.

Female healers took care of women's issues and health concerns, including childbirth and postpartum recovery. They also offered remedies for common childhood ailments and provided protection charms for infants and young children. As part of their healing role, female healers could protect and remove the *malocchio*, which was especially important for newborn babies' survival in a time of high infant mortality. Babies were also baptised soon after birth for extra protection.

Along with physical healing, healers addressed spiritual concerns, offering remedies for nightmares and sleep disturbances, anxiety, stress and emotional imbalances. They removed curses or negative influences, and provided blessings and purification rituals.

While their remedies and methods weren't mainstream medical practices, healers played an important role in the lives of their community. Their holistic approach to healing addressed not only physical symptoms, but also one's spiritual and emotional well-being.

The healers' special skills

Generally, folk healers have some or all of these skills and cures:

- Use magic to cure or cast protection spells, with their special knowledge of herbs.
- They are lineage healers.

- Remove the *malocchio*.
- Use inherited words, incantations and prayers.
- Protect victims against hexes and attachments, returning them to the sender.
- They are oracle tellers, using divination techniques such as cards to predict future events.
- They can astral travel.
- They can interpret dreams.
- Mark the body with signs.
- Use black magic, shape-shifting and other *maledizioni* (hexes).

What makes the healer special?

A common belief is that a healer born with special gifts is marked from birth with these traits:

- Being born in the caul.
- Being born with the umbilical cord around the neck.
- Being born on 24–25 December or 24–25 January.
- Being the third daughter.

A close friend told me this story of her mother, who was born with caul on her face:

'The baby was considered to be a gifted healer and have psychic ability. My grandmother kept the caul in a chest of drawers until it disintegrated. My mamma was shown the veil when she was a child. They said she was born with the veil (*nata con il velo*), which gave her special qualities and powers for healing (*nata con virtù*). My nonna was a healer who had *virtù*. She taught my mother to heal and reduce swelling on wounds when she was a young girl.'

We seldom hear these stories today because of the stigma associated with magical *stregoneria*. Unless we pass on their lived experiences, vital stories will be lost.

Passing down secret formulas

Healing formulas are passed on from one family member to another at significant times of the year such as Christmas Eve (24 December), New Year's Eve (31 December), St John's Eve (23 June) or St Joseph's Eve (18 March). The owner of the formula passes on the power along with the knowledge; once they have been transmitted, in many cases, the original owner ceases to practice. Often in some regions, only certain family members can receive the knowledge.

Folk healers are believed to be unable to die peacefully until they have passed on their knowledge. This includes *malocchio* cures and rituals. Once a ritual has been passed on, the spell words (*scongiuri*) are kept secret. They belong to that lineage of healers; it's only when a lineage ceases to practise that the words and complete ritual can be revealed to others. This is why there is still little documentation of spells, words and exact rituals today.

Types of folk healers and their cures

In the past, rural towns had several folk healers who could cure illnesses, such as with herbs, magic formulas and prayers. In case of serious magical attacks, people consulted sorcerers or real *streghe*. These practitioners overlapped, however, since almost any illness was regarded as the result of magic.

Most healers were women, as you would expect with women's traditional role of looking after their family and community. Their medicines, obtained from nature, were the only available remedies for the common folk. Many women who practised folk healing were midwives (*levatrici*) because they knew which herbs could help a new life to grow. Women were also death doulas, being at the side of someone dying and helping them to cross over peacefully – sometimes, they had the power to end lives.

Accabadora

In traditional Sardinian society, the dying had their own angel of death – the *accabadora* or *s'accabadora*. This name comes from the Sardinian word *accaba'*, which means 'to finish'. The *accabadora* was entrusted to be a mercy killer; she was responsible for ending the life of terminally ill or older individuals who were suffering and nearing death. Her role was one of compassion, and she was called upon when the person's family or community believed their suffering had become unbearable.

To perform the act of mercy killing, the *accabadora* would use a hammer, known as *su mazzolu* or *sa mazzocca*. She would use the hammer to strike a blow on the back of the person's head, causing immediate death. This method was considered to be swift and humane, aimed at relieving the person's suffering.

Naturally, the *accabadora* practice was highly secretive and shrouded in rituals and traditions specific to Sardinia. The *accabadora's* identity was usually known only to a select few within the community. As you would expect, her services were provided discreetly and with the utmost confidentiality. She arrived wearing a long black cloak with a hood covering her face (not unlike the image of death carrying a scythe), sometimes half-masked, carrying a large hammer to where the person was waiting.

She was the angel of death, highly respected for her skill. Like traditional lineage healers, this important role was passed down from mother to daughter. But she also faced accusations of being evil by the church and outsiders who didn't understand the custom. A witch museum called *Museo S'omo e sa Majarza* (Witch's House Museum) in Bidonì, Sardinia, exhibits the *accabadora* and her instruments, as well as the historical persecution of witches in Sardinia.

As Sardinia underwent significant social and cultural changes in the 20th century, the practice of the *accabadora* eventually disappeared.

Segnatura

Meaning 'signs or gestures', *segnatura* is the act of drawing symbols with the hand, such as crosses, over the ill part of the body, or over oil and water to remove the *malocchio*. The role of the *segnatrice/segnatore* (the gesturer) is that of healer and protector of the community. This term is mostly used in Emilia Romagna, but it's a common ritual in other regions.

Like all lineage healers, the *segnatore's* healing ability has been passed on from a close relative (usually a female) in a ritual that must be performed between sunset on Christmas Eve and sunrise on Christmas Day, usually around midnight. Traditionally, only a blood relative can receive the *segnatura* and only one family member can be initiated. The rituals are performed in one's local dialect and include syncretic elements with saint worship.

Once the newly initiated *segnatori* have learned the ritual, they must memorise the words that accompany the gestures to create the desired healing.

How the *segnatura* is performed depends on the region. Mostly, crosses are drawn on the body part that needs treatment, repeating the gesture three times until the end of the chanted prayer. Crosses can be drawn on the body directly with the fingers or applied with oil. The words are just as powerful as the gestures – they are considered sacred and are never revealed to anyone or written down.

Benedicaria

Translated as 'way of blessing', *benedicaria* is a traditional healing method concerned not only with healing, clearings and spirituality, but also on Catholic devotional practices. The practitioner is known as *benedetta* (female) and *benedetto* (male); like other lineage healers, it's a family-based spiritual tradition. Practices include cures for the *malocchio* and using candles, herbs, the rosary, novenas and Catholic prayers to various saints. The sacramentals are never disrespected because *benedicaria* use the same rituals for their healing, although the line might be crossed at times with this blending of the two 'ways'.

When removing the *malocchio*, the *benedicaria* primarily uses Catholic prayers. Divination tools such as scissors, a knife and an old-style key are placed on the body part where the recipient feels the pain. These tools are considered to hold magic properties; scissors and knives assist with cutting away illness, and materials such as iron or mirrors scare away or show the reflection of bad spirits.

Special prayers, which are unique to the family's tradition, are passed down the family line by the women. They are shared on two nights of the year only – at midnight on Christmas Eve and before St Joseph's feast day on 19 March.

Many cures show the *benedicaria*'s influence, none more than the cures attributed to saints.

Il male di San Donato and il male di San Valentino

Epilepsy is known as *il mal caduco* (the falling sickness) and is commonly called *il male di San Donato* (St Donato's sickness) in southern Italy or *il male di San Valentino* (St Valentine's sickness) in northern Italy. San Valentino is the patron saint of love, travellers and beekeepers. San Valentino is venerated as a healing saint who had cured an epileptic child. He was believed to have been imprisoned and executed by the Roman emperor Claudius II for his Christian beliefs. Some believe there were two Saint Valentines who were conflated, and thus their feast days are both on 14 February.

St Donatus, Bishop of Arezzo, was a martyr beheaded in the third century. He protected against epilepsy, which was once connected to neurological disorders caused by poor nutrition and intermarriage. Epilepsy was a greatly feared and misunderstood condition in rural Italy. Iron was used in amulets against attacks, and epileptics often carried iron keys or nails to ward off the illness (this technique also warded off negative energies). Because epilepsy was believed to have a supernatural cause, only the saints had the power to cure it.

Other pagan symbols that helped against epileptic fits were lunar crescents and frogs, which symbolised the agricultural season's cycles and moon's phases. The illness was also believed to follow the moon's phases, so it was cyclical. Eventually, with Catholicism, these symbols came to be associated with San Donato. In the amulets, the pagan symbols were combined with a figure of Saint Donato, who is depicted holding or standing on the crescent moon. Church prayers and veneration rituals slowly replaced the nature-based pagan amulets.

Il fuoco di Sant'Antonio

St Anthony the Abbot, born in Egypt, is invoked as a protector against *il fuoco di Sant' Antonio* (St Anthony's fire), otherwise known as shingles. This painful viral infection is caused by the varicella-zoster virus, which also causes chickenpox and creates the feeling of your skin being on fire. It is a serious condition, especially for older people.

Ways of asking St Anthony to heal and alleviate the pain and discomfort of shingles included votive offerings, wearing St Anthony's medal and collecting water from a spring dedicated to him. This water contained healing properties and was used for washing the affected area. Other methods included reciting special prayers and invocations to St Anthony.

In some regions, lineage remedies for alleviating the pain or curing St Anthony's fire have been passed down. The healer casts out St Anthony's fire by saying a prayer only they know then spitting on the infected area three times. Saliva is considered as having both healing and protective properties. In other regions, healers say a prayer nine times and make markings (*segnature*) on the body part to be healed. Then they disinfect the area with special local herbs known to be antibacterial.

● ● ●

Italian folk healers were known for their herbal knowledge. They came from the land − rural people whose ancestors had passed down their knowledge orally, who had lived in connection with nature's cycles and seasons. They relied on their intuition, hereditary cultural knowledge and family traditions to choose the appropriate herbs and methods for specific remedies and cures. Whatever plant or natural item they used, they did so with the understanding of the balance and harmony between the community and nature. As healers, they held that balance.

Hereditary herbs of protection

Healers use certain herbs and plants, along with spell craft in their methods and rituals, because of their protective and powerful properties. Each family has their own preferred plants and trees for remedies.

Garlic/l'aglio (*Allium sativum*)
Garlic is a natural antibacterial plant that was associated with the ancient mother goddesses Ecate (Hecate), Ceres (Demeter) and Cibele (Cybele), who helped mothers in childbirth and passed on the mystical knowledge of special herbs used for ecstatic flights (flying ointments). Garlic was used to cure energy parasites such as *vermi* (worms) and protect babies, who would have a whole head of garlic hung around their necks. When harvested around the June solstice, it has the highest potency. It was used in *l'acqua di San Giovanni* (St John's water).

Lavender/la lavanda (*Lavandula*)
This is used mostly to protect against the evil eye, offer a good night's sleep and provide abundance. When lavender is gathered on the night of the witches (*la notte delle streghe*), it has the maximum effect.

Juniper/il ginepro (*Juniperus*)
Rosemary/il rosmarino (*Rosmarinus officinalis*)
Thyme/il timo serpillo (*Thymus vulgaris*)
Juniper, rosemary and thyme are used to purify the home through smoke cleansing (*suffumigi*) and ward off venomous animals. Placing their fine, needle-like leaves at windows helps to protect the home from negative energies.

Butcher's broom/il pungitopo (*Ruscus aculeatus*)
Fennel/il finocchio (*Foeniculum vulgare*)
Sorghum/la saggina (*Sorghum*)

Magic filter plants such as sorghum, also known as millet; butcher's broom, which looks like a short bushy holly; fennel; and other plants with similar fibres, are used as protection against witches entering the home because they have to count all the individual strands first. Hung in bunches or as a broom, they ward off evil. The *guaritrice* is also a *fattucchiera*, whose role is to break hexes and prevent the *malocchio* or negative energies from taking hold, especially in young children who are the most vulnerable.

Sage/salvia verbenaca (*Salvia officinalis*)
Sage could cure insect bites and promote fertility, and its smoke is used for clearings (keeping away bad spirits). It is the witch's sacred herb and a healer uses it to access her intuition and hone her healing skills.

Trees of protection

In Italian folk magic, several trees are considered sacred and protective. They play essential roles in rituals, healing practices and protective charms. Some of these sacred trees are:

Holly tree/l'agrifoglio (*Ilex aquifolium*)
Elderberry tree/il sambuco (*Sambucus nigra*)

Holly and elderberry trees are said to protect against *fatture* (hexes/evil eye). When branches are hung out in the shape of a broom bundle on the front door, this prevents witches from entering the house and was supposed to prevent miscarriages.

Hazelnut tree/il nocciolo (*Corylus avellana*)

The hazelnut tree is a symbol of regeneration and fertility. It is another weapon to keep out negative energies. Healers use its branches for water dowsing.

Fig tree/il fico (*Ficus carica*)

The fig tree is believed to possess protective properties. It is associated with abundance, fertility and healing. Fig leaves are used in purification and blessing rituals.

Walnut tree/la noce (*Juglans regia*)

The walnut tree is considered a protective tree in Italian folklore. Walnuts and their shells are used in amulets and charms for shielding against negative energies and the evil eye.

Pine tree/il pino (*Pinus*)

The pine tree is associated with strength, endurance and protection. Pinecones and pine needles are sometimes used in protective amulets and charms.

Bay laurel tree/il lauro or l'alloro (*Laurus nobilis*)

The bay laurel tree is considered sacred. Its leaves are used in various rituals, including purification and divination.

Apple tree/la mela (*Malus domestica*)

The apple tree is associated with love, healing and protection. Apple blossoms are used in love spells and charms.

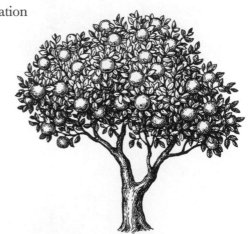

Almond tree/la mandorla (*Prunus dulcis*)
Almond trees are believed to bring luck and prosperity. Almond blossoms are used in rituals and celebrations.

Rowan tree/il sorbo (*Sorbus*)
Also known as mountain ash, the rowan is a protective tree in various cultural traditions, including Italian folk magic. It is believed to ward off evil spirits and negative energies.

Oak tree/la quercia (*Quercus*)
The oak tree is often referred to as the 'witch wood' for its protective properties against lightning. It is seen as a powerful symbol of strength and endurance because it can withstand severe weather conditions, including thunderstorms and lightning strikes. Some traditions plant oak trees near homes or in sacred areas to provide protection and promote security.

The oak's thick bark is resistant to heat. If an oak is ever burned to the ground, multiple shoots emerge. This fire-retardant tree acts as a green shield in front of your house, stopping embers from entering your home. As the fire passes through, fine embers fly and those trees that resist fire will help to stop those embers. Many trees will stop a fire because of the amount of moisture in the plant's leaf tissue.

Olive tree/l'olivo (*Olea europaea*)
The olive tree is deeply revered in Italian culture and folklore. It is associated with peace, fertility and prosperity, and is a symbol of longevity and divine

protection. Olive branches are often used in religious ceremonies and blessings.

Like salt, olive oil is used as a general cure for many ailments. If you have the *malocchio*, oil is dropped into water to remove it. Olive branches are used to protect the house from evil and lightning. When used in a *breve* (a small pouch) worn around the neck with salt, herbs, wolf's tooth and other amulets, olives fight off the *malocchio* and *fattura*.

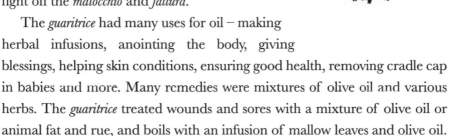

The *guaritrice* had many uses for oil – making herbal infusions, anointing the body, giving blessings, helping skin conditions, ensuring good health, removing cradle cap in babies and more. Many remedies were mixtures of olive oil and various herbs. The *guaritrice* treated wounds and sores with a mixture of olive oil or animal fat and rue, and boils with an infusion of mallow leaves and olive oil.

Witches' herbs

Rue, hemlock, belladonna, henbane, mandrake, wormwood – all these herbs are dangerous and can be lethal if administered incorrectly or the wrong dosage. Healers had the power of life and death. While a few small berries of belladonna can kill a child, the whole plant is deadly. Due to its hallucinogenic properties, this plant was used in witches' flying ointments. (For more information, see page 33.) There was a delicate balance of how to use it and how much to use – just touching belladonna can cause painful blisters and it should never be ingested. An experienced lineage healer knew how to use belladonna for other reasons – to induce numbness before surgery or relieve high fevers. For maximum potency, herbs were gathered on St John's Eve before sunrise. The ancestral healer knew who in the community needed which herbs and where to find them.

Healers today

Today's healers are discovering their environment is a natural pharmacy if one knows what and where to look. So many knowledge keepers are sharing their plant wisdom. No matter where you live, you can re-create the Italian herbal and sacred apothecary for magic and cures. Start planting the herbs a *guaritrice* would use, and gather local plants and flowers with wild crafting and foraging, while harvesting by the moon's cycles. (For more on foraging, wild crafting and harvesting by the moon, see pages 195–99.)

PART 2:

Practical magic

Chapter 5

Kitchen witchery

Traditionally, the path that leads to the kitchen was designed for easy access to the back garden. It was lined with lemon trees, geranium and lavender pots, and raised garden beds or tubs filled with bunches of flat-leafed parsley, rosemary, oregano and basil.

That was the way to my nonna's kitchen – her sacred space. It was filled with the aroma of home cooking and espresso coffee. It was not unusual to see her blessing the bread she baked, then throwing salt over her left shoulder for protection. If we had a visitor she suspected had given us the *malocchio*, she would throw salt around the kitchen and sweep it out the back door to cleanse the bad energy and purify the space.

In her cosy kitchen, garlands of garlic were strung around the kitchen bench to ward off evil spirits, curses and even the common cold. Hanging in the pantry were dried red *peperoncini* (peppers) used for protection, in cooking or tucked in a pouch as *portafortuna* (good-luck talisman) to keep the *malocchio* away. The *peperoncini* represented the *corno* (horn) that was a symbol of good luck in keeping the *malocchio* away.

Italian folk magic starts in the kitchen – this is where the real magic begins. It is the 'hearth' and 'heart' of the home; it is where love lives so it has incredibly strong energy. From this heart space, you can remove the *malocchio's* negative energy, create spells of protection, and use healing herbs for good health and well-being.

Building your folk-magic toolkit

Italian folk magic is not an organised or homogenous practice, so you don't need specific tools, equipment or rules to follow; however, you'll need some basic items if you wish to learn this ancient craft.

I always make sure I bless all the tools I'm using – the pots and pans, mini-cauldron, candles, ceramic bowl, scissors, knife, herbs, oil, saint medallions, key and straw broom – and I always remember to bless my hands by rubbing them with olive oil and saying a quiet intention to practise with integrity.

My shrine is dedicated to my ancestors and other unseen spiritual forces. I make offerings at the shrine, especially during family celebrations, feast days and death anniversaries. My nonna used to have a cauldron hanging on a chain in their open fireplace.

Straw/millet broom

I use my straw broom for banishment, cleansing, protection and as the threshold between worlds. I sweep a lot of salt with my broom! You'll find this type of broom at many garden centres – it looks like the stereotypical witches' broom. Keep it dry and for your use only.

Cauldron

In witchcraft, the cauldron represents the womb of the goddess, and holds offerings, sacred fire and more. I use my mini-cauldron to burn sage and sacred herbs, or for a protection spell that requires smoke cleansing. If you don't have a cauldron, use a special stainless-steel or cast-iron pot.

Utensils

Italian folk magic is meant to be simple, utilising whatever you have in the home. If you want to practise magic and not use your regular kitchen equipment, you can simply buy or find cast-iron pots and pans at second-hand stores. It's not fancy magic – you just need home-spun and home-grown utensils. Use what you have to hand – upcycle bottles and jars where you can.

Bowls

You'll need bowls to mix and hold ingredients when you create protection spells. Glass or glazed ceramic bowls are best for this because plastic absorbs oils, scents and colour dyes. I have a special white ceramic bowl as my *malocchio* removal bowl, which I use only for this purpose. I keep it away from all other crockery, and washed and dried individually with a special tea towel.

Jars and canisters

Dried herbs, incenses, resins, tinctures and infused oils all need to be stored, so using glass or ceramic jars are ideal. I use recycled jars, nonna-style. Keep clear glass away from the light and use dark-coloured glass where you can, to protect the herbs from fading and oils from going rancid.

Mortar and pestle

I prefer to use a stone mortar and pestle to crush dried herbs because it's easier to keep clean and its weight makes crushing easier. Get a reasonably large one – the small ones don't hold enough ingredients and create spillage – that's reserved for your use.

Knife and scissors

A sharp knife and scissors are essential to harvest, chop and prepare herbs. I use a pair of scissors to remove the *malocchio*; it's made of metal and is regularly cleaned and kept in a separate part of the cutlery drawer. You'll need a knife for some *fatture* (spells) and for cutting twine/string when hanging and drying herbs.

Candles

Use whatever candles you prefer – basic white candles, scented candles, tea-light candles or coloured birthday candles. I stick with using white candles. I'll decorate one with dried herbs, carving the name of the person I'm helping, and adding petals and whatever else the spell needs. But you can use any colour that has a special meaning or association for you. Of course, in the old days, they only had white candles, so they used herbs, flowers and oils to change the candle's intention.

COLOUR OF CANDLE	MAGICAL USES
WHITE	Multipurpose, blessing, cleansing, intention
RED	Energy, vitality, passion, health
GREEN	Money, success, growth, new love
BLUE	Healing, dreams, peace
PURPLE	Power, high spiritual connection
BLACK	Banishing, defence, strength

Cook with love

'Never cook in anger!' my nonna used to say. 'It will make the family sick.'

And she was right. Whenever I've cooked when stressed, angry or in a bad mood, the food doesn't taste the same. What's lacking is obvious – the love of food and cooking. The transfer of energy from the person into the food being prepared impacts those who eat it and the dish itself – its appearance, taste and texture.

Whenever you cook in a happy and cheerful mood, your food will turn out more delicious, but if you're feeling angry, frustrated, rushed or simply stressed (especially if you're hosting a dinner), the food won't taste anywhere near as delicious as it should. It's not a surprise that Italians invented the Slow Food movement, which promotes local and traditional foods that are made to be savoured in the company of friends and family – a direct protest against the hurried consumption of food (typified by the fast-food industry).

Bless your food

Our family didn't commonly say grace, but we blessed the food before serving it. Occasionally, someone at the table may have made the sign of the cross, but mostly the cook did the blessing – by giving the food her full attention and bringing love to it. My mother used to make the sign of the cross over any baking dish that needed to rise, such as focaccia, cake or pizza. Maybe it was a Catholic symbol of the resurrection of Jesus, or just a way to help the rising along.

List of herbs and their attributes

If you want to create magic in the cucina, focus on what you want to manifest in your home, then match this with the following essential herbs, spices and liquids in your pantry. (For more detailed qualities, see pages 69–73.)

COURAGE	Basil, bay leaves, chives, fennel, nettle, oregano, pepper
FERTILITY	Coriander, cinnamon, fennel, honey, mint, olive oil
LOVE	Basil, coriander, cinnamon, honey, lavender, oregano, rosewater, vanilla
PROTECTION	Angelica, basil, bay leaves, black pepper, cinnamon, fennel, garlic, mint, olive oil, oregano, parsley, peppermint, peperoncini (red peppers), rosemary
HEX BREAKING	Garlic, onion, rosemary, rue
PURIFYING	Bay leaves, cinnamon, salt, wine vinegar
SUCCESS	Bay leaves, mint, rosemary, saffron
MONEY	Basil, cinnamon, ginger, onion
HEALTH & HEALING	Angelica, coriander, chamomile, cinnamon, garlic, lavender, olive oil, poppy seeds

Kitchen essentials for protection

Herbs and plants are my talismans. They have healing, medicinal, protective and magical properties, and have been passed down for generations in my family and community. The basis of all Italian folk magic is using plants for their protective and medicinal properties.

The three most important items, which every Italian has in their home, are garlic, olive oil and salt. Most savoury dishes require one or all of these essentials. But apart from their delicious flavour, they also offer protection against the *malocchio* and other negative energies.

Other indispensable herbs mostly come from my garden to help protect myself and my family from negative influences, and offer medicinal benefits: basil, bay leaves, dill, fennel seeds, mint, oregano, parsley, rosemary, sage, rue, thyme and, of course, dried red *peperoncini*. (For a list of all protective plants and their properties, see Chapter 4.)

The essential magic cucina herbs

If you want to create magic in your kitchen, the following are the absolute essentials. As you use nature's bountiful gifts, you'll be blessed, refreshed, protected and nourished.

Basil/il basilico (*Ocimum basilicum*)
This bright green leafy herb never fails to enhance and flavour any food. Add basil to a ritual bath with rosemary and rue to break hexes and curses. Place basil on your windowsill and at your front door to remove negative energy. Add basil to the mop water for prosperity and negative clearing. To make a love charm, place a bundle of basil under your pillow to dream of your future love. Keep three leaves in your wallet to attract wealth.

Bay leaf/l'alloro (*Laurus nobilis*)
Use dried bay leaves for smoke cleansing instead of sage.
Add bay to your cooking to connect with the spirits.

Chamomile/la camomilla (*Chamaemelum nobile* and *Matricaria chamomilla*)
Use chamomile as a tea to calm nerves, aid digestion and help
you sleep. If you grow your own chamomile, boil it in a saucepan with hot
water, which gives it a much more intense flavour and effectiveness. If you
don't like the taste of chamomile, use it in a spray bottle with water when
cleaning your home for protection, or in bath water to attract or let go
of love.

Cinnamon/la cannella (*Cinnamomum verum*)
A great spice for prosperity and luck, add a cinnamon stick to a smoke-
cleansing bundle to cleanse your home and create a meditative space.

Dill/l'aneto (*Anethum graveolens*)
The dill's fine feathery leaves work like filters to absorb and remove *malocchio*
and other negative energies. Use it in cooking for courage and have it potted
near your thresholds (back and front doors) to keep out bad energies. Add
dill to your incense blend for deeper meditation. Add dill to sachets (*brevi*)
and use with spells that deal with love and romance.

Fennel/il finocchio (*Foeniculum vulgare*)
Hang bunches of fennel over your window and in doorways to drive away
negative spirits. Fennel helps with digestion when cooking with fatty meats
such as pork – that's why pork and fennel is so tasty and easy to digest.

Garlic/l'aglio (*Allium sativum*)

Hang a string of garlic in the kitchen to absorb negative energy and provide good health. You can grow your own garlic, then dry and braid. Garlic has antibacterial properties; one way to get its benefits is by soaking a few garlic cloves in oil.

Lemon/il limone (*Citrus* x *limon*)

While not a herb, it's vital to have one lemon tree or more in your garden. Add lemon juice to water for cleansing and purification rituals, which will absorb and break any negative energy. Dry and store lemon peels in a glass jar in your pantry for when you're out of fresh lemons – make magical potpourri and tea by adding orange peels (which are good for healing and prosperity).

Mint/la menta (*Mentha* spp.)

Drink an infusion of mint to relieve anxiety and revitalise. It's good luck to grow mint in your garden. My advice – grow it in pots because it overruns the garden bed. Use with mugwort for divination. Boil mint leaves and rinse your hair with the mint water to increase mental clarity and freshen your scalp. Peppermint is used in protection spells. Add mint or peppermint to a jug of water with ice cubes for a refreshing drink. Wash your front door with mint and water to cleanse it of bad energy and invite good fortune into your house.

Oregano/l'origano (*Origanum vulgare*)

Use oregano to flavour meat and tomato dishes for attracting love and wealth. It's easy to grow and dry. Oregano is popular in herbal infusions due to its healing properties – it is antiviral, antibacterial and antifungal. It is good for treating sore throats, infections, skin problems and digestive issues.

Parsley/il prezzemolo (*Petroselinum crispum var. neapolianum*)

With its high level of vitamin C, parsley is good on everything! Chewing fresh parsley will help with fresh breath, which is why it's used in Italian dishes that contain garlic. Make an oil infusion of parsley and use it to reduce the irritation of insect bites. Parsley is an ancient herb for warding off evil and communicating with the spirits. The flat-leaf variety has a more intense flavour and can be added to just about any savoury dish.

Red chillies/i peperoncini (*Capsicum* spp.)

Red chillies are from the nightshade family and resemble the *cornetto* (horn) that protects from the *malocchio*. Hung in doorways, chillies provide protection against the *malocchio* and break hexes. Use chillies in candle spells and charms to promote passion and love. Make your own chilli paste: add olive oil to chillies and preserve them in a glass jar for that spicy taste in your spaghetti arrabbiata.

Rosemary/il rosmarino (*Rosmarinus officinalis*)

Use rosemary for purification and banishing by adding it to a herb stick and burning it – rosemary helps with removing bad energies, breaking hexes and increasing your psychic abilities. Wearing rosemary (oil or a crushed sprig) or burning its essential oil will enhance your memory. Put a sprig under your pillow to keep nightmares away and remember your (good) dreams.

Rue/la ruta (*Ruta graveolens*)

The dark queen of herbs, rue is used in rituals and spells to deflect negative energy and hexes. It also enhances your intuition to receive spiritual messages. Hang sprigs of rue above entrances, and add to bathwater, sachets and amulets. Rue tea can help with stomach cramps and indigestion; used topically, its leaves can alleviate joint pain.

Sage/la salvia (*Salvia* spp.)

Use garden sage to purify and as an alternative to white sage. Bundle sage leaves with rosemary and use to smoke cleanse your home. Combine sage and salt and sprinkle over the front door to keep away the *malocchio*. Drink sage tea with a slice of lemon to calm your nervous system. As with all herbal and spiritual practices, treat sage with respect and mindfulness, recognising the cultural significance and symbolism associated with this revered herb.

Thyme/il timo (*Thymus vulgaris*)

When worn or slipped under your pillow, thyme will give you prophetic dreams. As a fumigant (smoke cleansing), it promotes good health and attracts fortune, love, courage and psychic enhancement.

Important note: while these herbs have historical uses in traditional medicine, they are not substitutes for professional medical advice or treatment. Always consult a healthcare professional before using herbs for medicinal purposes, especially if you're pregnant, nursing or taking medications.

Salt

No self-respecting Italian would omit salt from their magical tool kit. Salt is a cleansing and preserving agent, and it's so important when clearing your space. My nonna and zia threw salt everywhere – over their left shoulder if they spilled it to prevent bad luck, at the front door to stop negative people coming in, and on the ground to purify the home then swept outside. Ordinary **table salt** is fine to use, although you may wish to refine the type of salt when cleansing and banishing.

Rock salt is coarser; it's good to use outdoors and on thresholds where it won't wash away too quickly. **Pink salt** has a calmer, softer energy and creates a grounding effect. **Sea salt** is used to protect from psychic attacks, while **black salt** (sea salt with activated charcoal) is excellent in banishing spells.

There are so many ways to use this natural mineral that is part of our Italian heritage. Some say it's an ancestor with unparalleled power to cleanse, soothe and protect. I clean with it, sprinkle it, bathe with it, heal and protect myself with it, and use it in every way I can.

HOW TO MAKE BLACK SALT

Crush up and combine salt, activated charcoal, burnt herbs (choose protective herbs such as rosemary, oregano, sage and rue), black pepper and ashes from incense. Sprinkle the black salt around the four corners of a room. Place it in doorways for extra protection. (See also pages 216–17.)

Water

Used for blessings and purification, water is essential in *magia pratica* (practical magic). You can use normal tap water, but holy water is best. This is water that has been blessed by purifying the water with salt and praying over it, using any deity you are comfortable with. *Acqua di San Giovanni* (St John's water) is a batch I make for general blessings. I collect it once a year on St Giovanni's Eve (23 June). (For more information, see pages 270–76.)

Collecting rainwater or water from a stream or lake contains natural movement from the places it came from and can be used to enhance a spell. You can also leave water outside: under the full moon, it gains extra power and psychic ability, while under the sun's radiance, it gains vitality and strength when used as protection.

Olive oil

An absolute essential in any Italian household pantry is olive oil – it's the basis of Italian cuisine. You simply can't cook most dishes without good olive oil. It's been a staple of the Mediterranean people for thousands of years. Oil wasn't just used for food, but as a fuel source for lamps and for religious anointing – from kings and priests to baptism and before death. It is a magical elixir to work with.

Keep a separate glass bottle of oil for non-cooking purposes. I use organic, cold-pressed, extra-virgin olive oil from our olive grove, which was hand-picked the traditional way, and infuse it with herbs depending on the protection spell I want to cast. Store the bottle in a cool, dark place and let the herbs infuse with their essences. Shake daily and wait for a week or two until it reaches the desired strength. There is no right or wrong way to do it – trust your instincts.

How to make an oregano oil infusion

YOU WILL NEED

Fresh oregano leaves and stems
Carrier oil (cold-pressed, extra-virgin olive oil)
Glass jar, sterilised in boiling water for 10 minutes

METHOD

1. Gather a large handful of fresh oregano. Wash and air-dry it.

2. When dry, chop the sprigs and leaves, bruising them with a knife to release the oils. Place the oregano into a sterilised glass jar and fill three-quarters full.

3. Gently heat the olive oil (carrier oil) until lukewarm. Pour it over the oregano leaves. Stir the oil gently to coat the oregano. Allow to cool before sealing the jar.

4. Leave the oil jar in a cool, dark place and allow to steep for a week. You can strain the oil for a light flavour infusion to use on salads or in cooking, or you can leave in the oregano for a more potent remedy. Use it as an ointment for stiff joints, skin problems or gargling for a sore throat. (For more on how to use infused oil, see Chapter 7.)

Altars and sacred space

Traditionally, Italian folk magic practitioners don't have an obvious household altar as a magical display of spiritual practice. Most of us are limited by space and living with others. You don't need a grandiose altar. Instead, you can use a:

- ▶ special shelf or cabinet top in your kitchen or living room
- ▶ small footstool in the bathroom
- ▶ bookcase in the study
- ▶ planter stand
- ▶ windowsill
- ▶ corner of a dresser in the bedroom
- ▶ spot near the front or back door
- ▶ corner in the garden.

Some people love to create a grotto under a tree using statues of deities, such as Mother Mary or Diana, the three fates, or other fairy folk. This outdoor sacred space might have a small water bowl or bird bath or fountain. Perhaps it's simply a large stone in the dirt surrounded by your favourite plants. If you live in an apartment, set up a container garden on your balcony, or visit a place in your city park where you can achieve rebalancing and reconnection with nature. Sacred space doesn't need to be obvious to anyone but you.

My mother used a side table next to the large kitchen table. On it, she had photos of relatives who had passed on, a candle she lit daily, a small vase of flowers, a statue of Mary, rosary beads and a holy picture of Padre Pio. All these things meant something to her and let her connect to the spiritual and honour the ancestors. She also had extra items, including shells she'd collected from the beach, teaspoons with names from regional towns, a bottle of perfume and other random objects that were meaningful just to her.

I change my altar regularly. It's an old hall table I bought at an antique market. It's neither grandiose nor elaborate, and holds different meaningful objects depending on my spiritual mood and practices. Having a special place where you connect to your higher spiritual self means you can focus on and build up energy to protect your house and loved ones.

Keep your home and altar uncluttered. Your home is your sacred space; it's a place where you recharge and are nourished. If your home is cluttered and disorganised, it will reflect the energy you are experiencing and are operating from. Remove what you don't use. Change the décor with the seasons. Use colours that increase vitality, such as reds, greens and yellows, or blue for calmness. Clean your home regularly and purify it by smoke cleansing (burning garden sage/bay leaves or incense).

Smoke cleansing/fumigation

Always do smoke cleansing with the windows and doors open. Never do it too close to your pets and nowhere near babies, children or older people. If you have any breathing-related health issues, such as asthma, use alternative methods such as oil infusions or herb-infused water spritzes.

In Italian folk magic, smoke cleansing is called *suffumigio*, meaning 'fumigation'. *Suffumigi* are used for general cleansing and getting rid of *malocchio*, psychic fright and *fatture*. Traditionally, the healer gathered herbs from their local area and made them into bundles of fresh and dried plants. They are burned using a special method. The healer uses a ceramic or terracotta tile on which she places the herbs and embers (coals) from the fireplace. The herbs then burn and create smoke.

I typically use my ancestral herbs of rosemary, lavender and bay leaves, as well as sage from my herb garden because of its antimicrobial properties – this means it helps to ward off infectious bacteria, viruses and fungi. That keeps my house clean, fresh and cleared of negative energies.

I highly recommend drying your own garden sage to use on food and as a smoke cleanser. This is the simplest and quickest way: rinse the sage, remove excess water (I use a salad spinner) and dry it on a towel. Once it's dry, tie in bunches with red twine around the end of the stems, then hang upside down over a hanger (I use a clothes drying rack), out of direct sunlight. Leave it until fully dried.

For other smoke cleansings, I use a mix of dried and fresh herbs. This helps to keep the fumes down; peppermint and rosemary in particular burn more intensely. You can burn resins such as frankincense and myrrh in a metal or ceramic dish as you would incense.

Smoke cleansing your home will remove stale and bad energy and promote good energy. You are also performing a blessing with this sacred ritual. Burning sacred herbs and resins can cleanse a space energetically and physically. You can make your own herb stick using dried herbs from your garden and wrapping them in natural string or twine.

Here are some herbs from your kitchen garden that are alternatives to white sage:

- ▶ Bay leaves
- ▶ Cinnamon sticks
- ▶ Common garden sage
- ▶ Juniper
- ▶ Lavender

- ▶ Lemon balm
- ▶ Mint
- ▶ Pine needles
- ▶ Rosemary

Use rose petals or dried rosebuds for a lovely scent, adding love to any room.

> **Note:** *everyone is different and may have allergies to certain plants. If you notice a reaction to any herbs, stop burning them immediately.*

How to smoke cleanse your home with a herb stick

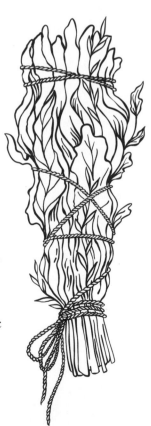

While there's no right or wrong way to do smoke cleansing, it's important to ground yourself first. Focus on your intention. Is it to clear out bad energy? Has there been tension or illness in the home? Have you been experiencing financial losses or breakages?

Use a lighter or candle to light the top of the herb stick. Allow the end to burn for a few seconds, then gently blow out the flame.

With the dried herbs smouldering, gently wave the stick around each room of your home. Gently wave it in circles so that smoke fills each room.

Always hold the stick's burning end over a ceramic bowl to catch falling ash and embers. As you visit each corner of a room, you may wish to say your intention out loud.

When finished, extinguish the stick by pressing it into the sides of the ceramic bowl.

If smoke cleansing your home isn't an option for whatever reason, you could instead use a spray filled with special herbs to cleanse your home's energy. Into a spray bottle filled with spring water (any pure water will be fine, such as cooled boiled water or moon water), add a sprig of rosemary, two sage leaves, some rose petals, 1 teaspoon salt, peel of one lemon and 1 teaspoon lemon juice. For a stronger scent, you may add some essential oils such as lavender.

JOURNALLING

Record everything in your journal and date it – your notes, recipes, rituals, research, spells, dreams, observations, sketches and other magical information that is important to you and your understanding of Italian folk magic. If you have Italian ancestry, your journal is where you can write down your family recipes and wisdom. It can be your very own grimoire (*il grimorio*).

What's your element?

Working with any type of magic means using the four elements – earth, air, fire and water. Before I began removing the *malocchio* and creating protection *fatture*, I noticed that when I used the element of fire, my protection and banishing spells were more powerful and swift to take effect. I'm comfortable with using fire because I appreciate its regenerative and cleansing powers. However, we need to balance the other three elements for our home magical practices. The kitchen is a mini-universe of magic and it's where our ancient Italian wise women practised their art. In our kitchens, we have fire (cooking appliances), water (taps and sink), air (exhaust fan/windows) and earth (food). Broaden your vista and look at the spaces in your home and neighbourhood where you can use these ancient principles.

Before you start any folk magic work:

▶ Bless your space.
▶ Have the right intention.
▶ Be in your integrity.
▶ Do no harm.
▶ Call in deities, saints, angels, spirits or ancestors to help.

Working with the elements

The four elements – earth, air, fire and water – are extremely powerful sources of energy that can boost spell-making and spell-breaking. Each element has an intrinsic power and has a specific relationship with magical purposes.

EARTH: TO CREATE

REPRESENTATION	Plants, trees, salt, stones, feathers, shells, dirt
HERBS/PLANTS	Sage, cedar, rosemary, rue
PROPERTIES	Healing, protecting, blessing, creating, feminine principle

Earth magic is one of the strongest forms – we use Mother Earth's apothecary for our health and well-being. To connect with earth, surround yourself with growing things, the scent of herbs and taste of spices. Tread barefoot in the dirt, listen to the sounds of nature, walk in the park and create a garden. Meditate with a focus of putting down roots to ground yourself and connect to the heart of the earth.

AIR: TO KNOW

REPRESENTATION	Wind movement in smoke, such as in smoke cleansing and incense
HERBS/PLANTS	Lavender, peppermint, anise, rosemary
PROPERTIES	Cleansing, protecting, banishing

Having knowledge means using magic wisely and with discernment. We are more than a conscious mind. Knowledge and wisdom are available to us if we open our minds to dreams, synchronicities and messages from the spirit world. To connect with air, take

a walk on a windy day or by the coast, where the breeze creates movement in the air and waves. Dancing and singing can circulate air in your body and create momentum. Hang windchimes or wind-catchers around your home.

FIRE: TO TAKE ACTION

REPRESENTATION	Candle or cauldron, pots, the colour red for passion and intensity
HERBS/PLANTS	Cinnamon, juniper, basil, peppers, garlic, nettle
PROPERTIES	Power, banishing, cleansing, creativity, protection, masculine principle

Fire is transformative and destructive. It is chaos and order. As we light our candles and remember our loved ones, fire is a conduit to the spirit realm. The cauldron from which we draw creative energy forms our desires and propels us to create. When working with the element of fire, know that it's quick to take action, so be sure of what you're doing when casting spells such as banishment spells. To connect with fire energy, light candles, meditate with fire, and light incense or herb sticks.

WATER: TO CREATE CHANGE	
REPRESENTATION	Bowls, jars and glass bottles of water
HERBS/PLANTS	Bay laurel, belladonna, chamomile, lemon, rose, thyme
PROPERTIES	Cleansing, removing curses, protection, creating changes, feminine principle

Water holds emotions, which is why using water and oil is an effective way to remove the *malocchio*. We use water for cleansing, blessings, purifications and initiations such as baptism. Water is in constant movement but, unlike fire, it's slow and steady. To connect with water, make herbal tea infusions, create oil infusions and perform bathing rituals to cleanse your energy and return you to balance.

The four elements are the foundation to magic and ritual because they are the root of all existing matter. Including them in your spiritual, magical and herbal practices will enhance all that you do energetically.

When cleansing your home, you may use some or all of the elements. I regularly bless my house with a smoke cleanse to protect me and my family from negative influences or spirits. My mother used to ritually clean the house on Catholic feast days. On New Year's Eve, she decluttered and scrubbed the house clean, removing the old dirt and rubbish to make room for the new. Christmas and Easter were big celebration days that required preparation for family feasts, so it was important to clean and tidy the house, and buy all the necessary ingredients for home baking and cooking. Like most children, I'd get new clothes for going to mass – the concept of newness and honouring our homes and ourselves was part of the ritual of these special feast days.

How to make a herbal blend protection for your house

YOU WILL NEED
Black pepper

Rosemary

Salt

Basil

Glass spell jar or sachet

METHOD

1. In a bowl, mix three parts table salt to one part each of the herbs and black pepper. As you do this, say aloud or silently, 'Protect my home and family from all potential harm, seen and unseen.'

2. Pour the mixture into glass spell jars or sachets hung near doors and windows. Sprinkle it under doormats or add to water when washing floors or the front door. Make sure you sweep up the salt mixture and dispose of in the rubbish bin.

3. If you wish to use the mixture on a candle, rub a little olive oil onto it. Then roll the candle in the herb mixture. Burn the candle in a fireproof container or pot. If using a bay leaf, write your intention on the leaf and burn it in the candle flame.

4. This spell uses the elements of earth (herbs), water (for a floor wash), fire and air (candle, bay leaf burning/smoke).

A witch's kitchen *benedizione* (blessing)

Bless this kitchen of air, fire, water and earth.
May all that is made here bring nourishment and healing,
and cause harm to no-one.
May it always be filled with love and magic.

How to hang your herb and plant bunches for house protection

Hanging a bunch of herbs and plants is a quick and holistic way to protect, bless and cleanse your home and those in it. Decide what fresh herbs or plants you need by setting an intention for your chosen spiritual or magical purpose – protection, blessing, cleansing, healing or other.

YOU WILL NEED

Plants and flowers (in odd numbers)

Red ribbon or string

METHOD

1. Gather plants with protective or healing properties. If you're not growing them in your garden, choose plants that are in their natural environment and free of pesticides. You can also buy them from a market but those you pick yourself will be energetically better.

2. Make an offering or say a prayer in your mind while harvesting or purchasing the plants. In Italian folk tradition, odd numbers are used for good luck, so choose five, seven or nine individual stems for your bunch. When planting ornamental bushes or trees in my garden, I use this odd-number method because it's geometrically more pleasing.

3. Tie the bunch with a red ribbon or string and hang them upside down. I do this with all my fresh plants – lavender, sage, rosemary all live upside down inside my large walk-in pantry. You can hang your bunch over doorways or your altar. After drying them, you can use them for smoke cleansing.

4. Say a prayer or invocation to ask for protection: 'May this house be protected from all negative influences.'

How to make protection oil

YOU WILL NEED

Carrier oil: olive (my favourite), coconut, jojoba, almond, vitamin E or other suitable oil

Herbs: basil, cinnamon, lavender, rosemary (or others of your choice)

1 small glass bottle or jar

METHOD

1. Fill a small glass bottle or jar with the herbs and add a carrier oil. Use fresh herbs where possible. Let your oil infuse in a dark space in your pantry for a few weeks, shaking it regularly. My last batch of oil had St John's wort, rose petals, peppermint and mugwort for enhancing intuition and protection.

2. When it's ready, dab the oil on your skin but do a patch test first. To anoint your candle for spell work, rub it in the oil, starting from the centre and moving to the ends.

Blessings for a new house

In Italian folk magic, blessings for a new house is not just important, it's essential. Usually the blessing is for newly married couples, so the notion of creating a family is enmeshed with the protection of a new home, bringing positive energies, prosperity and fertility to its occupants. In smaller Italian towns, people invite the local priest to go to their homes and perform a blessing with holy water for a new home and on feast days such as Easter and Christmas. This house-blessing tradition has regional and family variations, with some more influenced by Catholic symbols such as a saint icon or holy water, but the intention and method are essentially the same. St Joseph is usually invoked for protecting a new home. (For more information, see pages 260–64.)

You can perform a house spell to bless and protect a new home, bringing its inhabitants positive energies and prosperity. The spell typically uses symbolic elements, prayers and invocations.

How to create a blessing for a new home

YOU WILL NEED

White candle

Small bowl of salt

Bowl of fresh water

Olive oil (extra-virgin or pure)

Sprig of rosemary or basil (fresh or dried)

Small, clean cloth or cloth pouch

Small piece of paper and pen

METHOD

1. Find a quiet and peaceful area in your new home where you can perform the spell undisturbed. Light the white candle to create a sacred atmosphere.

2. Moving clockwise, sprinkle a pinch of salt in each corner of the room. Then walk around your home clockwise with the bowl of water, sprinkling a few drops in each room, while saying a simple prayer for cleansing and purification.

3. Stand at the entrance of your new home, holding the olive oil in your hands. Feel the positive energy and blessings flowing into the space.

4. Take the olive oil and, using your fingers, draw a small cross or any symbol you are comfortable with above the doorway entering the home. Recite a blessing or prayer, asking for protection, abundance and happiness to fill the home.

5. Hold the sprig of rosemary or basil between your palms. Focus on its energy and aroma, envisioning it as a symbol of abundance, prosperity and protection. Say a short blessing or prayer over the herb, infusing it with your positive intentions.

6. Place the herb in the centre of the cloth or pouch (also called a *breve, abitino* or *sacchettino*). Add a pinch of salt to represent protection and purification. Fold over the cloth or pouch to create a small talisman, sealing the herbs and salt within.

7. On the paper, write your intentions for your new home. Be specific about what you wish to attract, such as love, happiness, abundance or success. In the past, writing was not common; instead, people would recite a lineage prayer or incantation. Today, I prefer to write my intentions down, so they penetrate deeply within.

8. Holding the talisman and paper in your hands, close your eyes and visualise your intentions coming to life. Feel the energy of the spell growing stronger.

9. Find a special place in your home to keep the talisman and paper – hidden under a doormat, buried in a potted plant or placed in a drawer. What's important is that it remains undisturbed.

10. Thank the spiritual forces or deities you called upon during the spell for their guidance and protection. Express your gratitude for the blessings they've bestowed upon your new home.

> **Note:** the new house spell's effectiveness depends on your sincerity, belief and positive intentions. Italian folk magic embraces symbolism, prayers and positive energies to influence the environment. Customise the spell to align with your personal beliefs and traditions, and always perform it with respect and mindfulness.

Chapter 6

Herbal witchery

Plants and herbs are more than what we use in the kitchen – they can contain powerful properties. It's amazing to think that plants have survived for generations in their original state and all our ancestors used them, depending on which part of the world they lived. Today, we can all access these remarkable plants, dried or fresh, potentially growing them in our gardens. When using nature's apothecary, we need to be mindful of our intention – some plants are toxic while others are healing. Always remain in your integrity when using herbs and plants.

Glossary of herbs and magical plants

In this handy list of herbs commonly used in Italian folk magic, each herb has a brief description of its magical properties. Please note, the list is not exhaustive and the magical properties of herbs may vary based on regional traditions and individual beliefs. When working with herbs in any magical practice, make sure you research their properties, use them responsibly and respect the natural world. Always exercise caution and consult with knowledgeable sources before using any herb or plant. Some herbs may have medicinal properties or potential side effects, so be informed and use them safely.

ALFALFA	Money riches, favourable fortune, wealth attractor that draws money to you, expansion of wealth
ANGELICA	Dispelling, driving away, banishment, courage, protection
BASIL	Joy, love and affection, money riches, prosperity, protection, love, promoting harmony in relationships
BAY LEAF	Insight, wisdom, endurance, courage, success, divination
BELLADONNA	Psychic work, enhancing dream magic, astral projection
BIRCH BARK	Dedication, beginnings, guarding against psychic attacks, self-empowering
BLUE VERVAIN	Heart affections and love, astral projection, knowledge, growth and expansion
CALENDULA (MARIGOLD)	Success activator, increasing psychic awareness, dispelling negativity
CEDAR	Purification, protection, grounding, ancient wisdom
CHAMOMILE	Calming, healing, promotes sleep, relaxation, soothes
CINNAMON	Attracts and increases success, luck, wealth and prosperity, love, raises spiritual vibration
CINQUEFOIL (FIVE FINGER GRASS)	Its leaves have five points, representing blessings for love, health, wealth, power and wisdom.
CLOVES	Protection, banishing negativity, and promoting love and friendship

COMFREY	Protection; healing skin abrasions; safety and good health when travelling; preventing mishaps, theft and loss of belongings
DANDELION	Successful outcomes, enhanced psychic powers, prophetic dreaming, divination, wish fulfilment
DILL	Money, luck, sexual passion, protection, warding off negative energies and evil spirits
FENNEL SEED	All-round defence against evil spirits and malevolent forces, removing negativity from the home, psychic protection, cleansing
FRANKINCENSE	Spirituality, meditation, enhancing sacred rituals
GARLIC	Psychic protection, warding off evil spirits, cleansing
HAWTHORN BERRY	Good luck, fertility and love, happiness, connecting the heart and emotions
JUNIPER BERRY	Attracting love, increased visions and clarity, luck and prosperity
JUNIPER LEAF	Protection, clearing negative energy, removing spirits from the home
LAVENDER	Reducing stress and anxiety, relaxation, restful sleep, improving mental clarity, clearing and purifying stale air and stagnant energy, calming, sleep, attracting love and positive energy
LEMON BALM	Deodorising, freshening, purifying, cleansing energy and the home, psychic and spiritual enhancement
LEMON PEEL	Uplifting energy booster, aura cleansing, purifying, elevating the sensory body
LIQUORICE ROOT	Amorous love spells, amplifying passion and lust, heightening and strengthening personal power

MANDRAKE	Strong magic and spiritual properties; protection against all negative energies, entities, possessions, curses and hexes; enhancing magical workings
MARJORAM	Enhancing feelings of love, bringing harmony, easing grief, releasing emotions, attracting true love, calming
MUGWORT	Astral projection/travel, clairvoyance, perception, psychic capabilities, intuition, prophetic dreams, protection, dispelling negative energy
MYRRH	Purification, protection, enhancing meditation
NETTLE	Inner strength, removing and repelling curses and hexes, healing, purification, mothering herb of love and comfort, protection, banishing negativity, attracting abundance
ORANGE PEEL	Abundance, prosperity, luck, fertility, growth, success, uplifting
PARSLEY	Protection, purification, cleansing, clearing negative energies and spaces
PEPPERMINT	Cleansing, refreshing, soothing, healing, purification, relaxing, psychic development
PINE	Prosperity; success; good health; protection for the self, home and business
ROSE	Love, romance, charms, spells, female intuition, inner beauty and confidence, goddess rituals, associated with Mother Mary and Magdalene
ROSEMARY	Cleansing, purification, removing negativity, improving memory, protection, attracting love, relaxing for sleep
RUE	Warding off curses, exorcism, cleansing, clarity of mind, removing negative entities, protective charms (*cimaruta*)

SAGE	Strong cleansing and purification; dispelling negativity; protection and sealing of positive energy and vibrations to one's home, possessions, body, mind, heart and spirit; cleansing; purifying; removing negative energies; promoting wisdom
SANDALWOOD	Raising spiritual vibration, prayer beads and connection to the divine, ceremonial magic, meditation, boosts psychic powers, divination, strong protection against evil spirits and entities. Useful in exorcism spells and removing evil eye curses and hexes
ST JOHN'S WORT	Warding and fending off all evil intent, ghosts, evil and bad spirits and entities; protecting against and breaking curses, hexes, black witchcraft and black magic; banishing gloominess and depression; safeguarding one's home from natural calamities. Once used for exorcisms, it contains spiritual and mystical qualities and is connected with John the Baptist.
STAR ANISE	Clairvoyance, telepathic abilities, psychic awareness, prophetic dreams, good luck, successful undertakings, good fortunes. Representative of the cosmic stars (wishes upon a star) and amplifies the energy of moon-based spells and divinations. Wards off the evil eye and shields one from all harm.
THYME	Courage, strength, protection, purifying spaces, self-love, beauty, love and affection, attracting loyalty and true-heartedness in relationships. Used in all spell work with nature and nature spirits.
VALERIAN	Aiding restful sleep, calming and sedative, relieving stress and anxiety, quietening excessive mind chatter and over-wrought emotions. Also known as 'graveyard dust'.

VERVAIN	Bringing peace, love, joy and happiness to oneself; empowerment, purification. Used in celebrations, blessings, new beginnings, wisdom, knowledge and learnings of the 'old ways' and folklore magic.
WHITE WILLOW BARK	Heightening one's intuition, clarity and focus; removing negativity, bad intent, evil forces, curses and hexes. Used in all lunar spells and divinations, dream magic, healing rituals and spells.
WHITE SAGE	House blessings; increasing inner wisdom, visions and spiritual awareness; enhancing meditation; healing sadness, grief and loss
WITCH HAZEL	Comforting and healing; soothing emotional hurt, distress, sorrow and anger; healing emotional wounds; mending a broken heart; clearing away heartbreaking emotions
WORMWOOD	Psychic abilities, divination, contacting spirits
YARROW	Psychic abilities, protection, healing, enhancing intuition

Gut medicine

Our ancestors used many of the herbs and plants listed here for gut health and in cooking and drinks. They looked after their gut with medicinal herbs, but the common factor was bitters (*amari*) – bitter herbs and spices. These days, we tend to avoid bitter flavours; our brains interpret bitterness as a toxin, despite its potential medicinal properties. Just like a metaphor for life, in folk magic philosophy you need to take the bitter with the sweet.

Amaro

Traditionally, bitter (*amaro*) herbs are used to remove the *malocchio* and repel other negative energies. This is why they're known as witches' herbs. Not only are these bitter herbs good for gut health, stimulating the body's digestive system and promoting healthy digestion, but they are also believed to prevent intestinal diseases. Some bitter herbs target the liver and help protect its regeneration cells; they can also have carminative properties that help with releasing bloating and general toxins.

Amaro is a group of bitter Italian herbal liqueurs known for their bittersweet flavour. Amaro is made by infusing a combination of herbs, roots, spices and citrus peels in alcohol, many of which are associated with psychic and magical phenomena. Herbalist women used to create the herbal mixture, with recipes kept secret over many generations. Amaro liqueurs are traditionally used as a *digestivo* (digestif) taken after a meal to aid digestion. An *aperitivo* (aperitif) is taken before the meal to stimulate the digestive system – these are generally sweeter in flavour.

Amaro aperitivo (aperitif) and *digestivo* (digestif)

Campari and Aperol are both *amari aperitivi* made with bittersweet herbs, so they are lighter to drink and used in spritzers. Their red colour is appealing as a pre-dinner drink and is regarded as a lucky and protective colour, which wards off the *malocchio*. That's another good reason to drink these aperitifs.

My personal favourite *digestivi* are Strega, Sibilla and Centerbe. Strega liqueur is brewed in Benevento, the capital city of witches, and captures the aromatic notes of the Witches' Sabbath under the walnut tree. It's a sweet, bright yellow *amaro digestivo* with highly scented botanicals from saffron, mint and juniper berries.

Sibilla liqueur is produced in Le Marche and is a decoction of herbs, roots and barks prepared over a wood fire and sweetened with honey. A *sibilla* (sybil) is an oracle-teller – her prophetic power comes from the mysterious underworld. These elements create a magical and mystical experience for those who seek their medicinal benefits.

Centerbe liqueur, whose name comes from the Latin *Centum Herbora*, meaning 'one hundred herbs', contains about 100 species of wild mountain herbs, collected on the slopes of the Abruzzo mountains of Maiella and Morrone. Originally made from a secret recipe, it was later developed by a pharmacist in the early 19th century. Be prepared for a strong taste. Unlike the mellow yellow of Strega, this liqueur has an intense emerald-green colour and a high alcoholic grade. At home, we only drank a shot of Centerbe on special occasions because of its potency, but it's an excellent *digestivo*, infused with medicinal and magical plants traditionally used for purification, good health and warding off evil.

Amaro liqueurs can have more than 40 medicinal and magical plants. Everybody's favourite would have to be Limoncello – it is truly the drink of the gods on a hot summer's day. Its intense citrus flavour comes from areas in Italy where lemons grow on hillsides by the sea, like in Campania and Liguria. Folklore associates the lemon with love magic, perhaps because the lemon is both sweet and bitter (like love), and also with clearing negative energies. Most Italians have a recipe for Limoncello liqueur. It may seem easy with four basic ingredients – lemons, alcohol, water and sugar – but no matter how hard we try in our family, we can't capture the delicate balance of *dolce-amaro* (bittersweet) it requires.

Common Amaro herbs

Many Amaro recipes contain bitter herbs such as gentian root and wormwood, which stimulate digestion and support the digestive system. Chamomile and fennel have calming effects on the stomach and help alleviate indigestion or bloating. Artichoke leaf and dandelion root and leaf support liver function and promote liver health. Some herbs and spices used in Amaro are rich in antioxidants, and have relaxing effects and other benefits, such as anti-inflammatory or immune-enhancing properties.

These common Amaro herbs stimulate the body's digestive system: angelica, anise seeds, artichoke leaf, asparagus, bay leaves, bergamot, birch, calendula, cardamon, chicory, coriander, dandelion, dill, elderberry, elderflower, fennel, gentiana lutea flowers and root, hawthorn flowers, hypericum, ivy, juniper, lemon, liquorice, mallow, milk thistle, mint, motherwort, myrtle leaves, nettle, orange peel, peppermint, raspberry leaves, rosemary, saffron, tarragon, thyme, wild rose, wormwood and more!

Amaro is often associated with ancient herbal wisdom and folk remedies passed down through generations. In this context, it is not only used as a beverage for enjoyment but also as a symbolic or ritualistic element in various magical practices. It may be incorporated into rituals for healing, protection or spiritual enhancement, depending on regional customs. In certain practices, Amaro is used as an offering to spirits or ancestors.

Amaro is valued for its potential health benefits, cultural significance and connection to the natural world using herbs and botanicals. As with any herbal remedy or magical practice, use Amaro with respect, moderation, and consideration of your individual health conditions and sensitivities. Always consult with a healthcare professional if you have any specific health concerns or are taking medications.

How to make your own Amaro

The ingredients and proportions can vary, depending on the recipe and your preference.

YOU WILL NEED

1 large, clean airtight glass jar or container

1 bottle (750 ml/26 fl oz) high-proof alcohol, such as vodka or grain alcohol

Assorted dried herbs, roots, spices and citrus peels (e.g., cardamom, chamomile, cinnamon, fennel seeds, gentian root, orange peel, wormwood)

Sugar, maple syrup or honey (optional, to sweeten)

METHOD

1. Select dried herbs, roots, spices and citrus peels to create your desired flavour profile. Traditional Amaro recipes often include bittering agents such as gentian root and wormwood, as well as aromatic spices and herbs.

2. Place your chosen ingredients in a large clean, airtight glass jar or container. Pour the high-proof alcohol over the herbs until they are fully submerged.

3. Seal the jar tightly and store in a cool, dark place away from direct sunlight. Let the mixture steep for at least 2 weeks, but you can leave it longer for a more intense flavour. Shake the jar gently every few days to help the flavours meld.

4. After the steeping period, strain the infused liquid through a fine mesh strainer or cheesecloth into a separate container. Squeeze the herbs to extract as much liquid as possible.

5. Taste the Amaro infusion to determine if it needs sweetening. Some recipes call for adding a simple syrup made from equal parts water and sugar, or you can use honey. Sweeten to your preference and mix well.

6. Pour the finished Amaro into clean, sterilised bottles with tight-fitting lids. Store the bottles in a cool, dark place to allow the flavours to continue to meld.

7. For a smoother and more well-rounded flavour, you can age the Amaro for another few weeks or even months before enjoying it.

Warning: the alcohol content in Amaro can be high, so consume it responsibly. Feel free to experiment with different herbs and ingredients to create your own unique Amaro recipe.

Chapter 7

The *malocchio* (evil eye)

Much of Italian folk magic and healing revolves around the evil eye, *malocchio*. This is where someone can harm another person with their eye (gaze). The idea that a single glance or jealous intention can cause harm sounds like ancient magic, but the belief has never been more popular. Amulets to ward off the evil eye and curses from other ancient cultures, such as the Turkish *nazar* (eye) have become mainstream in the fashion industry and home goods markets, ranging from jewellery, clothing, towels and homewares. The *nazar* is universally recognised as a protection amulet. Italians have their own amulets to ward off the *malocchio*. (For more information, see pages 142–47.) Even in this high-tech modern world, amulets are used for protection.

Malocchio herb essentials for your pantry

These herbs are commonly used for protection against the evil eye and are found in most kitchens. (For more information, see chapters 5 and 6.)

BASIL	Basil is my favourite herb. Use it to cleanse your home by hanging it over your front door, putting it on your windowsill, burning the dried leaves, making a tea or using it as a floor wash.
BAY LEAVES	Burn the dry leaves to purify your home. Place a leaf under your pillow for protection and, in your dreams, to reveal the identity of who gave you the evil eye.
CHILLIES	Hang fresh or dried *peperoncini* in your kitchen to burn up and scare away the *malocchio*.
CLOVES	With their phallic shape, cloves can act like a *cornicello* to ward off the evil eye.
DILL	Dill helps to dispel *malocchio*-caused nightmares and insomnias. Holding dill in your hand is a natural protective amulet. You can carry dill seeds in a pouch with you or leave them under your pillow. Add some lavender for a relaxing sleep.
GARLIC	Garlic wards off all evil, including vampires. Eat it, hang it around your neck, place it in each corner of your house or simply hang in garlands in your kitchen.
LEMONS	Like salt, lemon halves or wedges will absorb negative energy in a room. Add lemon juice to your bath, handbasin or even drinking water to ward off the *malocchio*.
OLIVE OIL	Oil is a tool for divination and has anointed kings and been part of religious ceremonies since ancient times. You may wish to anoint yourself when removing the *malocchio* or bless yourself when you're feeling under negative attack energetically.

PARSLEY	Parsley is a staple in Italian cooking. Our family has always grown it in our garden to use when relationships are in trouble. To protect your relationship from the *malocchio*, tie a bunch of parsley with a red ribbon and place it under your mattress at the end of your bed.
ROSEMARY	Plant rosemary around your house or in a pot by the front door. Cut sprigs and place them under your pillow to remember your dreams. Use it for cooking or burn the dried herb to clear negative energies.
RUE	Rue is not common in my region, so I don't grow or buy it, but it is powerful when used in protective magic and hexes. Hang a sprig of rue on your front door and replace it regularly. Beware that rue can be dangerous for pregnant women because it can bring on a miscarriage and it's not safe for young children.

Smoke cleansing

Smoke is sacred in many cultures because it cleanses and purifies the energy fields that surround us, including our auric field (the energy that emanates from our body).

You can burn the following herbs and woods for removing negativity, protection and good luck:

- ▶ Herbs: basil, bay leaves, lavender, mint, rosemary, rue, sage
- ▶ Woods and resins: cedar, frankincense, juniper, pine, sandalwood

> **Note:** some people may have an adverse reaction to the smoke from these herbs. If you are pregnant, do not inhale smoke from any herb or plant.

What is the *malocchio*?

People often ask me, what is *malocchio* exactly? Is it a real negative energy? Can anyone fall victim to it? What are the consequences of being cursed? How do you break free from its negative influence?

The *malocchio* is a bunch of negative thought forms; this negative energy is transmitted to the recipient through a stare or glance. In other words, it's the belief that a malicious glance can 'curse' someone, causing them harm via physical symptoms, emotional issues or a series of things going wrong. The most common symptom is the sudden onset of a headache right after the *malocchio* was cast, but it can also manifest as stomach aches, feeling dehydrated or fatigued, things going wrong in your life, appointments getting cancelled, flights being delayed, feeling emotional overwhelm, erratic responses, and mostly a general sense of doom – that things aren't quite right in your life. In Campania, throwing the *malocchio* at someone is known as *jettatura* ('j' is pronounced 'y') and the person throwing it is a *jettatore*.

When a person falls ill, a way to explain the *malocchio* and other psychic causes is that there is a subconscious energetic transference. The eye can send and focus energy along energetic lines not visible to the physical eye. In rural traditions, spirits can weaken iron content in the blood of their victims, resulting in fatal illness. The psychic link between the sender and victim is so strong those fascinated (called *il fascino*) by the spell are unable to help themselves.

Compared to a *fattura* (spell) or *maledizione* (curse), symptoms caused by *malocchio* are typically mild to moderate. A mild case may be a sudden streak of bad luck, or objects flying out of your hands and crashing on the floor. Headaches, specifically behind the eyes, or swelling behind the eyes is a sure sign of the evil eye. Other symptoms include fatigue, depression, anxiety for no reason, obsessive thoughts and loss of focus. (For detailed symptoms, see pages 115–17.)

What happens when the *malocchio* is cast

The *malocchio* is cast in several ways. The most common way is when it's unintentionally cast by someone who gives you a compliment or praise. This could be verbally, face to face or even on social media. How many times do we feel we're missing out? Although you're happy for your friends to be travelling overseas, lounging by an outdoor pool drinking cocktails, part of you thinks, *It's not fair – I want to have it too.* These negative thought forms could be transmitted to the blissfully unaware holiday maker.

Beware of the following phrases. Although they seem positive, behind them lurks feelings of envy and insincerity. The supercharged energy is projected through the 'eyes' and hurled at the unsuspecting victim (who is distracted by the compliment). They let their guard down … and the *malocchio* is cast!

Congratulations on your beautiful new home! You must be so happy!
You look amazing!
What a beautiful baby!
I wish I could dance like you!

These types of compliments stem from insincere praise, because the praiser secretly wants to have those things themselves. They may have feelings of envy, greed or jealousy. That's why Italians are wary of boasting and bragging in front of other Italians, in case they're given the *malocchio*. We don't know someone else's emotional state, and their emotional wounds are likely to affect us and our health. Babies and young children are particularly susceptible to the *malocchio*; the easiest way to counteract its effect is by blessing the baby with '*Dio ti benedica*', meaning 'God bless you'. You can do this as many times as you want; it might be you as a parent or grandparent who unintentionally cast the *malocchio*, unleashing harm on the vulnerable victim. If someone else compliments a baby without the blessing, spit (dry spit is fine) three times while making the *mano cornuto* gesture behind your back. And never forget to have some amulets and red string tied to the baby's stroller or cot. (For more information, see Chapter 8, on page 167.)

They say the eyes are windows to the soul. So it is with the *malocchio* – some regions hold a belief that some people possess a natural evil eye and their gaze delivers negative energy. In the past, people with unusual eye colours were seen as harbingers of *malocchio*, especially if they had two different-coloured eyes, which suggested the person had black magic powers.

Another way the *malocchio* can affect a person directly is by intentional confrontation. This type of *malocchio* casting comes from someone who is jealous, envious or angry at you. They may perceive you to be successful, and have things they don't have – a relationship, job, financial security or good looks.

Consider this scenario. You are happy in your relationship, but your husband's ex-wife is still feeling angry, even though she wanted the divorce. Despite dating, she hasn't found anyone to have a committed relationship with … and maybe her ex-husband wasn't so bad after all. She blames you for 'having him to yourself' while she is all alone. She is jealous, bitter and resentful of your happiness.

You are at your mother-in-law's funeral, which the ex-wife is also attending, feeling she has the right to be considered part of the family. You can feel her eyes burning into the back of your head. She stares at you as she gives your husband an awkwardly long hug. She doesn't try to hide her envy – this intentional, malignant stare is more than enough to cast a powerful *malocchio*. She projects negative energy through the portal of her eyes.

What if your friend keeps joking about how many babies she can pop out, while you have been longing for a child and are doing IVF without success? Even though you might be genuinely happy for her, part of you is jealous and wishes it could have been you.

Anybody can intentionally or unintentionally give the *malocchio*.

How the *malocchio* began and why

The evil eye is a widespread belief spanning the Mediterranean and North Africa, as well as the Middle East and Central Asia – the eye of Horus, *hamsa* and *nazar* are all talismans used for protection.

So, why is the evil eye still a prevalent belief? And why does Italian folk magic centre around this one ritual?

The *malocchio* is essentially the 'envious' eye – an emotional response to feeling a sense of having 'limited good'. Historically, the good things in life were believed to be in limited quantity, especially in harsh times. So, the 'good things' you had were rationed; usually, they were at the expense of your neighbour. In times of uncertainty, when survival often depended on uncontrollable events like the weather, earthquakes and illnesses, people used beliefs and rituals to help explain and manage their environment. This gave them a sense of control over their lives. If the evil eye was responsible, they reasoned, they could use special rituals and words to remove it and guard against it in the future.

In the hot, dry climate of the Mediterranean, moisture was considered favourable because it meant fertility, whereas dryness was associated with barrenness. This also applied to the body – people regarded youth as lubricated (wet and supple) while old age was dry and brittle. Bodily fluids such as semen, milk and blood were symbols of reproduction and nurturing. Even today, terms like 'shrivelled up', 'dried up', 'bone dry' and 'washed up' reinforce the view that dryness is linked with a lack of vigour.

People who were in a state of wetness (fertility) were more vulnerable to envy and the evil eye, so it was especially important to protect babies, pregnant women, brides, nursing mothers and even young livestock. To protect against the evil eye's dryness curse, you had to dry-spit (making a 'p' sound with the lips three times) after admiring someone or something. This spitting action shows that you had lots of bodily fluids and were therefore fertile.

Traditionally, those with the most cause to be envious were thought to cast the evil eye deliberately. Therefore, people often avoided priests (who had renounced sexuality), hunchbacked men and women, and anyone with a disability that excluded them as desirable marriage material. In Naples, these people were believed to be the casters, or *jettatori*, of the evil eye.

Animals were also subject to the evil eye's curse. Especially in rural areas, envy was frequently considered to be the cause when animals fell to sickness or died unexpectedly. In agricultural societies, people's livelihoods depended on their livestock to survive. This was true for crops too. If your crops had a low yield or blight, the evil eye was responsible. Many pet owners today have an amulet or medal of St Francis (patron saint of animals) on their pet's lead or collar for protection.

Countless spells could ward off and cure the evil eye. Generally, many cures for the *malocchio* involved water. After dropping any of these materials – wheat seeds, salt, oil or molten lead – into a bowl of water, the diagnosis depended on whether eye forms emerged. To be cured, the diagnosis was essential as were specific prayers and incantations. Most rural Italian women could do this in the home because children were usually most vulnerable to a *malocchio* attack. Despite using amulets and blessings as prevention, more complex cases required a healer with specialist knowledge to intervene.

If you're not a lineage healer and want to learn how to remove *malocchio*, you may wish to follow the way of the *benedicaria* – using prayers and rituals in line with the Catholic Church. Alternatively, you may prefer to enlist the help of deities, spirit guides and ancestors with your own individual incantation.

Symptoms of the *malocchio*

How do you know if you have the *malocchio*? When is a headache just a headache? When is a series of bad luck simply a coincidence of unfortunate events? Maybe it's random fate that some people never get lucky, or maybe you have the evil eye.

The evil eye can manifest in many ways and its symptoms can indicate that you're its victim. *Malocchio* symptoms include both physical and non-physical manifestations:

Physical symptoms

- ▶ Headaches (sudden onset), especially when located around the eyes and temples
- ▶ Stomach ache
- ▶ Lack of appetite
- ▶ Hair loss (in clumps)
- ▶ Eye twitches
- ▶ Bruising (unusual shapes)
- ▶ Insomnia: unable to sleep for several nights in a row

- Itching: needing to scratch body parts that have no obvious sign of rash or insect bites
- Loss of sex drive or impotence
- Sore throat
- Yawning
- Sweating
- Teeth falling out or cracking

Non-physical symptoms

- Sleep paralysis
- Nightmares
- Feeling a high level of anxiety
- Panic attacks
- Feeling overwhelmed and sad
- Feeling overemotional
- Feelings of oppression
- Dropping/losing items
- Breaking things all the time
- Fighting with your loved ones
- A series of bad or unlucky events happening all at once
- Lacking concentration and focus
- Things getting delayed or events/appointments being cancelled
- Your bedsheets ripping

> **Note:** many of these symptoms may also be linked to medical conditions. If you have a persistent ailment, pain or trauma, you should always consult a healthcare practitioner first.

If the *malocchio* is sent due to jealousy of love, the afflicted person's symptoms will include inexplicable thoughts of attraction to the caster and cause disagreements with their current partner. The afflicted person will dream of the caster, so it's important to remember your dreams.

Other signs of the malocchio

- ▶ A dead bird outside on the windowsill
- ▶ Seeing more than one dead animal carcass on the road
- ▶ Finding dead fish in a waterway
- ▶ Blood in eggs
- ▶ Fruits that rot quickly
- ▶ Finding worms in your food
- ▶ Driving behind a funeral procession

How to diagnose if symptoms are due to the *malocchio*

As isolated ailments, these symptoms seem fairly non-specific and normal. So, if you have the occasional nightmare or miss a medical appointment, this does not point to the *malocchio*.

The *malocchio* is a spiritual sickness that presents as many different symptoms. In my view, it doesn't hurt to check if you have the *malocchio*. You'll know if you have it once you drop the oil in the water. (For more information, see page 120.)

If you want to know whether you have it, first do a simple diagnosis.

What are your symptoms? If it's a headache and you feel lethargic, that could be normal but if you can see a pattern or repetition where you feel unwell – both mentally and physically, you can pinpoint the curse. The *malocchio* usually presents as a pattern of loss of small problems that build into issues and make your life miserable. It takes time to find the source of envy – the clue is looking at your emotional state and recent events in your life.

Malocchio strikes us both at our happiest and most vulnerable times. You could be recovering from an illness when your spouse decides to leave you. Maybe you're working on an important project at work, but you lose your mojo halfway through, resulting in delays and obstacles. These are signs of the *malocchio*. Ask yourself, who is envious of my life and achievements? What have you done to protect these important things in your life? Have you boasted unintentionally? Who has the most to gain from your misfortune?

After working with the *malocchio* for some time, I've come to know the difference between random, normal events and ailments, and those that are not. Physical symptoms such as headaches, fatigue, yawning, falling or tripping over regularly, short bouts of recurring illnesses, and a general feeling of not being well that lingers for no apparent reason – all indicate a *malocchio* may be at play. Added to these physical ailments, psychological factors such as feeling low, being unable to have positive feelings, crying and disagreeing with others. People have described it to me as like having a dark heavy energy around that makes it feel impossible to move on with life. One young woman was having small car accidents: denting her car at the gate post, getting a flat tyre, breaking a door handle and losing her car keys. Another person couldn't keep a job for more than three months and had to move house because she couldn't afford to pay the rent.

These all point to the possibility of having the *malocchio*. As a practitioner, it's important to remove your judgement and focus on the negative work the *malocchio* is doing. Your job is to remove it and support the victim during and after the removal by having regular check-ins.

Before you begin

Take some time to ground yourself and let go of any personal worries. Sit in a quiet space or stand at the window and clear your mind. Rest your body and relax. Cleanse your space by decluttering, tidying up and cleaning, then smoke cleanse with your most powerful protective herbs – white sage, dried bay leaves and dried rosemary leaves.

Have the best intentions for the person you're healing from the *malocchio*. You may wish to remove the *malocchio* from yourself too. The preparation method is the same. Invite your spirit guides, angels or ancestors to help you. Our spirit allies, such as angels, saints, ancestors and deities, are ready to give us assistance from the spirit world. Light a candle to them and offer them gifts on your altar: 'I call on [name] to …'

Wash your hands and purify with salt by sprinkling it on the floor where you will be breaking the curse. Dab your hand with olive oil and anoint the other hand.

Say three times:

Bless these hands
May they heal and protect.

Removing the malocchio

Oil and water method

Using oil and water is the most basic and common traditional method to remove the *malocchio*.

YOU WILL NEED

Bowl of water (white ceramic is best)

Olive oil

Spoon or small bowl

METHOD

1. Fill the spoon with olive oil, then gently dip your index finger into the oil.

2. Recite a prayer or incantations of your choice (see following methods).

3. Let the oil drop from your fingertip into the bowl.

4. Inspect the water closely to see if the drops are intact or dispersed.

Removing the malocchio

(*FROM MY ANCESTRAL LINEAGE*)

This method of removing the *malocchio* is how my zia taught me. Her mother taught it to her and she to me; it comes from the region of Molise. I have only included half of the words because the rest are unique to our lineage and are what I now use. It's only when the healer is no longer practising that they will share the words with anyone.

Each Italian region and individual families have their own way of removing the *malocchio*. New elements may be added to the method over time, according to how the practitioner works best.

This method is easy and reliable and has yielded excellent results over time. I don't normally remove *malocchio* on myself, but know some people who self-diagnose and cure. Note that it has Catholic folk magic elements (*benedicaria*) in the prayers/invocation.

YOU WILL NEED

Cold water

Olive oil

White ceramic bowl

Small cup or tablespoon

Female key (old-fashioned key that is hollow in the centre)

METHOD

1. Ask the person to be diagnosed to sit at the kitchen table. If you are doing this remotely, make sure you have spoken to the person previously (for their voice imprint) and have a photo of them (for visual recognition) while you are doing the ritual.

2. Pour a small amount of oil into the cup or tablespoon.

3. Pour water into the ceramic bowl until three-quarters full.

4. Make the sign of the cross on yourself, saying, 'In the name of the Father, the Son and the Holy Spirit'.

5. Dip your index finger in the oil. Let one drop fall into the bowl of water at a time, with three drops of oil in total.

6. Watch how the water and oil interact. If the oil drops remain intact as three separate drops, the person does not have *malocchio*. If the oil disperses, they have *malocchio*.

7. Use the key to tap on the bowl in a cross formation. Rotate the bowl and repeat the tapping. The sign of the cross must not touch the same position.

8. While you tap the key, say the following invocation three times. I have used my Molisano dialect because ancestral words carry their own energetic signature.

Uocch' contra maluocch'
(Occhio contra malocchio)
Crepa l'invidia e schiatt' ru maluocch'.
(Crepa l'invidia e schiatta il malocchio.)

Eye against evil eye
Crush envy and banish the evil eye.

9. Using the oil and water from the bowl, make the sign of the cross on the person, saying, 'In the name of the Father, the Son and Holy Spirit'.

10. Drain the water down the sink or pour it in the garden where nobody will be walking over it.

11. Repeat this procedure three times. Each time you do this procedure, examine the pattern the oil makes in the bowl to determine if the person has the *malocchio*. When you have finished, make the sign of the cross on yourself.

UNDERSTANDING THE OIL SHAPES

If the oil drops maintain their shape and remain visibly intact, there is no *malocchio*. In normal chemistry, when water and oil are mixed they form two separate layers. Oil should float on top of the water because oil molecules stick together.

If the oil drops disperse and spread across the surface of the water, with the droplets getting bigger and bigger or mixing with the water, then the *malocchio* is present. If drops are in the shape of an eye or series of eyes, that is another sign of the *malocchio*.

If the drops completely vanish once they're in the water, this is a sign the *malocchio* is present.

Words to banish the malocchio

Zampa d'urs (orso) e cor di leone
L'occhi che vedono fanno pronto
Cresci, cresci malocchio malenato
Come un falso Cristiano
Al mare ti andiamo a buttare.

Bear paw and lion's heart
The eyes that see are ready
Grow, grow twisted/deformed evil eye
Like a false Christian
We will throw you to the sea.

METHOD

1. While saying the words, make the *tre croci, tre volte* (three signs of the cross three times).

Words to banish the malocchio (from Campania)

Malocchio calpestato a terra, lascia questa creatura.

Evil eye, trampled to the ground, leave this creature.

METHOD

1. Say these words three times as you do the oil and water ritual.

Removal method from Calabria

YOU WILL NEED

Glass

Water

Tablespoon

Oil

METHOD

1. Fill a glass three-quarters full of cold water.

2. Pour oil (olive or vegetable) onto the tablespoon. Dip your thumb into the oil and drop four drops in a cross formation.

3. If the person is *fascina* (bound by the *malocchio*), the oil droplets will clump then disperse in large dops on the water's surface.

4. Repeat the procedure until all the oil is used.

Note: this method has no prayer or incantation to recite. However, methods may vary in other parts of the region. All prayers and incantations are passed down through oral tradition; therefore, nothing is in writing to ensure accuracy or consistency. The words themselves are not important; what really counts is the intention and power behind the action and the meaning.

Make sure you dispose of the water and oil in a place where nobody will step on it, because it's bad energy. In our Molisano tradition, the water used to be thrown into the fireplace hearth.

Removal ritual from Le Marche

As was the norm, the *malocchio* ritual from the Le Marche region was handed down to the women in the family. A friend from Le Marche shared her family's story with me. Her paternal grandmother, who was both a healer and midwife, taught the method to her oldest daughter. The older sister then passed down the ritual to her youngest sister before she left for Australia, so the tradition would continue. This is a perfect example of the continued influence of ancestors despite the Italian diaspora and assimilation process.

YOU WILL NEED

Olive oil

Metal spoon

Luma (little lantern with a wick)

Water

Bowl

Salt

METHOD

1. Place some olive oil on a metal spoon or *luma*. Light the *luma* to heat the oil.

2. Place a shallow amount of water in the bowl with a sprinkle of salt.

3. Dip your index finger in the oil, holding finger downwards so oil drops slowly into the water.

4. Once a droplet hits the water, observe the oil to check for *invidia* (envy from the *malocchio*). *Invidia* is present when 'eyelets' of oil spread and multiply in the water. Intense *invidia* eyelets can sometimes spark or jump.

5. Make the sign of the cross on the person's forehead, heart, arm, legs and upper back while reciting special words (not spoken out loud). This is the *segnatura* healing method. (For more information, see pages 49–50.)

6. Continue the ritual until the oil remains in a single drop without spreading. If a person has a lot of *invidia,* repeat the ritual the next day or the day after.

7. As per lineage healing tradition, the words used in ritual are generally not shared with others unless the tradition passes on to the next person/healer.

Yawning and prayer with malocchio

When yawning is one of the symptoms of the *malocchio* being cast, there is a *benedicaria* way of finding out who sent it to you. This way to reveal the *malocchio* caster was given to me by a friend from Basilicata.

The victim of the *malocchio* says these two well-known Catholic prayers: the Our Father and Hail Mary. If they yawn while saying the Our Father, the person responsible for giving the evil eye is a man, and if they yawn while saying the Hail Mary, the person is a woman.

The power of three

Place a bowl over the person's head. Make the sign of the cross over the bowl then recite the following incantation:

Chiamo la Madonna e Gesù Cristo. [Name of the person who is affected] si sente male [Saint name] aiutami. Caccia che m'guardato storto.

I call Mary and Jesus Christ. [Name of the person who is affected] is feeling unwell. [Saint name], help me. Throw out the one who gave me this evil stare.

Benedicaria prayers for removing the malocchio

The *Sub Tuum Praesidium* is the oldest known prayer to Mary. It is used in special Catholic rituals and also for removing *malocchio* from children and pregnant women.

We fly to thy protection,
O Holy Mother of God;
Do not despise our petitions
in our necessities,
but deliver us always
from all dangers,
O Glorious and Blessed Virgin.

Prayer to the Holy Spirit

Uno mi ha ferito.
Tre mi hanno salvato.
Mi hanno guarito le tre persone della Santissima Trinita': Padre, Figlio e Spirito Santo

One has hurt me.
Three have saved me.
The three persons of the Holy Trinity have healed me: Father, Son and Holy Spirit.

Touching the forehead to detect the malocchio

This is the simplest way to detect the evil eye. The practitioner places the palm of their right hand against the forehead of the affected person. Standing behind the person and avoiding their eyes, the practitioner says her prayer or incantation. If either the practitioner or person yawns, or their eyes begin to feel watery, the evil eye is present.

Charcoal method from Campania

YOU WILL NEED

charcoal disc

censer

frankincense

METHOD

1. Light a charcoal disc and place it in a censer. (You can make one by using an empty bean or tomato can and a piece of wire.)

2. Place a pinch of frankincense on the charcoal and allow to burn. When a generous amount of smoke appears, open the windows and let smoke cleanse your house, reciting this incantation:

> *Uocchie, maluocchie e frutticiell' e ll'uocchie,*
> *Aglio, fravaglio, fattura ca nun quaglia,*
> *Corne e bicorne, cape'e alice e cape d'aglio.*
> *Scio', scio' ciucciuve'.*

> *Eyes, evil eyes and iris round and coloured as small fruits,*
> *Garlic, small fishes, cure which can't be worked out,*
> *Horns and double horns, head of anchovy and clove of garlic.*
> *Shoo, shoo, bird of ill omen.*

Coal and water method from Abruzzo and Molise

YOU WILL NEED

Cooled coals

Bowl

Water

METHOD

1. Take cooled coals from the fireplace or outdoor fire. Place three small pieces of coal in a white ceramic bowl filled with water. Drop each one individually.

2. If the coal pieces sink to the bottom, the *malocchio* is present. If they float, there is no *malocchio*. If some sink and others float, it's best to assume some level of *malocchio* is present. You may use the same technique with the water and oil method previously described.

Matches and water method

YOU WILL NEED

3 matches

Bowl of water

METHOD

1. Light the first match. Focusing on the flame, say the name of the person with the *malocchio* or the situation needing a remedy. Toss the match into a bowl of water.

2. Light the remaining two matches and drop them into the bowl.

3. Wait for a few minutes then look in the bowl to see how the spent matches are placed.

4. If the matches are clumped together, crossed over one another or have all sunk to the bottom of the bowl, the *malocchio* is present. If the matches are spread out or have stuck to the sides, the evil eye is not present.

Water and wheat method

YOU WILL NEED

Grains of wheat or similar

Glass of water

METHOD

1. Water and wheat can be used in the same way as the water and
    olive oil method. Each healer will use their own method of prayers,
    incantations or blessings and make a mark on parts of their bodies.
    To check for the *malocchio*, a single grain or grains (odd numbers of
    up to 11 grains), are dropped into a glass of water.

2. If the grain or grains lie horizontal in the water, the *malocchio* is not
    present. If the grain(s) are vertical, the evil eye is present.

Ovomancy – using eggs

A common practice is using eggs as a form of negativity cleansing and removing the evil eye. The egg is believed to absorb and capture negative energies, which allows the healer to read the patterns formed within the egg to diagnose the type of *malocchio*.

Egg and water method

This is the same method as the water and oil, except with the egg being substituted for oil.

YOU WILL NEED

Glass of water

Egg

METHOD

1. Fill up a glass of water at room temperature.

2. Set an intention or say a prayer if you're using *benedicaria*: 'With this cleanse, may all toxic energy be absorbed and removed from their body.'

3. Run the egg over the person's head, ears and face, or anywhere else on their body that needs healing in small circles. Move from head to toe slowly and calmly to focus on releasing negative energy.

4. Crack the egg open carefully and drop its contents into the glass of water. Some prefer using warm water to see more clearly. The egg white will spread and form shapes in the water, and the yolk may remain intact or disperse in patterns (just like the water and oil method). Let the egg settle for about 5–10 minutes.

5. Look through the glass from the side not above. Observe the patterns and shapes formed by the egg white and yolk in the water. These

formations hold messages and insights relating to the person's well-being, health or spiritual state. Based on patterns you observe, you can interpret whether the person is affected by the evil eye or if any negative influences or energies are at play (see the following box). Then you can offer advice on protective measures needed.

6. Flush the egg and water down the toilet.

Egg on body method

YOU WILL NEED
Egg at room temperature (free range if possible)

METHOD

1. Roll an egg all over a person's body so it can absorb the negative or toxic energy within that person. Pay special attention to any area they say feels painful or uncomfortable.

2. After doing this with the egg for about 10 minutes, crack the egg and throw it down the toilet, flushing away its remains. The negative energy is now gone.

MEANING OF EGG SHAPES

BUBBLES	Large bubbles suggest the egg has absorbed a lot of negative energy.
COBWEBS IN THE WHITES	You're tangled in a confusing situation (web of deceit).
FACE	Seeing a face in the yolk means someone is envious of you and potentially has given you the evil eye.
NEEDLES OR SPIKES	People around you are taking away all your energy.
SNAKES	These are always considered an ill omen and warn of danger or gossip.
WEDDING DRESS	This could mean a special event like a wedding or that a woman has cast the evil eye.
NORMAL	If the water and egg look normal, there is no negative energy or *malocchio* present

There are numerous regional variants when it comes to removing the *malocchio* – secret words (*scongiuri*), prayers, incantations, tools and formulas have been passed down through family lineages and kept secret. The power of the words and ritual was in the cultural tradition and lineage that was passed down, which meant a great deal to the healers in a particular community.

If you wish to remove the *malocchio*, the words, intention and method should appeal and resonate with your personal belief system, while also respecting the traditional ritual.

Who gave me the *malocchio*?

You will need to trace back your movements from when you first felt the *malocchio's* symptoms. Who was the last person you met and what was the conversation about? Where in your life has there been ongoing tension? Who stands to gain from your stress? Although the *malocchio* is mostly not intentional, I always delve deeply into my relationships with those around me to understand what may be missing in someone's life – what do they feel is scarce and that I have in abundance?

Healers who can understand evil eye shapes and their meanings are specialists in this area and can tell someone who has cast the *malocchio* and other details. While I don't have this expertise, I can work out who has cast the *malocchio* by studying the shapes of the oil drops in the water.

EMBRYO AND YIN AND YANG SHAPE	The victim had the *malocchio* from her boyfriend's mother, who did not approve of their relationship and didn't think she was good enough for her son. The shape suggested a curse (evil eye) for the victim not to get pregnant, so she would go and seek another partner elsewhere.
LOT OF SMALL EYES	This case suggested the *malocchio* was cast by a woman who had lots of small envies. Small circles and jewellery motifs suggest the *jettatore* is a woman, but my interpretation was also of small daily envies. The caster was someone the victim knew and had weekly contact with, who always commented on something she 'liked' about the victim's house, husband, children or job.
SNAKES	This shape demonstrates that envy is intense (poisonous) and dangerous to the victim, but it could also point to sexual jealousy. Sometimes it could suggest that the *jettatore* is a man or the envy is over a man.

Each practitioner/healer will have their preferred method in working out what part of the victim's life is being impacted, and who was most likely to be the *jettatore*.

How do I know the *malocchio* is gone? How do I stop it coming back?

With the oil and water method, repeat the ritual until the 'eyes' in the water are normal. Continue praying and asking for help until the affected person yawns, sneezes or begins to cry unexpectedly. This is a visible emotional release of the built-up negative influence. The energy should be lighter, and the victim should feel immediate improvement.

If the person is not present, return to the bowl with oil and water. Using a sharp, pointed knife or a pair of scissors, stab and slash through the oil. Repeat until the oil and water are mixed and the small eyes (oil droplets) no longer appear. That means the *malocchio* has 'burst'. You've burst its evil stare. You might say an incantation like: 'May this blade cut through the eyes of the *malocchio* and never return.'

Pour the water and oil down the kitchen sink then wash out the bowl and dry it. Do the ritual again to test if the *malocchio* has gone.

I have a special bowl for *malocchio* removal, which is energetically cleared each time and will not affect me or my family. I would be worried if I 'ingested' any negative energy from a bowl in which I served food.

The best way to know if the *malocchio* has been removed is if the person is feeling better, with a renewed sense of energy and purpose and a general sense of 'lightness'. Some use a pendulum to get a 'yes' or 'no' answer on whether the *malocchio* is gone.

Protection against the *malocchio*

Amulets and charms can be worn as protection against the *malocchio*. Each one works a little differently, but they all stop the evil eye from targeting you.

Some people wear charms and pendants daily as their primary source of protection. In this case, you should select a charm that is sturdy, such as gold, silver, bone or coral. You may wish to carry additional charms in your pocket or wallet, pin them to the visor of your car, attach them inside your clothing, or hang them on a keychain.

The most popular evil eye amulets are *cornicello* (little horn); *mano cornuta* (horned hand); *mano fica* (fisted hand) and *cimaruta*. (For full descriptions, see pages 157–59.)

Wear something protective at all times – tie a small bow or red ribbon to your undergarments, wear red clothing or jewellery whenever you can, or apply red lipstick or nail polish. Keep rosemary sprigs in your bag, next to your phone, near your bed and in your car. Do you have a saint medal you can use in your car or on the key ring?

Men can touch or grab their crotch after receiving a compliment, especially one relating to their health and virility.

The *breve* or *abitino* is a small pouch you carry with you, put under your pillow or mattress, or keep in your home. Fill it with any of these protective items:

▶ 3 pieces of grain
▶ 3 pinches of salt
▶ 3 pebbles collected from the middle of a crossroad
▶ 3 pieces of blessed palm or olive leaf (usually blessed on Palm Sunday)
▶ 3 pieces from an Easter candle from church

Protection for children

▶ Give your loved ones a protective pendant. Children can have a protective charm or saint's medallion pinned inside a piece of clothing.

▶ For babies, a protective item could be pinned to their pram or stroller.

▶ Tie a piece of red string into a bow or knot then pin it inside your child's clothing. Adults can pin a red ribbon underneath their clothing or wear it as a bracelet.

▶ Sprinkle a little salt around your child's bed and inside their pockets.

▶ Place a clove of garlic in each corner of your child's bedroom to smash negative vibes.

▶ Unicorns, reindeers and other horned stuffed animals are a good substitute for the *cornicello* and keep away the evil eye.

Protecting your home

▶ Scatter salt on your front doorstep or under your door mat. Sweep it away from the house weekly. This will remove any negative energy absorbed in the salt from your house.

▶ Hang braided garlic and a bunch of chillies in the kitchen, preferably near the window.

▶ Place a mirror near the front door, so it is seen immediately upon entering. This will reflect the evil eye and it won't get the opportunity to enter.

▶ Instead of knocking on wood, touch a piece of iron.

It's more difficult to protect your office without the objects being visible, but I have some amulets on my desk for protection (containing black tourmaline to ward off evil), an Archangel Michael medallion in my drawer, and dried or sometimes fresh rosemary leaves in my work bag. Whatever it takes.

Make sure you extend all your protection remedies to your material possessions – cars, bicycles, motorbikes, scooters, tractors, ride-on mowers, caravans, or boats – by hanging medallions, charms, amulets, charm bags and anything else that repels bad energy.

Malocchio herbs and remedies

To help protect those from whom I've removed the *malocchio* and to generally keep the *malocchio* away, I use these herbs: basil, bay leaves, garlic, mint, parsley, rosemary and sage. The following recommendation is for someone who has been experiencing bad headaches, depression, things in the house breaking and a feeling of doom.

These are just some things I do because I believe they work, but you do it your own way that makes sense to you. If your mind or that of the victim thinks it's being protected and that you can 'fight' back these envious people around you, then you will change your perspective and become stronger in your power. It doesn't matter if you believe it or not, it's based on negative energy and when we are feeling vulnerable, tired or deflated, people's envy can penetrate through our conscious minds and cause us all sorts of grief. As long as you can shift your energy and be in your power, things will start to improve.

How to use herbs to remove malocchio

YOU WILL NEED

Sea salt or Himalayan sea salt (not iodised or table salt)

2 pots of basil (supermarket ones are fine)

Fresh rosemary

Dried bay leaves

Dried sage stick (optional – can use the bay leaves instead)

METHOD (SALT)

1. Keep the salt next to your bed for seven days, changing nightly.
    It doesn't have to be much salt. Dispose of the salt in the bin.

METHOD (BASIL)

1. Place one pot of basil at the entrance of your home (inside the front door) and one on your kitchen window – this is for protection. After seven days, you can consume as much basil as you want until it's finished. I love basil on my windowsill all year round.

2. Infuse basil leaves to drink as a tea. Have one cup a day for seven days. Use three basil leaves for each drink until you get accustomed to the taste. If you don't like it, don't drink it. You can use the basil infusion as a foot wash or face wash instead.

3. To make basil tea, pour boiling water over a normal tea bag (green or black tea). Add three basil leaves and immerse. Take out the tea bag. Leave basil leaves steeping for longer. You may add sugar, lemon or flavouring.

4. Basil not only protects you from negative energy, but it also gets rid of what you no longer need in your life (especially people) and helps with depression.

METHOD (ROSEMARY)

1. Buy a rosemary plant or fresh bunch from your greengrocer. Put one sprig of rosemary under your pillow for seven nights. It will calm your nervous system.

2. To make rosemary-infused oil, pour extra-virgin olive oil into a small jar and add three or four sprigs of rosemary. Leave it overnight. Rub the infused oil on your temples. This will help with headaches. You can also use the oil as a salad dressing or in cooking.

3. Rosemary is a powerful herb for protection against evil, memory and restoration; it cleanses the spirit and helps to relieve stress.

METHOD (BAY LEAVES)

1. Bay leaves are highly regarded as cleansers of bad energies, promoting achievement and success. Bay will protect your home and your romantic relationship.

2. To use bay leaves, burn dried leaves (one leaf at a time) in a saucer, letting the smoke move around in each room of the home. It's similar to sage because it is a purifier. You can do this once at the beginning of the week and once at the end (twice in seven days is enough).

3. When you cleanse your home with bay leaves or herb stick, say these words of protection or choose your own words:

May this space be cleansed and blessed,
And may all those who dwell here be protected.
I now release into smoke all the bad energies and negativities in my life.
I fill myself with love, good health, and positive energy.
So it shall be.

Is the *malocchio* still real today?

The *malocchio* is not an outdated concept or an old wives' tale. I have lived experience, and don't doubt that negativity is sent from multiple sources daily, especially since we live in a world filled with stress and uncertainties. I carefully avoid feeling envious if I'm on social media because we all know people post only the best parts of their lives. I believe negative thought forms exist and the stronger the emotion, the more harmful it is to the person it is aimed at. Just like people experience emotional heartbreak as a physical manifestation, resulting in broken heart syndrome, it's not a stretch to believe that negative emotion can have a detrimental effect too.

We're all capable of giving and receiving the evil eye. It is disconcerting to think that something as normal as a person's 'glance' can affect us, and that we cannot control that person's emotions or thoughts. All we can control is how we choose to protect ourselves from this toxic energy. One way is to be informed and learn the practices and techniques our ancestors used to keep ourselves as safe as possible, and to empower ourselves by choosing not to be part of the 'comparison' game where resentment and jealousy eventually manifest into something that harms someone's well-being.

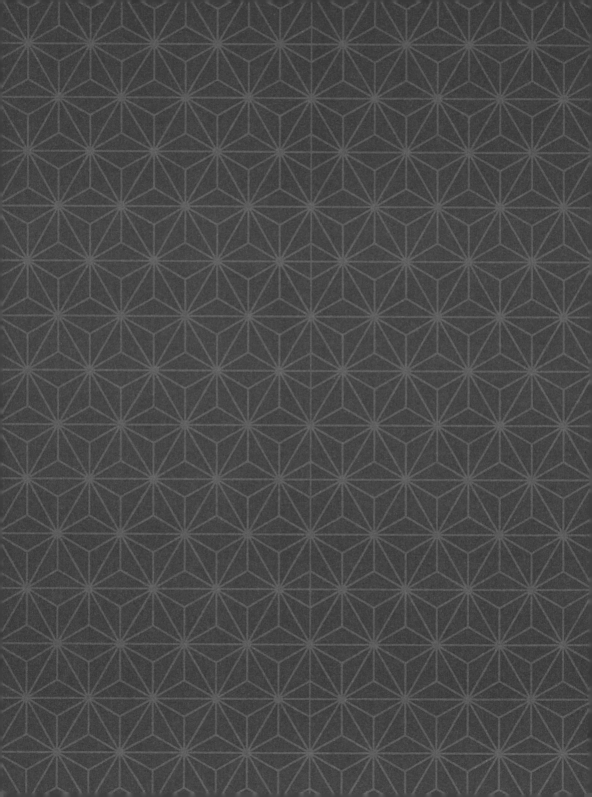

Chapter 8

Portafortuna – charms, amulets and superstitions

We wear charms, amulets and talismans as symbols of what is meaningful to us at a particular time in our life – charms with animals; 21st birthday key symbols; faith, hope and love symbols; a cross; saint medallions; precious stones with special significance; religious and culturally significant charms; and personal charms that comfort and protect the wearer.

Charms and amulets aren't unique to Italian folk magic – people have used them since prehistoric times to ward off evil, bring luck and protect the wearer from harm in deflecting attacks of negative energy. Talismans are slightly different in that they are worn to 'attract' good luck, health, abundance and desired outcomes.

In Italian folk magic, amulets were designed to protect babies, nursing mothers, pregnant women, farm animals, the family and the home. People lived in close relationship with the natural world. For survival, this meant having fertility, children, good health to work on the land and enough food to eat – all without evil spirits and negative energies endangering their way of life. Understandably, their amulets and talismans were from nature with symbols of their world – iron, salt, trees, branches, dirt, flowers, stones, herbs, corals and animals.

In a traditional Italian household today, warding off the *malocchio* is the highest priority; protection from its negative energy is key to a stress-free life. Many amulets, charms and talismans are readily available to all who seek protection from the evil eye.

If you're wearing a charm every day to ward off the evil eye, then choose gold, silver, horn or bone – these hardy materials can be worn any or all the time. Some occasionally use charms but have additional protection at home, such as holy water, garlic, herbs, chillies, altars and holy pictures. Many have protective charms on their key rings, in their car or in their wallets. And if you don't have any charms handy, you can make hand gestures behind your back, such as the *mano cornuta*, to keep yourself safe from the *malocchio*.

In the kitchen

You may see braided garlic hung in the pantry, by the front door or (as my parents did) in the garage. As well as having protective properties against evil spirits, *malocchio* and spells *(fatture)*, garlic has medicinal benefits that assist in protecting against viruses and bacteria.

HERBS	Basil, oregano, parsley, rosemary and rue are my go-to *malocchio* herbs. I put fresh herbs in pots on the windowsill or by the front door, or more conveniently dried bunches on the wall or in the pantry. You can use these herbs in several ways for the best possible outcomes against the *malocchio*. (For more information, see pages 144–47.)
HOLY OR BLESSED WATER	Holy water is usually blessed by a priest or comes from a holy pilgrim site, such as Lourdes. You can also make blessed water at home from flowers like *Acqua di San Giovanni* (St John's Water) or medal water, which uses a saint to inspire the blessing. Both methods promote blessings and good energy. When you're feeling unwell, you can wash your face and hands in it.
OLIVE OIL	An essential staple natural product, olive oil is used in blessings, *malocchio* removal, infusions and healing.
***PEPERONCINI* (LONG RED PEPPERS)**	Threaded or strung on a cord, these peppers ward off the *malocchio* and bring good luck due to their red colour and *corno* (horn) shape.
SALT	This is the most powerful means to protect from and repel evil, both in black magic and against the *malocchio*. Remember to sprinkle salt in your home, sweeping the bad energy outside away from your front door, and throw salt over your left shoulder to get rid of anything with evil intention.

At home

When in an Italian household, it's inevitable you'll encounter folk magic Catholic objects, such as a crucifix or cross and rosary beads. Not only are these used in prayer, but also to protect people and their property. Saint icons, prayer cards, saint medallions and scapulars are all part of having the protective presence of a patron saint.

BLESSED OLIVE BRANCH	Olive branches or 'palms' that have been blessed during Palm Sunday celebrations are said to ward off any evil.
BROOM	Placing the 'bristle' broom outside the front door keeps the 'witches' and any negative energy away.
HORSESHOE	A horseshoe is lucky because it is made from iron. (For more, see *tocca ferro*, page 173.)
***IL BREVE* (THE SHORT)**	*Il breve* is a small fabric bag/pouch made of felt or soft woollen fabric sewn on two sides, which is worn around the neck next to the skin. *Brevi* may contain beneficial herbs such as rue and lavender, as well as garlic, salt, stones, ashes from burnt olive branches used on Palm Sunday, flowers grown near churches, animal hair, pieces of wood, and other amulets. You may place the medallions of saints whom you wish to petition and any other small offerings inside, depending on your intention.
KEY	The key (old-fashioned type with a hollowed centre) is used to remove the *malocchio*. Wearing or carrying an old key or hanging them above the door if they are made of iron is good for protection.
NAILS	Nails made of iron help with spells as well as ward off misfortune.
NEEDLE	A needle is used for sewing *brevi* or *abitini* and for piercing the *malocchio* 'eye' when doing the removal ritual.
RED THREAD OR STRING	The colour red represents vitality and fertility and therefore discourages the *malocchio*.
SCISSORS	Place scissors under your bed, opened in the shape of a cross, to cut and repel spiritual attacks made against you while you sleep.

Abitino (little suit)

In our Molise region, *il breve* was known as *abitino* (little suit). The word *abitino* refers to a small article of clothing or tiny garment often used as a protective charm or amulet. The term *abitino* is derived from the Italian word *abito*, which means 'garment' or 'clothing'.

Abitini are typically made with great care and attention to detail. They are believed to hold protective and magical properties. Usually crafted from fabric, these small garments may be adorned with symbols, charms or other magical elements. *Abitini* are often worn or carried as personal talismans or amulets to provide protection, bring luck or ward off negative influences.

The specific design and symbols used on an *abitino* can vary, depending on the individual's beliefs, intentions and regional traditions. Some common elements include religious symbols, protective signs, sacred herbs or stones, and phrases or prayers that invoke blessings and protection.

Abitini are an integral part of Italian folk magic, reflecting the deep-rooted belief in the power of charms and amulets to safeguard individuals from harm and bring positive influences into their lives. These tiny protective garments are cherished possessions, which are often passed down through generations, carrying the wisdom and blessings of the ancestors and their folk traditions.

How to make a breve or abitino

You may wish to use a ready-made *sacchettino* (charm bag/small pouch).
You can also raid your mum's crystal cabinet, where she probably keeps the
wedding bonboniere sugar almond bags. Or you can make your own *sacchettino*
imbued with your energy that can be passed down to the next generation.

YOU WILL NEED

Materials to make a small square bag measuring 4 x 4 cm (1 ½ x 1 ½ inches)

Red thread or yarn

Dried herbs and flowers of your choice

Saint medallion (optional)

Pinch of sea salt

METHOD

1. Sew the bag on three sides with the red thread, leaving one side open.

2. Fill the bag with the dried herbs, medallion (if using) and salt then sew it shut.

3. Make a loop and fasten the bag to a ribbon or fine leather strip and
    carry it around your neck. You can use the loop to fasten the bag to
    the inside of your clothing with a safety pin. Or you can simply carry
    it in your pocket – whatever is most meaningful to you.

4. This is a protective amulet. The aim is for you or someone in your
    family to wear it on the body to keep safe from harm (physically and
    energetically) when it's most needed.

Jewellery and charms

Jewellery, made of gold or silver and semi-precious
stones with various charms, is used as visual protection
against the *malocchio*.

Cimaruta (*sprig of rue*)
This iconic charm has a unique and delicate design. It is worn as
a necklace or hung above a baby's crib for protection. The traditional
cimaruta is fashioned after a leafy sprig of *rue*. Various protective symbols are
attached on the rue's design, each with a special meaning.

The main symbols are the moon, serpent and key, which represent
Diana (Artemis), Proserpina (Persephone) and Ecate (Hecate), respectively.
Most popular designs include these symbols: the rue flower, crowing rooster,
frog, sacred heart, fish, dagger, owl, vervain blossom, plumed medieval
helmet, rose, cherub and eagle.

Corallo rosso (*red coral*)
Coral is used in Campania in general protective amulets against bad spirits,
sorcery and nightmares, as well as to attract love. Because of its red colour,
coral symbolises regenerative qualities, which makes it a popular gift for
brides, mothers and babies. Wearing a coral twig as a pendant or brooch is
also used as a charm against the *malocchio*.

Corno/cornicello
The *cornicello* (horn) is a single horn with a distinctive twist, which is used as
jewellery in gold, silver, red coral or other semi-precious stones. It represents
the sexual potency of the mature male herd animal, usually the goat or ram.
When worn by men, the *cornicello* is a phallic symbol, which can overcome

any *malocchio* due to its sheer masculine power. But unlike the male genitals, the *cornicello* is pointy and can pierce the energy being sent. Therefore it pierces the '*occhio*' – the eye of the envious person who has sent it.

Traditionally, *cornicelli* were carved out of red coral or made of gold or silver. Because of its blood-red colour, coral has long been associated with virility and good fortune. Although many claim the amulet represents one of the devil's horns, the *corno* symbol existed before Christianity. The Roman horned god Faunus had a wild nature and interest in fertility.

Earrings

Gold earrings and noisy jewellery were designed to keep the *malocchio* away. In Abruzzo, the *sciacquajje*, meaning 'fool' in the local dialect, were large, jangly half-moon earrings with small dangling parts. The women wore them so their jingle would distract and keep the evil eye away.

Il gobbo (*the hunchback*)

This odd charm in the shape of a hunchbacked man with one horn leg is considered a powerful charm for luck and protection against the evil eye. It is usually worn on a key ring with other charms, and used to be worn on bracelets, necklaces and watch chains.

The *gobbo* is a well-dressed little man wearing a suit and top hat, and his bottom half is a *corno* (horn). He has a horseshoe in one hand and makes the *mano cornuta* sign with the other. It was considered a good omen to rub a hunchback's hump; gamblers believed that touching it would bring them a lucky streak. It was thought that people with physical disabilities would divert the *malocchio* away from them.

La coccinella (*the ladybird*)

The *coccinella,* or ladybird charm brings luck in love and romance; women wear it as a charm mostly on bracelets and as pendants. The red colour helps to ward off the *malocchio* and is the colour of passion and romance. In nature, the ladybird eats the 'bad' bugs, which could consume a farmer's entire crop, so it was easy to see why they were thought of as a sign of good luck.

Mano cornuta (*horned hand*)

Mano means 'hand' and *corno* means 'horn'. The charm represents a hand gesture used for *malocchio* in which the index and little fingers are extended while the middle and ring fingers are curled into the palm, which looks like the horns of a bull. The horned hand is a masculine gesture to ward off bad luck and the *malocchio*. The reasoning is that the *malocchio* is attacking the genitalia and this charm will counteract the evil (impotency intention) being thrown.

Mano fica (*fisted hand*)

The clenched fist with a trusting thumb is known as *mano fica*, which resembles female genetalia. The pendant or charm represents this hand gesture in which the thumb is thrust between the curled index and middle fingers in an obvious imitation of heterosexual intercourse.

Whether made as an apotropaic gesture or worn as an amulet, the *mano fica* is used to protect against the evil eye and infertility, like men wear the *mano cornuta* to protect them against impotency.

Nazar (*eye charm*)

While not a traditional protective Italian charm, the *nazar* has become fashionable in Europe from its Turkish, Middle Eastern and Greek origins. Its meaning is that the powerful eye of God will overcome negative influences directed your way, returning them to sender. The eye's design, usually in white, black and bright blue colours, is an iconic and easily recognisable symbol of the evil eye.

Silver and gold

The Neapolitan custom of making *cornuto* charms from silver (sacred to the moon goddess Luna) and blood coral (sacred to the sea goddess Venus) is connected to the surviving influence of ancient pagan worship.

Su coccu (kokku)

In Sardinia, the *su coccu* amulet wards off the evil eye. It is usually a round-shaped black stone, such as onyx or obsidian, set between two little silver cups. The black stone represents the 'good eye' and can neutralise, absorb and even break a *malocchio's* negative energy. As a baby's amulet, the *su coccu* was often a brooch given as a gift from the godmother or grandmother to be pinned on the baby's cradle. For a single person wanting to attract love, a red coral *su coccu* is highly recommended.

Wooden bracelets, saint medallions

While wooden bracelets depicting saints and the Madonna have recently become popular, people have been carrying medallions of certain saints (from St Benedict and St Christopher to St Jude) for years. Because St Christopher is the patron saint of travellers, for example, many keep a St Christopher medallion in their cars.

Nature amulets

Amulets from nature are varied, including plants, woods, seeds, flowers, herbs, garlic, chillies and seahorses.

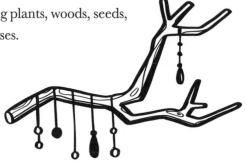

ANIMAL PARTS	Wolf teeth, dog bones, badger hair, deer horns and serpent heads or skin all repel evil and offer protection to the wearer.
BADGER HAIR	Like dogs, badgers (*tassi*) are considered clever for knowing how to escape danger, so their hair is used as a filter against negative energies, especially the *malocchio*. Badger hair was hung on barn doors and the *commare* (godmother) gifted badger hairs to the new mother. Badger hair was also combined with juniper wood and carved into a cornetto shape. It was considered a powerful amulet.
BROOMS AND BROOM-LIKE PLANTS	Handmade brooms and plants that grow in a broom-like shape have a special power to filter out negativity and are used in all entrances to the home.
DESICCATED SEAHORSES	A seahorse dried indoors or in the shade, tied to a ribbon and worn as a pendant was a sure way for a new mother to have ample breastmilk.

DOGS	Dogs are natural enemies of witches unlike cats, which are known as witches' familiars. Because dogs have protective instincts, they can detect if a shape-shifting witch is using a double during their night flights or carrying out *fatture*. Dog skulls, hair and other parts have been used to protect homes and people. Dogs would be buried under the floor of a room on the ground floor so its body acted as a filter – the witch had to count each hair and tooth before entering the house.
HOLLY (*ILEX AQUIFOLIUM*)	Holly is known as *legno stregonio* (witch wood), and is carved into crosses to protect against witchcraft. Other protective trees include the oak, walnut and elder.
***LEGNO STREGONIO* (WITCH WOOD)**	Witch wood is a natural phenomenon that occurs on some trees, especially willow trees and holly. Natural cavity openings in treetrunks are made fertile by birds that nest in them, dropping seeds or berries. Elder trees sometimes grow in the cavity from this natural fertilisation. Elder trees seeded in this way are considered to have potent fertility magic. Women take a piece of this wood and wear it on their bodies during pregnancy for protection.
***PIETRE DELLA SAETTA* OR *PIETRE DEL FULMINE* (LIGHTNING STONES)**	These iron-infused stones were thought to have fallen from the sky during storms and are believed to have protective powers against strokes.

PIETRE STREGONIE (WITCH OR HAG STONES)	With a naturally occurring hole, hag stones are normally found near water. They are valuable because it's commonly believed that magic cannot work on moving water. Because the holes in hag stones are made by the force of water, the stones retain its protective influence. Hag stones are used for rituals and spell work, to counteract spells and hexes cast by witches and to ward off illness and nightmares. They are a powerful, protective talisman against hexes and negative spirits when worn or carried.
RED CORAL	Red coral is used in protective amulets against bad spirits, sorceresses and nightmares, especially in Campania. It is also used to attract love. Because of its red colour, it symbolises regeneration. Red coral is a popular gift for brides, mothers and babies.
SEA SHELLS	Shells symbolise the goddess of love Venus (Aphrodite) and good fortune in love. The sea snail *Astrea rugosa* supposedly watches out for evil, trapping it in its spiral. It's known as *occhio di Santa Lucia* (St Lucy's eye) – the eye is its protective shell.
STONES	Natural stones can have apotropaic qualities, and are carried in the pocket as protection or used in other amulets.

These natural symbols may be part of ancient superstitions, but they have survived until today for a reason.

How to create your own amulet

Creating your personal amulet is a wonderful way to infuse your energy and intention into a magical object for protection, luck or other purposes. Amulets carry specific energies; you wear or carry them with you to attract positive influences and repel negative ones.

YOU WILL NEED

Charms

Ribbon, leather or chain

Beads

Gemstones or natural items

Saint or angel medallions

METHOD

1. Determine the purpose of your amulet. What do you want it to bring into your life? Whether it's protection, love, abundance or any other intention, be clear about your goal.

2. Select a symbol or charm that aligns with your intention. Common symbols include the *cornicello* (for protection), *cimaruta* (for protection), *mano cornuta* (repelling negative energy), or *mano fica* (for good luck).

3. Choose the materials you want in your amulet. You may need a small pendant or charm of your chosen symbol, a chain or cord to wear it,

and any additional items such as beads, gemstones or charms that resonate with your intention.

4. Before working with your materials, cleanse them of any negative energies or influences. You can smoke cleanse them with herbs like sage or pass them through incense smoke.

5. Hold the pendant or charm in your hands and close your eyes. Focus on your intention and imagine your desired outcome. Infuse the amulet with your energy and intent, visualising it radiating with positive vibrations.

6. Add any additional beads, gemstones or charms that hold significance for you or relate to your intention. Consider the colours and materials you use, because they can amplify the amulet's energy.

7. Say a short blessing or invocation over the amulet, asking for the spiritual forces or deities you believe in to empower the amulet with its purpose.

8. When your amulet is ready, wear it as a necklace or bracelet, or carry it with you in a pocket or purse. Keep it close to your body so it can work its magic throughout the day.

9. Over time, your amulet's energy may need to be recharged or cleansed. On nights of the full moon, place the amulet in the moonlight to recharge its energies. You can also cleanse it with smoke or blessed water when needed.

10. Listen to your intuition and use the amulet as you feel guided. Trust in your intention and belief as you carry your amulet with you.

11. Remember, the potency of your amulet comes from your belief, intention and connection with its purpose. Personalise the amulet to suit your individual beliefs and cultural heritage, infusing it with your energy.

Superstitions

Amulets and talismans listed may sound primitive to us today, but Italian culture is rich with superstitions for good and evil. The Romans used the word *superstitio* to describe religious cults such as the Druids and early Christians because of their excessive religious belief. Due to this excessive nature, they were banned by the Roman Empire. In our modern world, we may disregard traditional fears as something set in place before science or during eras of hardships, but many are still taking superstitions perhaps not seriously but at least with a grain of salt.

Here are some well-known Italian superstitions – many of which originated from folk magic.

Animals

- ▶ Avoid hurting or killing a bat because it will bring you bad luck.
- ▶ Killing a cat will bring you seven years of bad luck.
- ▶ A cat washing its face or grooming itself is believed to bring good luck and favourable outcomes.
- ▶ It's bad luck for a black cat to cross your path. You need to turn back and start on your path again.
- ▶ If you hear a cat meowing or an owl hooting, you will receive bad news.
- ▶ Hearing a cat sneeze brings good luck.
- ▶ Owls, bats and peacock feathers inside the house are bad luck.
- ▶ Hearing a rooster crowing means you'll receive good news.

Babies

New babies are gifted an amulet for protection against the *malocchio* from their godmother. This is usually a red ribbon on a gold safety pin that's pinned inside their clothing or somewhere in their bedding.

Never cut a baby's hair until the child is one year old.

Be careful with bread

Italians love bread so much that it's a sacrilege to drop it. Growing up, we rarely threw stale bread away – my mother had plenty of ways to use it dipped in milk, added to hearty chicken soup or toasted for coating *cotolette* (crumbed cutlets). If you drop bread, you must immediately pick it up, kiss it and eat it, so you'll never experience hunger.

Never place a loaf of bread upside down. This shows disrespect and can attract bad luck. It's bad luck to leave a knife in a bread loaf.

Bed

It's unlucky to leave a hat on a bed. In the past, a priest would go to the bedsides of the sick and dying to administer their last rites. They would normally take off their hat and leave it on the bed next to the dying person. So a hat on the bed is a reminder of a death scene and therefore considered bad luck.

If you put a photo of a loved one on a bed – when tidying, packing or doing housework, for example – this will bring them bad luck. Other unlucky items you should keep off the bed are clothes hangers, hairbrushes and shoes (of course, the last is a hygiene issue too).

A bed should never face the door because this replicates the position of a coffin in a church. This is also a feng shui principle in the Chinese tradition.

Blessing a new home

A new broom is a common first gift in a new home to sweep away evil spirits. Sprinkling salt in the corners of the home will purify it. People would invite the local priest to their homes before Easter to bless them with holy water.

Candle

Don't let a candle burn itself out. Extinguish it before it is finished, preferably with a candle snuffer.

Carry a fava bean

Dried fava beans are lucky; they are thought to attract money and wealth. Carry one in your wallet so you'll never run out of money. People keep one in the pantry so they will never run out of food.

Clothes

If you accidentally put on your clothes inside out or backwards first thing in the morning, you'll have good luck or receive good news for the day.

If you left your washing out on the line at night after sunset, the spirits can get into them and haunt you.

Coins

It's good luck to throw coins into a well or a fountain. It's also good luck when you build a new home and leave some coins in the foundation or concrete slab.

Don't cross silverware

Crossing your cutlery predicts conflict in the house. Crossed forks, knives and spoons are an omen that people are being at cross purposes – arguing and disagreeing. It also indicates you will have crosses (hardships) to bear in your life.

Don't give an empty wallet or handbag as a gift

Make sure you add some notes inside so the gift's recipient will never be penniless. It works like the law of attraction in which abundance attracts more abundance.

Don't give a sharp object such as a knife or scissors as a gift

Due to its ability to cut, if you give this as a gift, it risks cutting or severing friendships. To prevent any misfortune, the gift's recipient should 'pay' for the item using a token coin as payment.

Don't spill salt or oil

Spilling salt is bad luck; historically, salt was of great value. Even today, we can't live without salt. The remedy for spilling salt is a strange one – throw a pinch of salt over your left shoulder. Normally, this is where the devil is supposed to be standing and he caused you to spill the salt in the first place!

It's also bad luck to spill cooking oil. Cover it with salt and wipe it up immediately. Don't forget to throw the salt over your left shoulder to avoid misfortune. This superstition probably dates back to times when olive oil was considered a luxury.

Don't sweep over or under someone's feet

Because brooms clear negative energies and anything else in their way, you could sweep away good fortune or even money. Sweeping over the feet of someone single means they will never marry.

Don't use an old broom in a new house

Take care when moving house – this is an in-between time when you're making a lifestyle transition. You don't bring in the old 'rubbish' (and old issues) you have swept away in the past into the new sacred space you are entering. Buy a broom once you're in your new place, not before. Also get rid of the dustpan, handle and mop, only buying new ones once you're in your new house. It's considered bad luck to sweep your house after dark.

Place a straw broom upside down at your front door to keep the *streghe* away. (For more information, see page 21.)

Eat lentils on New Year's Eve

On New Year's Eve, eating lentils at midnight will bring you luck for the year. The lentils symbolise coins.

Eggs

Never discard halved eggshells. Crush the shells in your palms before throwing them away, so you won't attract negative energy into your home.

Front door or kitchen

To prevent the *malocchio*, place braided garlic and a bunch of hot red peppers (*peperoncini*) either by the front door or in your kitchen.

Itchy nose

When your nose itches, it's either *pugni* or *baci*, meaning 'punches' or 'kisses'. This means you don't know what's coming.

La Befana

No housework should be done on 6 January, known as the Epiphany in the Christian calendar. According to legend, the Wise Men asked La Befana, a kindly old witch/crone, to accompany them to see the infant Jesus. She refused, saying she was too busy and had to clean her house, so she missed this miraculous event. Each year, on 5 January, La Befana goes from house to house, leaving gifts and looking for the Christ child.

Left hand

When your left hand is itchy, you will receive money, but if it's your right hand, you will pay money.

Love and weddings

You will dream of the man you'll marry if you place a few sugar almonds (*confetti*) under your pillow. It's similar to today's version of placing some wedding cake under your pillow for the same reason.

No birds in the house

Having a bird inside the home brings bad luck. Peacock feathers look like multiple evil eyes and are capable of cursing a home's residents. Paintings of birds should also be avoided.

November

Avoid getting married in November, traditionally known as the month of the dead (*mese dei morti*). This is generally regarded as a time of mourning for those who have passed on, not a time of celebration.

Number 13

Italians consider the number 13 lucky and even wear a lucky charm of 13. The number 13 is also associated with the lunar cycles, and is thought to bring prosperity and abundant life. But make sure you don't set the table for 13 people, like in Jesus's Last Supper – that's considered unlucky because of its association with Jesus's betrayal and death.

Number 17

The number 17 is considered unlucky because, in Roman numerals, 17 (XVII) is an anagram of the Latin word *VIXI*, meaning 'I have lived'. Another translation is 'My life is over', which suggests death and therefore bad luck.

Nuns

Seeing a nun crossing your path is bad luck.

Palms

Palm Sunday is an important Catholic feast day, celebrating when Jesus had palms laid at his feet as he walked by. Usually substituted with small olive branches, people keep these long after they've been blessed at mass on Palm Sunday. Once dried, the branches are burned and mixed with some incense to use as protection against the *malocchio*.

Pregnancy

It is bad luck to announce a pregnancy before three months.

A pregnant woman with a craving should not touch her body or the baby will be born with a birth mark in the same body part that was scratched. Brown birthmarks indicate a craving for coffee, while red marks indicate foods such as strawberries or wine.

Pregnant women should avoid looking at things they find ugly or distressing, and avoid seeing the terminally ill or people with physical disabilities or this could transmit negativity to the unborn child. Instead, they should focus on positive and beautiful images and experiences.

If a woman's pregnant belly is low and round, she will have a girl. If the belly is high and pointy, she'll have a boy.

A pregnant woman should not cross her legs or her baby will be born breech.

Seeing an empty hearse

Spotting a hearse with no coffin inside is an omen that your own death is approaching.

Spider

Killing a spider will make you lose money. Seeing a spider at night is a sign of money arriving.

Toasting

Never raise a toast with a glass full of water because it's bad luck. Don't cross arms when you clink wine glasses together. Also, look your fellow toasters in the eye when clinking glasses and make sure you take a sip before setting your drink down.

Thursday

Never trim your toenails and fingernails on a Thursday.

Tocca ferro (*touch iron*) to avoid bad luck

Instead of touching wood, Italians touch iron for good luck (*tocca ferro*), an abbreviation of *toccare ferro di cavallo* (touch horseshoe), which dates back to when horseshoes were thought to ward off devils, witches and evil spirits. This is why we still carry around horseshoe charms or something made from iron, just in case. If you lived on a farm, crossing the iron hoe on the outside of the front door would protect you from bad, damaging storms.

But what happens if no iron is around? A man may do a quick grab of his crotch (*tocca palle*), which will work just as well. This stems from the old belief that symbols of fertility can thwart the *malocchio*.

Tuesday and Friday

Never get married, travel or begin a new venture on a Tuesday because this day is considered to be cursed.

Di Venere e di Marte non ci si sposa e non si parte (On Venus and Mars don't get married, and don't leave) means you shouldn't get married or go on a big trip on the days of Venus (Venerdì/Friday) and Mars (Martedì/Tuesday). Some Italians also say, '*e non si da principio all'arte*', which recommends that you shouldn't start any new artistic projects on these days if you want them to succeed.

Friday is also considered unlucky because *Venerdì Santo* (Good Friday) was the day of Jesus's death. Don't wear something new for the first time on a Friday. Never celebrate on a Friday unless it's the exact date of the occasion. Never get married, begin a trip or move house on a Friday.

Walnut tree

Walnut trees bring good luck and longevity, so each time you move to a new home, plant a young walnut tree.

Wearing red underwear

Women wearing red undergarments will have luck in love.

Wedding rings

Wedding rings are considered to have mystical powers. Traditionally, they were blessed by the priest and marriage vows were seen as an unbreakable bond.

Young single women should never wear a ring on their left ring finger or they won't get married. They should not try on a married woman's ring either.

The consequences are that the single woman won't get married and the married woman will be widowed.

Using a pregnant woman's wedding ring to tell if her baby is a boy or girl is a well-known and regularly used method. Tie the expectant mother's hair or a ribbon around her wedding ring. Hold it over her belly like a pendulum. Move it around, asking 'Is it a girl?' and' 'Is it a boy?' Each time, watch how the pendulum moves. If it moves in circles, she will have a girl. If the pendulum moves up and down, she will have a boy.

While we may not hold all these superstitions, they are part of the fabric of Italian folk magic culture that weaves its magic in our otherwise humdrum existence. The same goes for the following sayings, which have been uniquely constructed over the centuries to reflect the diversity of the Italian people.

Popular Italian sayings

When we were growing up, the nonni always had a saying about something that applied to our lives. The same goes for all grandparents, who applied wisdom to situations. Of course we didn't understand the concept of *Sempre avanti mai indietro* (Always forward never backward) or *Chi va piano, va sano, e va lontano* (Whoever goes slowly, goes safely and far). As a child, I just wanted a simple answer, not a philosophy. Part of being philosophical comes from their worldview, which was shaped by their difficut lived experiences.

Here are the most popular sayings that reflect the spirit of the Italian lifestyle.

IN BOCCA AL LUPO!
Good luck!

Meaning: to wish someone good luck 'in the mouth of the wolf', similar to 'break a leg'. Both phrases were originally used in opera and theatre. But what is confusing is the response you're meant to give to this: *crepi il lupo* ('may the wolf die'). A fairy-tale fear of the wolf or werewolves considered scarily dangerous in Italy? A logical explanation would be that it may have originated with hunters wishing each other well in dangerous situations.

FIDARSI È BENE MA NON FIDARSI È MEGLIO.
Trusting is good, but not trusting is better.

Meaning: while trust is important in life, you don't have to be overly optimistic; a little extra attention may save you a lot of trouble later on.

FINCHÉ C'È VITA, C'È SPERANZA.
Where there's life, there's hope.

Meaning: we should always have hope and not despair despite challenging circumstances. This expression is sometimes used ironically with those who continue to hope even though it is useless to do so.

LE BUGIE HANNO LE GAMBE CORTE.
Lies have short legs.

Meaning: lying won't get you anywhere because the 'short legs' of lies means they can't go a long way to convince people. You'll get caught before you get too far into your web of lies and deceit.

OCCHIO NON VEDE, CUORE NON DUOLE.
The eye doesn't see, the heart does not hurt.

Meaning: what you don't know won't hurt you.

CHI HA TEMPO NON ASPETTI TEMPO.
Who has time, shouldn't wait for time.

Meaning: don't put off tomorrow what you can do today.

LA NOTTE PORTA CONSIGLIO.
Night brings advice.

Meaning: sleep on any important decisions and make your choices in the morning with a fresh mind.

AL CUORE NON SI COMANDA.
You can't rule the heart (love is blind).

Meaning: a person who's in love doesn't see their partner's faults the same way others do.

L'OSPITE È COME IL PESCE DOPO TRE GIORNI PUZZA.
A guest is like a fish that, after three days, stinks.

Meaning: don't overstay your welcome.

TRA MOGLIE E MARITO NON METTERE IL DITO.
Don't put a finger between wife and husband.

Meaning: never interfere between husband and wife.

CHI DORME NON PIGLIA PESCI.
Those who sleep don't catch fish.

Meaning: you snooze, you lose.

L'APPETITO VIEN MANGIANDO.
Appetite comes with eating.

Meaning: when you begin to eat, even if you're not hungry, it will increase your appetite. This is a favourite saying of relatives when you visit and say you can't possibly eat a five-course meal, then they hit you with this wise saying!

L'ABITO NON FA IL MONACO.
The clothes do not make the monk.

Meaning: clothes don't make the man – don't judge a book by its cover.

The origins of rituals and superstitions have been shrouded in mystery, yet they have been practised by Italians from all regions in one form or another for countless generations. *Stregoneria* and pagan rituals were banned by the Christian Church. Over the millennia, these traditions were modified and blended into a Christian world to survive. The fact that these superstitions are still with us today is a credit to how practical and earth-based they were, and how they still hold up today. Luck, prosperity and fear of ill fortune still top our list of superstitions – who walks under a ladder and doesn't pause for a second, hoping it won't bring them bad luck?

It may be simply psychological, but I feel safer with my amulets and talismans to protect me from the unknown dangers of this world – the *cornetto*, saint medallions, holy water, salt, plants, herbs, candles … in fact, just about everything in this chapter.

Chapter 9

Hexes, cures and remedies

What can cure can also kill. Poison is both magic and power. A healer must walk in the liminal place between life and death. Powerful plants can teach and heal in the right doses, but they can also kill. Healers have always had this power over the lives of their community, which is why they were both feared and revered. The healer/medicine woman/herbalist can use their gifts for the benefit of others or to profit from people's very human failings.

Some 'healers', known as *fattucchiere*, practised black magic spells and hexes, also called *fatture*, to obtain desired results. So there is always a duality, a conflict of sorts between medicine and spell craft.

Although many folk would claim they don't believe in spells because they're Catholic, they were still naturally following the more pagan and animistic origins of their ancestors through healing remedies and using plants and herbs.

La fattura/le fatture

When I looked up *fattura* in the dictionary, it gave various meanings: bill, invoice, manufacture, make, cut, model, design, and charm or spell. The common meaning is that something is made (like a spell or hex) and something is taken away or owed (invoice or bill) in payment, like the money from the person wanting the *fattura*, or the energy of the victim. In other words, *fattura* in Italian folk magic means 'spell' and is sympathetic magic, meaning the victim isn't aware of it, and it aims to bring damage and pain to the victim's physical body.

The spell is made using a sympathetic double for the victim's body, which can be in the form of a poppet (*puppia*). A poppet is a type of 'magical' doll or effigy made from cloth or fabric that is fashioned to resemble a human form. It is based on the principle that like attracts like. By using a poppet that resembles the target, the practitioner can connect with that person on an energetic level and direct the magic accordingly.

Poppets may be hand sewn or made with other practical ingredients, such as corn husks, which are then stuffed with items, such as herbs and personal items (like hair or nail clippings), to bind the individual to the poppet. The *puppia* represents a specific person intended to receive a magical intention.

Added to the spell are words of evil intent and acted out with the help of a baneful spirit. Lemons with pins stuck in them were commonly used for this type of hex, but also if a spurned lover wanted revenge or had other strong negative intentions, such as greed or jealousy. Basically, the *fattura* aims to harm a bodily organ and even cause death.

The *fattucchiera* would normally visit the victim, pretending it was a social visit, then hide the poppet somewhere inside their home. There are also edible poppets; a *fattucchiera* would need to be particularly sly to slip the *fattura* into the victim's food or drink. If this fails, then she would rely on black magic and negative spirits to put the *puppia* into places where people wouldn't look. A *fattura* can only be broken by a *fattucchiera* – so, a *fattucchiera* was both the spell-caster and spell-breaker.

What is *la pupatta*?

For New Year, my mum used to make a sweet biscotto pastry in the shapes of a woman wearing an apron (called *la pupatta*) and a rooster (*il gallo*) to represent fertility and good fortune. They can be considered edible poppets and could be used for evil intent, but our family enjoyed the food for its festive meaning. As a child, biting into the soft dough on a cold winter's New Year's Eve was magical. People watched fireworks and music played all over town, especially the *zampoganiari* (bagpipers), who would come down from the Abruzzo mountains to play their bagpipes and welcome the New Year. In Abruzzo, dolls made out of pastry (*pupe di Pasqua*) were given to children on Easter morning. Girls would receive peasant-girl-like dolls and for boys it would be horse-shaped dolls.

How to use a puppia

A *puppia* (poppet) is different from a *pupatta* because it was primarily used for spell work and black magic. *Pupatte* or *pupe* (biscuit dough dolls) were enjoyed as part of an annual feast day. However, you could argue that poppets can be used in a positive way as part of healing rituals to aid a person's recovery.

How to make an ethical poppet (puppia)

YOU WILL NEED

Poppet

Herbs

Crystals

Saint medallions

Dried flowers

Shells

Positive affirmations

Anything else of significance to the person

METHOD

1. Fill the poppet with herbs or items with healing properties and charged with positive energy to promote the person's well-being. This may be crystals, saint medallions, dried flowers, shells, positive affirmations – whatever might help the person to feel better.

2. The poppet can also represent a person seeking protection or a loved one. When charged with protective energy, it serves as a guardian against negative influences or harm.

3. Once the poppet is filled and stitched closed, perform a consecration or blessing ritual to activate its magical properties. During this ritual, you may invoke deities or spiritual forces, call upon your ancestors, or recite prayers.

4. Remember, using poppets or any other magical tools should always be done with positive intent and respect for people's free will. In *stregoneria,* as in any magical practice, it's crucial to approach spell work with mindfulness and responsibility for the energy you're directing.

Legature

Legature, or binding spells, are used in black magic to tie someone to you or tie them apart (breaking them up). Knots are used both for magic and physical cures. You could use them in a revenge spell by turning the spouse who rejected you against their new spouse. Hair *legature*, for example, is a serious hex. You should make sure that all shed hair is removed and discarded so no-one can obtain it to use in a spell. Knotted hair is unlucky because a *fattucchiera* can create a break-up spell with braids and *trizzi* (tangled dreads).

I recall how my mother was absolutely vigilant about brushing and cutting our hair at home, which was burned in the fireplace. It was the same for fingernails. Someone's nail clippings can be used for spells of love or revenge. You should never give a *fattucchiera* an opportunity to collect hair or nail clippings to use in a poppet.

Psychic fright and worms

When you had a psychic fright or 'the frights', this was thought to bring on an infestation of worms. Or simply having stomach pain was thought to be worms. *Avuta n'a paura* (meaning 'having a fright' in our dialect) was a primitive and simple diagnosis because no medical information was available to distinguish one condition from another. A ruptured appendix, for example, would present with similar symptoms as having worms. The 'frights' might be caused by living people, ghosts, shocks or a *fattura*. Today, it's recognised as a trauma or post-traumatic stress disorder. Symptoms include insomnia, vomiting, loss of weight, high fever, delirium, strong abdominal or stomach

pains, anaemia, choking, and having jitters. In Sicily, jitters are called *lu scantu* and are said to affect the intestines.

In our Molise region, the frights was called *verminara* and the treatment, other than a *malocchio* ritual, was to drink a hot infusion (like a tea) from the plant *malva* (marrow, or *Malva sylvestris*) to ease the pain. Mallow is a spreading bush with palm-looking leaves and purple-pink flowers. It grows naturally on lawns and fields. All parts are edible either raw or cooked. As a tea, mallow is antibacterial and helps with colds, bronchitis and sore throats; soothes burns, bruising and swelling; and helps urinary tract infections, nausea, and stomach and digestive upsets. *Malva* is used for all sorts of ailments in central Italy. I'm only now just beginning to recognise its properties and appearance. Who knew it grows just about anywhere?

It's difficult for us in our modern world to understand *vermi* – why were Italians obsessed with it? I was confused too. What is the connection between treating an intestinal worm infestation and a condition known as psychic fright? From my understanding and speaking to older Italians, it seems that worms, or parasitic infestations generally, are more than just a physical issue; they can also be perceived as a spiritual infestation or energetic imbalance.

From a spiritual perspective, worms may be associated with negative influences or spiritual disturbances. Negative energies or entities might be attracted to or manifest as parasitic infestations in the body. In such cases, the healers approached the issue from both a physical and spiritual perspective to restore balance and remove the infestation. To address this, rituals for cleansing and protection methods would remove and prevent the recurrence of worms, and protect the individual from spiritual harm.

A friend of mine remembers that when she was a child, a special healer removed her 'worms' by running her hands over her body, expelling them. My friend thought it was physical worms because she lived on a farm; she was around animals and dirt and may not have practised good hygiene.

I asked my zia for clarification about 'real' versus 'psychic' worms. She explained that people used to believe that everyone had parasites, but it took something out of the ordinary to make them active and cause harm. So, getting a fright created a weakness in the body at that moment, which gave the worms a chance to jump and become active.

Treatments

How could we treat this complex condition? First, the traditional healer would have used medicinal herbs for the physical treatment and suggested purifying baths. Plants were used to cure almost anything – the most effective were mallow, rue and verbena. Other herbs and plants used for psychic fright were bay leaves, bitter drinks (pomegranate juice and lemon), coffee, dog rose, garlic, marjoram, mint, olive leaves, parsley, rosemary and St John's wort.

For a psychic fright manifesting as a form of worm infestation, the healer would use various methods – smoke cleansing, invocations, rituals, gestures, spells and plants. They may recite prayers or invocations to specific saints, deities or spiritual forces associated with healing and protection to seek their aid in removing the infestation and restoring spiritual balance. Depending on how serious the infestation was, they may have performed a form of exorcism.

How to diagnose parasitic worms (vermi)

This technique has several variations. My nonna told me this one, which was used in central and southern Italy:

1. Coat the rim of a cup with olive oil and garlic.

2. Place it on the child's navel, rim facing down.

3. If the cup sticks (has suction), worms are present.

How to get rid of psychic fright

Bread water (*acqua panata*) is used for getting rid of psychic fright. It's connected to the idea that Italian rural folk saw bread as something holy and respected, because it was an essential part of their diet and survival. I've heard older Italians refer to bread as '*santo pane*'. Because they went without food during the wars, any small amounts of bread enabled them to live. They even have a saying that someone is good like bread (*è buono come il pane*). Bread is part of the Catholic ritual of the holy Eucharist, so to 'undo' the goodness of this bread by dissolving it makes it unholy. This then becomes a way of fighting evil with evil.

1. To make *acqua panata*, roast bread in an open fire or a gas flame like toasting marshmallows.

2. Place in cold water until the bread has completely broken down and looks like a cloudy paste.

3. The affected person drinks a glass of this water.

PROTECTION FROM WORM INFESTATIONS

BREVE	The _breve_ (cloth pouch) could carry protective amulets – garlic cloves, saint medallions, animal teeth, small stones, salt, olive leaves, herbs, coins and anything else considered an apotropaic (protective) item against evil or illness.
GARLIC	Because children or babies were mostly affected by worms, care had to be taken. Many regions used non-invasive methods like a bulb of garlic tied around the baby's neck. The smell was thought to encourage the worms to leave the body. Garlic was the hero of protection and antiviral infections. In psychic frights, healers would put a clove of garlic and a saint medallion inside a _breve_ to give protection against magic hexes.
HERBAL REMEDIES	Other herbal remedies were mallow and sometimes rue (please note, rue can be a toxic herb that is not suitable for everyone).

Herbal remedies for vermi

To make a drink from mallow (_malva):_

1. Crush the leaves.
2. Pour hot water over them.
3. Steep, strain and drink.
4. To make a poultice from rue (_ruta_) or other appropriate herbs:
5. Use the soaked leaves wrapped in a cloth or handkerchief over the affected area like a poultice.
6. Make an oil fusion with rue and rub it on the affected areas to alleviate the _verminara_ pain.

FOR OTHER ILLNESSES

Herbal preparations were regarded highly in Italian folk magic; people believed plants could cure everything. For centuries, all that was available for medicinal purposes were home remedies passed down from mother to daughter. Before Italy introduced free public medicine in the 1970s, folk medicine was the only option. Over time, folk remedies blended with Western biomedicine and today we're witnessing a revival of this relationship.

The cultural affinity of blending other elements such as prayers, spells, talismans, charms, magic and religious rituals create a rich tradition of healing the folk magic way.

In general, to protect against illness, people placed a *breve* filled with herbs on the left side of their chest under their clothes, containing semi-precious stones, ashes from sacred fires, flowers grown near churches or images of saints. Extra healing properties were granted if the *brevi* contained pregnancy stones (*pietre della gavidanza*), red-spotted jasper to stop bleeding (*pietre del sangue*) and star stones (*pietre stellare*) with tiny star-like spots and crosses, which offered magical protection.

Here are some ailments with cures using more than just herbs. While these cures are not recommended today, in the past they were the main form of treatment for minor ailments in rural villages.

COLIC	Babies with colic would be treated by holding them upside down by their feet while reciting the Lord's prayer. Once the baby was lifted the right way up, they were expected to be fine with the colic gone.
CONSTIPATED BABY	Carefully inserting the tip of a parsley stem into a baby's anus was a popular method of relieving constipation.

DANDRUFF	In the case of recurring dandruff, soap made from pig fat, soda, olive oil and lemon peel was an effective treatment.
EAR INFECTION	Breastmilk (from feeding a male baby) was thought to relieve ear infections.
HEADACHE	Sliced potatoes were applied to one's head and held in place by a headband. Soaking the headband in vinegar beforehand was thought to be more effective.
HIGH BLOOD PRESSURE	Olive leaves were crushed and mixed with water, then imbibed.

Medallion water cure (*l'acqua di medaglia*)

In almost all regions of Italy, this cure is considered a therapeutic medicine. It uses water, coarse salt, wheat grains, special gestures (*segnature*), special words only known to the healer, and a saint or Our Lady medallion. It can be used on several illnesses and can also help remove the symptoms of the *malocchio*.

Poultice for healing infections (from Le Marche)

YOU WILL NEED

Bread

Soap flakes

Honey

Cotton bandage

METHOD

1. Chew the bread to moisten it with saliva. Then make a paste by adding soap flakes mixed with honey. Mix it together, so it resembles a thick, sticky dough or paste.

2. Place the mixture over the wound to draw out the pus and infection. Apply a cotton bandage to cover.

3. Leave the poultice on overnight for splinters, boils and other infections. Keep the bandage on until pus leaks from the wound and the splinter is drawn out.

4. Depending on the type of wound, you may need to repeat the process a few times.

Plant cures

My ancestors lived in one region for hundreds of years. The local plants and foods contributed to their health through their diet and herbal remedies. Any medicinal cure was passed down through families orally in the *paese*. Regardless of what plants or remedies they used, a blessing, prayer or powerful words always accompanied the treatment. The region of Molise is known for its wild beauty as well as its wheat products (*Pasta Molisana* is world renowned), cheeses, salami, wine and truffles. It's a gourmet paradise today, but in bygone eras it was not always so productive. The *magare* had to find whatever herbs or plants were growing in places that weren't too remote, such as the *bosco* (woods) and the *montagne* (mountains), where wolves were said to roam.

These cures and remedies from the ancient healers have evolved over time with increased herbal and modern medical knowledge. When using plant medicine, Italian folk healers relied on their intuition, cultural knowledge and family traditions to select the right herbs and methods for specific ailments. They used ethical harvesting and sustainable practices to maintain the balance and harmony between people and nature. Our ancestors understood that plants have magical and natural properties, and held them with the utmost respect and gratitude, giving back to nature through offerings and eco-friendly practices.

Foraging and wild crafting

While our nonni and those before them all foraged and practised wild crafting, today we're seeing the return of this honourable method of harvesting plants. Foraging and wild crafting involve gathering and using wild plants, herbs and other natural materials found in the local environment.

Foraging refers to searching and collecting wild food resources from nature, including edible plants, mushrooms, berries and nuts. It has been a way of life for centuries, as people relied on the land's fertility to supplement their diets. Foragers were knowledgeable about seasonal changes and the habitats and signatures of different plants, which allowed them to sustainably harvest wild foods throughout the year.

My nonni's house in Molise backed onto the *bosco* – a large tract of common land filled with trees such as apples, figs, pears, mulberries, cherries, peaches, plums and nuts (almonds, walnuts, chestnuts, hazelnuts); mushrooms and truffles; berry bushes; and herbs and edible plants. As a child, I loved having the freedom to run wildly in this forest and pick whatever I wanted and eat it (with some supervision). I loved white mulberries and would eat them until I made myself sick.

Wild crafting is different from foraging because it involves gathering all types of natural materials – including herbs, flowers, roots, bark and other plant parts – for purposes other than just food. These can be used in rituals, healing practices, spells and making amulets. Each plant is believed to have unique magical and medicinal properties, and is gathered with care and reverence to preserve the plant's energy and potency.

SOME MATERIALS FROM WILD CRAFTING

BERRIES	The edible ones (please make sure you know the difference), such as blackberries are tasty in pies or eaten as they are.
DEAD BRANCHES AND TWIGS	These can be used as broom handles, walking sticks or floral arrangements/decorations.
FALLEN LEAVES	These make a great display for your grimoire or scrapbook.
MUSHROOMS	Leave mushrooms alone – it's too risky.
PINECONES, ACORNS, SEED PODS	All these can be used on your altar, in prosperity spells and for burning in your fire pit during winter.

Pick wildflowers such as yarrow, daisy, cornflower, mallow, native orchid, wild rose and others from your region. You can dry them and add them to your journal or grimoire with a note on their magical uses. Add dried petals to your home-made smoking stick, or make oil infusions and add to oil essences.

The practice of foraging and wild crafting is a beautiful way to connect with the land, honour ancestral knowledge and integrate nature's healing properties into everyday life for health and magical practices.

Some popular herbs and plants from our ancestral homeland may also be found in wild places in the Italian diaspora. They are each filled with nutritious goodness, but it's wise to forage with a local who is familiar with the area's wild plants and herbs (*erbe selvatiche*). Remember, our ancestors lived in the same landscape for generations and had information passed down to them about edible wild plants.

Porcini mushrooms (*porcini*)

These usually grow under pine trees but the tastiest are supposed to be near chestnut trees. Many other types of mushrooms are not unique to Italy, such as oyster mushrooms (*cadoncelli*) and chanterelles (*galletti*). The most poisonous and dangerous mushroom is the death cap (*Amanita phalloides*). Ingesting only half a cap can lead to death. You need to be well informed about the different types of mushrooms before you go foraging.

Wild borage (*borragine*)

This is a versatile green. Its leaves can be eaten raw in a salad or steamed as a substitute for spinach or soft greens. Its sweet-tasting flowers can be used as a dessert decoration, and its seeds pressed to extract oil. In Liguria, borage is used as a filling in a ravioli pasta called *pansotti*.

Wild cardoon (*cardoni or cardi*)

A winter vegetable, only the stalks of the cardoon are used. It can be boiled in salted water, fried, preserved in oil or made into a soup.

Wild fennel (*finocchietto*)

While wild fennel doesn't grow a bulb, it produces attractive fragrant fronds as well as seeds to use in cooking.

Rampion bellflower (*raponzoli*)

This is used as a substitute for spinach and cooked lightly steamed with a drizzle of olive oil.

Wild dandelion (*cicoria*) and wild chicory (*cicoriella*)

These are found in open fields or meadows pretty much everywhere. Wild dandelion is a versatile and nutritious vegetable, its leaves used in main courses, side dishes and even in pasta sauces, as well as some desserts. You can make a dandelion tea from just the flowers for a milder, sweeter taste. Wild chicory looks similar and is less bitter than dandelion. Roasted chicory root is used as a caffeine-free alternative to coffee. Not for the coffee purists, but good for your health.

Other plants you can forage

- ▶ Wild asparagus (*asparago*)
- ▶ Mallow (*malva*)
- ▶ Nettles (*ortiche*)
- ▶ Wild oregano (*origano comune, origano meridionale*)
- ▶ Wild anise (*anice*)
- ▶ St John's wort/hypericum (*erba di San Giovanni/iperico*)
- ▶ Sorrel (*acetosa, acetina*)
- ▶ Yarrow (*achillea, millefoglie*)
- ▶ Plantain (*piantaggine*)
- ▶ Chard (*bietola*)

> **Note:** make sure you correctly identify plants when foraging for food. Mushrooms especially are easy to mistake because some poisonous varieties look similar to edible varieties but can be fatal if eaten. Make sure you have reliable information for the area you're foraging in or find a local person or guide who specialises in your area's native plants to help you. Never eat anything you aren't sure you've correctly identified.

Bitter greens from the garden

My parents' vegetable garden contained bitter greens that provided us with a healthy gut and an appreciation of the *amaro* taste in vegetables. If you've grown up in a typical Italian household, you'll recognise these vegetables, which would have originally grown in the wild. Here are some of my childhood memories of bitter greens on our family table:

- ▶ Pasta with cooked *rape/rapini* (broccoli rabe)
- ▶ *Carciofi* (artichokes) stuffed with breadcrumbs, grated parmigiano, oil, parsley and steamed, then baked
- ▶ *Cavolo nero* (kale) cooked in minestrone soup or boiled then fried with garlic and oil

Our summer salad mixes would never have the mild flavours of iceberg or cos lettuce; instead, we had the bitter and peppery *cicoria* (chicory), *scarola* (escarole), *arugula* (rocket) and *radicchio* (type of chicory).

Other traditional Italian foods are also considered healing remedies. Basil, garlic, olive oil, onion, oregano and rosemary are the most commonly used ingredients in the cucina, which support the immune system as part of the healthy Mediterranean diet.

Cime di rapa cooked in pasta

Here's a simple recipe for *cime di rape* cooked in pasta. Delicious, nutritious and basic, it's part of the *cucina povera* (peasant food) style of cooking.

YOU WILL NEED

1 bunch of *cime di rape* (broccoli rabe or *rapini*), or other bitter greens such as kale, silverbeet or Swiss chard

Orecchiette or penne pasta

Garlic

Olive oil

Chilli

Anchovies (optional)

Salt

METHOD

1. Wash and trim the *cime di rapa*.

2. Cook the orecchiette in salted boiling water. Drain, reserving some of the cooking water.

3. Gently fry the garlic in oil with the chilli and anchovies (if using). Add the *cime di rape* and cook until wilted. Season to taste.

4. Add the cooked pasta into the frying pan with the *cime di rape* and a little pasta water. Add grated parmigiano or pecorino. *Buon appetito.*

Herbal remedies

Foragers and wild crafters didn't use plants and herbs for food only – they created herbal remedies, tinctures, teas and poultices for various ailments and health concerns. Here are some modern ways to re-create these ancient healing cures and remedies.

Herbal teas and infusions

Herbs such as chamomile, lemon balm, peppermint and thyme can make soothing and healing drinks. These teas have calming, digestive, and immune-boosting properties.

Herbal inhalations and steam treatments

Steam inhalations infused with aromatic herbs, such as eucalyptus or thyme, can relieve congestion and respiratory discomfort. Breathing in the herbal steam helps to clear the airways and promote easier breathing.

Poultices and compresses

Poultices made from crushed or ground herbs can soothe and heal skin conditions, bruises and muscle aches. Compresses using herbal infusions can be applied topically to reduce inflammation and promote healing. For sprains, healers once used beaten egg whites wrapped around the sprains like a plaster.

How to make
herbal poultices

Italian healers created healing poultices or amulets using specific herbs, stones or symbolic objects to promote healing and protection. These items were believed to carry the energy and properties of the elements they represent. Poultices are useful in treating insect bites, wounds and rashes.

YOU WILL NEED

Calendula

Plantain

Yarrow

METHOD

1. Blend or chop the fresh plants and herbs into a paste.

2. Fold the paste into a fine muslin cloth to form a packet large enough for the affected area.

3. Apply to the area, using a bandage to keep the poultice in place.

4. Apply a new poultice every two hours if the injury is serious or leave it overnight if it's less serious. Seal with plastic to avoid leakage.

How to make
herbal tinctures and remedies

Tinctures are made from steeping herbs in alcohol or vinegar to extract their medicinal properties. They can be taken orally or applied topically to address specific health concerns.

YOU WILL NEED

Glass container or jar

Dried or fresh herbs

Alcohol or cider vinegar

Strainer or muslin

METHOD

1. Fill a clean, dry glass jar with one-third of the dried or fresh herbs (fresh herbs should be wilted for 24 hours before using).

2. Choose herbs that have the healing properties you require. (See herbs list on pages 95–100.)

3. Cover the herbs with an alcohol of your choice (must be above 80 proof). I use

brandy, but you could use grappa, vodka, gin or rum. You may prefer to use apple cider vinegar.

4. Secure the lid. Label the jar with the date and herbs used. Store in a dark room or cupboard away from direct sunlight for 4–6 weeks, shaking the jar every few days for even distribution.

5. After 6 weeks, strain or squeeze out the herbs using muslin cloth and bottle your tincture.

Note: while these remedies are based on traditional practices, they are not a substitute for professional medical advice or treatment. Always consult a healthcare professional for any health-related concerns. When using herbs or natural remedies, ensure you understand their properties, potential interactions and any contraindications before use.

Coughs, colds and eye complaints

Treating an eye stye

Eye stye, or *orzaiolo*, is named after a grain of barley because its shape resembles an eye stye. The most common way of removing an eye stye was a sympathetic sewing ritual over the affected eye. In this ritual, the healer makes a sewing movement over the closed eye with a thread and needle, or with a saint medallion, adding prayers for maximum effect.

Here are two more methods:

1. Using nine barley grains, roll them over the affected eye, so it absorbs the negative energy. Repeat nine times.
2. Rub a gold wedding ring briskly in your palm. When warm, apply gently to the stye.

Treating conjunctivitis

Most remedies for conjunctivitis included warm chamomile tea. The most accessible cure was a warm wash of water and salt. This salt wash was used for just about anything – irritated eyes, toothaches or gum problems, sore throats, skin or nail infections, muscular and arthritic complaints, allergies, and post-baby treatments.

Treating colds and sore throats

For colds and sore throats, healers used mostly herbs and plants found in the colder weather. Other than drinking warmed wine or similar, most rural Italian folk used whatever was available in their region. My nonno would have our regional dish, *lo scattone* – a ladleful of fresh pasta and its starchy water mixed with red wine – to help cure his cold. Steam inhalations infused with aromatic herbs, such as thyme, are still used to relieve congestion and respiratory take back to previous pageBreathing in the herbal steam clears the airways and promotes easier breathing.

In central and southern Italy, the mallow plant was a good all-rounder in poultices or hot tea infusions. To make an infusion of mallow leaves, place them in a saucepan and bring to the boil. Once boiling, inhale the steam.

Other types of healing

For those living in southern Italy, life was perilous. Protective magic – whether using herbs, rituals, spells, amulets, or prayers to saints, angels or spirits – was a means of ensuring their survival and well-being. Life revolved around appeasing the spirits and living a highly syncretised life with folk Catholicism. One way to bridge the gap between ancient pagan rituals and Catholicism was to dance in honour of the saints on feast days. It wasn't just any dance. It was the *tarantella*. This dance has ancient origins and is connected to the orgiastic rituals of Bacchus (Dionysus), the god of wine.

Tarantìsmo

The *tarantella*, or dance of the spider, is a lively and rhythmic folk dance that has been popular for generations. It originated in southern Italy, particularly in Puglia, Calabria and Sicily. The dance has quick, upbeat movements and is often accompanied by traditional music played on tambourines, accordions and mandolins.

Apart from the joy of dancing the *tarantella*, the dance is considered to have healing properties and was once used as a form of therapy or cure for tarantism (*tarantismo*). Tarantism was believed to be caused by the bite of a tarantula spider, which led to symptoms such as restlessness, anxiety, hallucinations, sweating, trembling and an uncontrollable urge to dance.

Sometimes it had the opposite effect; the *tarantata* (usually a woman) entered into a state of shock and general malaise, from which she could only wake up through music. The cure for *tarantismo* involved performing the *tarantella* as a form of therapeutic release.

The dance was a way for the *tarantate* to expel the spider bite's venom or toxins from their bodies. The dance's intense and vigorous movements helped to release pent-up emotions, stress and anxiety, which would have promoted emotional and physical healing.

The *tarantella* also served as a way for the community to come together and support those affected by tarantism. People surrounded the victim and joined in the dancing, while musicians played until they found the correct rhythm to cure the *tarantata*.

Today, the *tarantella* dance is more a cultural and artistic expression than a cure for *tarantismo*. It is performed during various celebrations, festivals and traditional events in southern Italy, carrying on the region's rich cultural heritage. In Puglia, they dance to the rhythm of the *pizzica* (bite) − a type of *tarantella* originally from Salento. I enjoy listening to the *pizzica* songs by the group Canzoniere Grecanico Salentino and it's heartening to see the resurgence of this ancient folk-dance tradition with young artists using the ancient rhythm of the spider bite dance to create new versions.

At its heart, the *tarantella* encourages collective healing and a connection to ancestral music and traditions. This method of healing has been underestimated until recently. It's only now that we understand how moving the body can have a powerful healing effect that can be as effective, if not more, than other Western medicine alternatives.

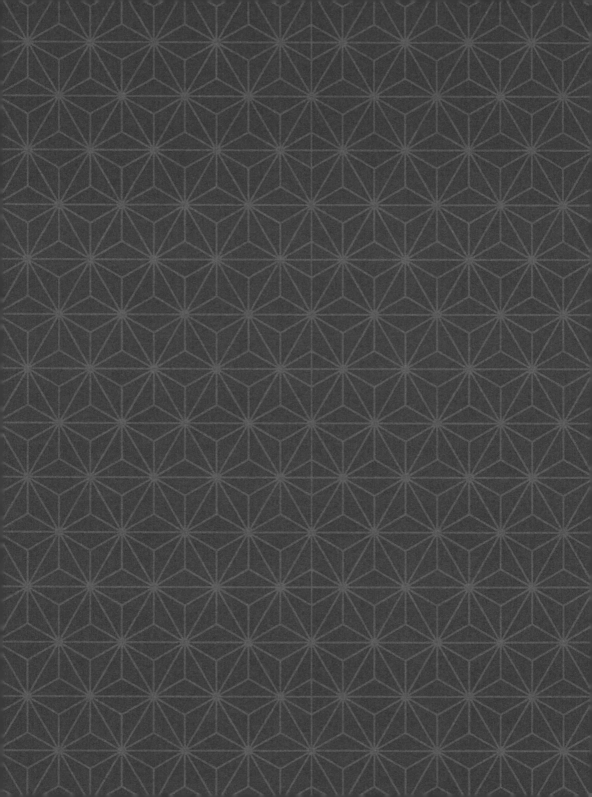

Chapter 10

Spells and love potions

Casting a spell in Italian *magia* or *stregoneria* involves focused intent, ritual actions, specific ingredients, such as herbs, candles, charms, words and symbolic objects. Although poppets (*puppie*) can be used as part of white magic, they were originally designed as binding (*legature*) practices and to restrict or contain the energy or influence of a person, situation or spirit. That goes for lemon-and-pin curses, and love philters containing menstrual blood or semen.

A *fattura* is a hex or spell that usually intends to control (as in a love break-up or lust spell) or wish someone bad luck. Again, these types of controlling hexes are not ones I would encourage anyone to practise. The use of charm bags (*abitini* or *brevi*) is a much more widely used method of spell-casting.

The *scongiuri* are spells with words or invocations; the term can also mean exorcisms. As you can imagine, because the term *strega* was derogatory, spell words in any dialect have not been shared other than through lineage healers. If these spells are still in use, they are not available for sharing.

I have collated some common spells and created modern versions, adapted from the *stregoneria* tradition. The intentions contained in these spells reflect the basic needs of common folk – protection, money, love and health. In the Italian diaspora, it's difficult to find a village healer who practices *stregoneria* and is willing to share her spells and incantations.

If you want to experience the flavour of these spells, this chapter provides you with some basic methods adapted from the ways of the *benedetti, guaritrici* and *streghe* (including herbs, *brevi*, salt, food, invocations to saints, smoke cleansing and a modern 'freezing' spell). Remember, the practice of creating spells, especially for protection, began in the kitchen from simple everyday herbs and items, for a very simple reason – survival. (For basic herbal spells, see Chapter 5.)

You may wish to add personal touches to make these spells your own, perhaps based on the old ways mentioned in this book or your ancestry. But however you create your *scongiuri*, keep it simple.

Before you begin spell-casting

1. Set your intention

Clearly define the purpose of your spell and set your intention. Be specific about what you want to achieve, ensuring your intention is positive, ethical, and aligned with your highest good and the good of others.

2. Choose your spell

Select a spell that aligns with your intention and is appropriate for your level of experience and comfort. You can find existing spells in books or online resources, or learn from an experienced practitioner within the Italian magical tradition.

3. Gather your materials

Collect the necessary ingredients and tools for your spell, including specific herbs, candles, oils, crystals or other symbolic objects that correspond to your intention and type of spell.

4. Prepare your space

Create a sacred space for your spell-casting, perhaps an area in your home or outdoors where you feel comfortable and undisturbed. Cleanse the space to remove any negative energies, using sage, incense, rosemary, bay leaves or any method that resonates with you.

5. Ground and centre yourself

Take a few moments to ground and centre yourself through deep breathing or visualisation. Focus your mind on your intention and connect with the energies of the elements and nature.

6. Perform the ritual

Follow the steps of your chosen spell, which may involve lighting candles, burning herbs, chanting incantations or performing specific actions. Pay attention to each step, staying focused on your intention throughout the ritual.

7. Visualise and embody the outcome

As you perform the ritual, visualise the desired outcome as if it has already happened. Feel the associated emotions, such as joy, gratitude or relief. Embody the energy of the outcome you seek.

8. Give thanks and release

Express gratitude to any deities, spirits or energies you invoked during the ritual. Release the spell's energy, trusting it will work in alignment with your intention.

9. Observe and trust

Observe the results of your spell with an open mind and heart. Remember, magic works in mysterious ways. The outcome may not always be immediate or apparent. Trust in the process and have faith that your intention has been set in motion.

Important note: always practise spell-casting with respect, responsibility and ethical consideration. Harming others or attempting to control someone's free will is not aligned with the principles of positive magic.

Protection spells

You don't perform protection spells, magic and rituals to bring harm or ill intent to persons; they protect you, your home, business and belongings from evil-eye curses, negative energies and entities, and all ill-intent curses. Using salt, fire, candles and herbs in spells can be powerful and versatile.

Simple protection spells with charms

1. A simple protection spell could be a charm or *brevi* recited with intention and belief. Sprinkle protective herbs, such as bay laurel, rosemary, rue or St John's wort, in doorways or carry in *brevi*.

2. Recite the following words:

    Con questa preghiera, ti invoco o Santo Patrono. Proteggi e custodisci questo luogo e chi vi risiede. Scaccia via le ombre e allontana le energie negative. Concedi la tua luce e il tuo vigore come scudo.

    With this prayer, I invoke you, Holy Patron. Protect and guard this place and those who reside here. Chase away the shadows and banish negative energies. Grant your light and strength as a shield.

    O Santo Patrono, proteggi da ogni male e pericolo. Fa' sì che la nostra casa sia un rifugio sicuro e sacro. Che ogni minaccia si allontani e non possa avvicinarsi. Concedi la tua benedizione, la tua protezione, la tua pace. Così sia.

    O Holy Patron, protect from all harm and danger. May our home be a safe and sacred refuge. May every threat be kept away and unable to approach. Grant your blessing, your protection, your peace. So be it (or Amen).

3. This charm can be recited while visualising a protective shield around the space or those you wish to protect. Together, the words and intention create a sense of safety and security, invoking the blessings and protection of a holy patron or spiritual figure.

Remember, the spell's power comes from your belief, intent and connection to the spiritual forces you are invoking.

Approach the charm with sincerity and reverence, trusting in its protective qualities. As with all magical practices, personalising the spell to fit your specific beliefs and traditions can make it even more meaningful and potent.

Protection from nightmares spell

If you want a good night's sleep, dill is the answer.

YOU WILL NEED

Dill seeds

Sea salt

Small sachet

METHOD

1. Grind the dill seeds and the salt together and pour them into the sachet.

2. Say a prayer to your favourite deity, nature spirit or folk saint – many invoke Archangel (Saint) Raphael (angel of healing) to protect them from nightmares.

3. Place the sachet under your pillow to repel nightmares, attract good dreams and have a relaxing night's sleep.

How to make black salt

Salt is used in various rituals and ceremonies, as well as remedies, cures and especially to form a protective boundary around one's home. Salt is said to absorb and repel all degrees of negative energy, evil eye curses, ghosts and spirits. Black salt is more powerful than sea salt; it is used for protection, banishment and fighting off baneful magic. (See also page 74.)

YOU WILL NEED

Birch (bark)

Cumin (optional)

Dill seeds

Fennel seeds

Rosemary sprigs

Sage

Coarsely ground black pepper

Crushed eggshell powder (optional)

Small pieces of charcoal

Sea salt, rock salt or Himalayan salt

METHOD

1. Heat the herbs, spices and eggshells with the charcoal until they burn. I use my cast-iron mini-cauldron (iron is for good luck), but you can use any heatproof dish or steel pan. Burn until only ashes are left.

2. Once they have cooled down, scrape the ashes out of your cauldron and place in a mortar. Grind down any larger pieces then mix with salt of your choice. Use two parts ash to one part salt. Store in a clean airtight glass jar and store in a dark place.

3. Sprinkle some black salt at the entrances and exits of your home, as well as by windows, drains, air or heat vents.

Salt spell no. 1

YOU WILL NEED

Salt (preferably sea salt or Himalayan salt) or black salt

Small glass jar or container with a lid

White candle

METHOD

1. Pour the salt into the glass jar, holding the intention of protection in your mind. Light a white candle and let the flame pass over the jar's opening, symbolically sealing the protective energy within.

2. As you do this, recite a short incantation for protection: 'Salt of earth, protect and guard, keep away all harm and ill regard. By the power of fire and light, protect this space both day and night.'

Salt spell no. 2

YOU WILL NEED
Bowl

Salt (preferably sea salt or Himalayan salt)

METHOD

1. In a bowl, place the quantity of salt needed for your protection ritual (whether it's for sprinkling around the perimeter of your home, by your entrance doors or in each room).

2. Place the prepared bowl of salt on a windowsill or in a window space where the sunlight and moonlight rays will 'touch' it. Leave for 24 hours to absorb the sunlight's and moonlight's energy.

3. When you're preparing to disperse the salt around your home, bless and say a prayer over your prepared salt to magnify your intention, such as healing, purifying or protection. If it is for protection, say: 'I ask the protective energy of this salt to form a boundary and protect my home from all negative energy and ill intent.'

4. After 24 hours, your salt is ready to be sprinkled in small amounts in the areas you want to protect and clear away negative energy. Allow the prepared salt to remain in those areas – it does not need to be cleaned away.

Smoke-cleansing protection spell

Whether using a smoke-cleansing stick or incense stick, the 'smoking' (directing the wafting smoke around your body or through your house) gives you a three-fold circle of protection. In *suffumigi* (Italian-style smoking), it was traditional to burn both fresh and dried herbs on a ceramic or terracotta tile – even a roof tile. You light small pieces of coals on the tile then burn the herbs with it. You may wish to adopt this style of smoke cleansing to honour the *stregoneria* tradition.

YOU WILL NEED

One or several herbs (common sage, pine, mugwort, rosemary) and flowers (such as lavender) bunched and tied together securely, or a crafted smoke-cleansing stick. You may use a resin such as frankincense as an incense.

Fireproof dish or bowl

METHOD

1. Light the herb bundle, allowing it to smoulder and produce smoke.

2. Walk around your space, carrying the burning sage in a fireproof dish or bowl. Focus on cleansing the space of negative energies, paying particular attention around doors, windows and mirrors, and inside cupboards..

3. As you do this, say: 'With this smoke, I cleanse this space.' You may also ask for Archangel Michael's protection.

Front door protection spell

You'd typically do this on the first day of the new year or any time you need to 'wash away' bad energy from entering your home through the front door. Spiritual-practising cultures often refer to doorways as portals or passageways, which bridge the outside and inner sanctum worlds.

YOU WILL NEED

Large bowl or bucket

Filtered, spring or moon water (see page 75).

Choose a herb or essential oil with 'protection and cleansing' properties for house blessings. Herbs that match well for house spells and blessings are cedar, fennel seed, juniper leaf, pine and white sage. The best protective and cleansing essential oils to use for this spell are eucalyptus, lemon, peppermint, rosemary, tea tree and thyme.

Clean cloth

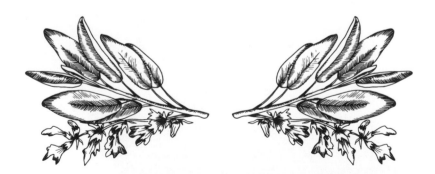

METHOD

1. Fill a large bowl with filtered water.

2. Place a handful of protective herbs or several drops of protective essential oils into the water bowl. You can even add both herbs and oils if you like.

3. Dip the cloth into the herb- or oil-infused bowl and wash down your front door, including the screens, handles, locks, frame and bottom lintel.

4. As you wash down your front door and entrance, you can also say a house-protection blessing to add a further layer of protection for your home.

5. Allow your newly washed front door to dry naturally.

6. Using a broom or besom made from natural wood fibres is useful to 'sweep away' and clear negative energy from your front entrance.

Simple oil protection spell

YOU WILL NEED

Basil

Cinnamon

Lavender

Rosemary

Carrier oil (olive oil, vitamin E, coconut, jojoba)

1 glass jar or container

METHOD

1. Infuse the herbs in a glass jar or container and leave in a dark space for several weeks. Shake it every few days to mix the flavours.

2. You can apply it on the skin (after doing a 24-hour patch test on skin). Use the oil for anointing candles or any spell work that requires defensive and protective magic.

Banishing spells

If you want to remove someone from your life, you'd use a banishing spell. A typical one blocks or pushes someone away. A freeze spell makes someone stop bothering you − this could be a persistent ex-boyfriend or a negative person who 'dumps' their problems on you. Before freezers were available, the *fattucchiera* would bury the offender's *puppia* (poppet) in the ground, and possibly cut areas such as the mouth to indicate they didn't wish to be communicated with any longer.

Banishing spell using freezing

This spell stops people's energy from bothering you. Note, it doesn't affect who they are or cause them any harm, it just freezes their negativity towards you personally, not their negativity towards anyone else.

People affect you with their negativity in two ways:

1. If they have something against you specifically.

2. If they are negative and angry at everyone, but you're the one they dump on and you get the brunt of it.

YOU WILL NEED

Plain, clean, square piece of white paper

Black permanent marker

Small piece of black string

Small food storage container that seals

Water

Freezer

Best time to perform: five minutes after the hour, during the waning moon

METHOD

1. Write or print the offending person's name in the centre of the paper with the marker.

2. Draw a thick circle anticlockwise around the name, thinking of banishing energy as you draw. You can say: 'I banish your energy,' or 'I banish your presence from my life.'

3. Tie a knot in the middle of the string. Fold up the paper with the piece of string placed inside it like a bookmark.

4. Put the paper and string in the empty container. Pour water on the paper, so the paper floats but is still surrounded by water.

5. Seal the container and put in the freezer. Wash your hands in cold water. Leave the container in the freezer for as long as the person is around you then a month longer.

6. Once you no longer need the freezing energy, remove the container from the freezer and let it thaw.

7. Take out the paper and let it dry.

8. Once dry, burn it.

Money spells

Cinnamon is not only a centuries-old favourite cooking spice, but it's also a tool to attract wealth, abundance and prosperity. When you consume or handle this spice, those same energetic properties flow freely throughout your body and spirit.

Lemons contain powerful cleansing and protective properties. When performing spellwork combining lemons with ground cinnamon, your blessings will attract good luck, favourable fortunes, wealth and abundance from the cinnamon, while instilling a powerful protection essence from the lemon, protecting your money from any negativity, evil eye or bad intent.

Bay laurel is protective and brings in wealth. Its leaves were used for crowning Olympic champions and Roman emperors. Basil is another prosperity herb with added properties of love and protection. The following spells can bring these wealthy attributes to your life when you set the intention of wanting abundance 'for the need and not for the greed'.

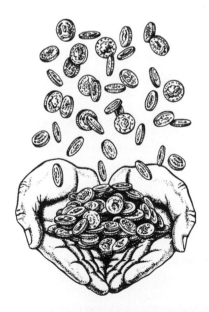

Lemon and cinnamon

YOU WILL NEED

Lemon

Ground cinnamon (grind a cinnamon stick in a mortar and pestle)

METHOD

1. Cut the lemon in half.

2. Sprinkle a generous amount of ground cinnamon on one lemon half.

3. Rub the cinnamon-coated lemon half on your palms – first the right palm, then the left palm.

4. Rub your lemon-cinnamon-coated palms together while you visualise or speak your blessing of attracting money's flow and abundance to you.

5. Stand or sit down, turning both palms to face upwards.

6. Remain still and quiet for a minute or so while you continue to visualise good luck, good fortune and money flowing to you, as well as your life being abundant on all levels.

7. After completing your abundant visualisation and blessing, wash the remaining cinnamon and lemon off your hands.

Bay leaf money spell

YOU WILL NEED

Dried bay leaf

Marker or ink pen

Tweezers

Fireproof bowl

Lighter or matches

METHOD

1. Choose a large bay leaf with enough area to write some words and symbols on it. Place the bay leaf on a flat dry surface.

2. Using the marker, you can write out the exact amount of money you're calling in, or simply write the words 'Abundance', 'Wealth', 'Money' on the bay leaf. Once you have written your word or amount, draw some dollar signs in the unwritten space.

3. Using your tweezers, pick up the bay leaf by the stem.

4. Holding it over your fireproof bowl, light the bay leaf at the tip end (opposite to the tweezers) with your free hand. As the bay leaf burns, set your abundance intention by visualising wealth and abundance flowing to you, or speaking a wealth and abundance blessing: 'With this fire, bless my wealth and prosperity.'

5. You can sprinkle the bay leaf ashes in your garden.

6. Alternatively, instead of burning the bay leaf, once you have written your word and symbols on it, place it in your purse/wallet and carry it for 8 days. Then take out the bay leaf and bury it in your garden.

7. You can also place the bay leaf on the inside sole of your left shoe (the left side is the 'receiving' side), so when you walk, you're 'walking' towards abundance and prosperity.

8. Leave the bay leaf in your shoe for nine days, then remove it and bury it in your garden.

Love spells

When casting love and romance spells, remember that everyone has free will. The real purpose of love and romance spell work is opening yourself up to the possibilities of love and bringing more romance into your life. This includes romancing yourself and raising your own levels of self-love, so you can begin to attract that which you are. It's best to cast love spells, rituals and charms on a Friday night because Friday is associated with Venus, which signifies tenderness, love and courtship. But don't forget that, in Italian folk tradition, it's bad luck to get married on a Friday.

Love philters (*filtri*), also known as love potions, are used for attracting love or as aphrodisiacs. I wouldn't recommend using menstrual blood or semen as part of the brew, but some potions contain ingredients that can allure love.

LOVER-LY INGREDIENTS

APPLES	Known to be symbols of love and longevity. Add apple blossoms to love *brevi* to attract love. The simplest spell is cutting an apple in half and feeding it to the person you're attracted to so they will fall in love.
COFFEE AND CHOCOLATE	Other major love foods are coffee and chocolate – both said to elevate desire and romantic energy.
FIGS	Reported to be one of Cleopatra's favourite fruits, figs are associated with sexuality and female genitalia due to their erotic shape. *Mano fica* (literally meaning 'fig hand') represents the sexual act in a charm to protect from the *malocchio*. Saffron was Cleopatra's other favourite herb.
HONEY	With long history as an aphrodisiac, honey is known as the nectar of the gods. It 'attracts' suitors – who doesn't like some sweetness in their relationship? The word 'honeymoon' (*luna di miele*) comes from wishing newlyweds a 'sweet marriage' – a fertile and compatible one. Honey can sweeten an existing relationship.
POMEGRANATES	A fruit sacred to Venus (Aphrodite), pomegranate is associated with fertility and connected to the goddess Proserpina (Persephone), who was abducted by Pluto (Hades). Because she ate six seeds, it meant she had to spend six months of the year with Pluto in the underworld. The pomegranate's red colour is associated with passion, love and fertility. It may be used in love spells or rituals to enhance romantic relationships.
SEEDS	These have great sexual potency. Fennel is a common ingredient in love spells to awaken love. Dill seeds strengthen existing love. Coriander seeds help to maintain faithfulness, while caraway seeds encourage lustful thoughts.

LOVER-LY INGREDIENTS

STRAWBERRIES The strawberry's heart shape symbolises the goddess
Venus (Aphrodite). Legend says that if you share a double
strawberry with someone special, it will turn into true love.
Use strawberries in fruit smoothies so love is never too far
away – especially as a reminder to love yourself.

Herbs of love, spice of life

Other herbs and spices used in folk magic love potions include:

- ▶ Angelica
- ▶ Anise
- ▶ Basil
- ▶ Bay leaves
- ▶ Cardamon
- ▶ Chamomile
- ▶ Cinnamon
- ▶ Cloves
- ▶ Coriander
- ▶ Cumin
- ▶ Lavender
- ▶ Lemon
- ▶ Lemon verbena
- ▶ Mint
- ▶ Rose petals
- ▶ Rosemary
- ▶ St John's wort
- ▶ Vanilla
- ▶ Violet flowers

Enchanted love

Create the intention of a romantic evening and infuse your energy into the love potion. Mix your potion on a Friday (Venus's day).

YOU WILL NEED

2 cups orange juice

Juice from 2 limes

2 basil leaves

6 mint leaves

Sweetener (e.g. caramelised sugar)

METHOD

1. Combine all the ingredients in a large jug.

2. Serve chilled in tall glasses decorated with extra mint leaves. You could coat the glass rims with caster sugar.

3. Give the potion to your loved one when they arrive home.

Spellbound

Make this winter passion brew to help you find the love of your life.

YOU WILL NEED

6 fresh mint leaves

½ cup rose petals

1–2 teaspoons ground cloves

Pinch of nutmeg

½ cup mixed lemon and orange peel

4 cups spring water

1 bottle red wine

METHOD

1. Mix all the ingredients together in a saucepan. Bring to the boil and simmer for 15–20 minutes.

2. Serve warm. Drink half a glass nightly until consumed. When you drink, say: 'Bring me my true love.'

LOVE POTION NO. 3

Lover-ly tea

Celebrate love and feel-good vibes with this relaxing tea.

YOU WILL NEED

1 part lavender

1 part jasmine

1 part rose petals

1 part orange peel

Pinch of cinnamon

Honey

METHOD

1. Mix all the herbs together in a jar with a lid.

2. Put 1 heaped teaspoon of the herbal blend in a cup and pour 1 cup boiling water over. Let steep for 5 minutes.

3. Sweeten with honey as desired. Strain, sip and relax.

Magical self-love

YOU WILL NEED

Rose quartz

Rosemary

Cinnamon

Pink Himalayan salt

Pink rose buds and rose petals

Pink ribbon

Pink candle

Lighter or matches

METHOD

1. Put the first five ingredients in a jar with a lid. Sit with the jar and the intention of self-love. Say three times: 'I ask for love of myself to come. I open my heart to myself.'

2. Close the jar and tie the pink ribbon around it from top to bottom.

3. Position the candle on the lid over the ribbon and light it. Let wax drip over the lid to seal the spell.

Passion love oils

You can add essential oil blends that entice love to your bath, oil burner or use as body oil. Always mix them with base oils (almond, jojoba, olive, apricot, avocado) and test a small area on your body before using any of these blends. These oil blends also work in room sprays and with water as body splashes.

PASSION DEWS	
FOR SENSUALITY	Chamomile, lavender, orange blossom, jasmine, patchouli
TO HELP HEAL A BROKEN HEART	Bergamot, rose, neroli
TO OPEN UP TO A NEW LOVE	Rose, sandalwood, jasmine

Pink candle spell

Love and romance spells using pink candles are among the most popular love spells. Pink candles are often used in love spells because they symbolise love and spirituality.

YOU WILL NEED

Two pink candles
Fireproof dish
Essential oils
Thick pink ribbon

METHOD

1. Place the pink candles on the fireproof dish. (Small candles will burn down quicker.)

2. Anoint the candles with an essential oil that represents love, such as bergamot, jasmine, orange blossom, patchouli, rose, rosemary or ylang ylang.

3. Tie the pink ribbon around the base of both candles.

4. Carefully light the candles. As you gaze upon their flames, visualise an image of you and your desired love partner together. Spend time imagining the love relationship, pleasure and loving life you will share with each other.

5. Now say a love prayer and repeat it three times: 'I open my heart and mind so I will recognise my love partner. I ask that my love partner now comes into my life so we can live our lives together.'

6. Allow the candles to safely burn out. Bury the melted candle wax in your garden.

● ● ●

I listed love spells last for a reason – they can be effective but will take time, effort and focus for the spell caster. You must have clear intentions, mental focus and the required ingredients. Most importantly, you cannot use a negative energy to put a spell on someone to make them fall in love with you against their free will, or break them up with their current partner. The spell will backfire and can be turned against you.

While love marriages are now common, most of our grandparents and some of our parents had arranged marriages, or were pressured to marry someone their parents recommended. Marriage was for survival – having children and a partner to work alongside until your old age. The benchmark for partner selection was not what it is today. I've included self-love here (unheard of 60 years ago) because we live in different times. Today's relationships are much more unpredictable.

These spells are intended as examples. You can modify them to suit your specific intentions and beliefs. Create your individual rituals to invite love into your life. When performing any spell work, make sure you have positive intentions, respect for the elements and a clear focus on your desired outcome. Always practise magic responsibly and in harmony with the natural world, like the wise women of Italy.

PART 3

Spiritual practices

Chapter 11

Working with saints and angels

There is a special relationship between Catholic saints and Italian people. I've been surrounded by saints my whole life – our house was filled with icons, images, statues, holy water from Lourdes in the moulded plastic shape of a Madonna, rosary beads, crucifixes, the Last Supper hanging over our dining table and the strangely disturbing heart of Jesus image that lit up above my parents' bed.

Those of Italian heritage and of a certain age will know what I'm describing. Who are the saints and why do they have such influence on Italian Catholics? Saints are explained as being real humans who lived holy lives and continue to live on spiritually after their physical death. They are venerated for their healing miracles and martyrdom, and it's only through their intercession that we're given what we request. The saints serve as mediators between the spiritual and material realms, offering comfort, protection and hope to those who seek their aid.

Many folk saints are invoked and venerated because they are relatable to the real problems Italian people face that put their lives and survival at risk – from persecution and protection from the weather or natural events to relationships and health. These saints offered devotees a connection to their shared experiences. According to tradition, if you're named after a saint, you're protected by that saint. So, choosing a name for your child is more important than simply liking the sound or trend of that name. Most people in my generation were named after their grandparents or the town's patron saint, which makes your family and home town easy to work out. This ancestral identity is something we've lost today in our individualistic-driven society.

My zia was terrified of thunder and lightning, right up until she passed away. Even as a child she would pray to St Barbara, who protected against thunder, storms and lightning strikes. My zia's worst fear came true when her brother, my zio, was hit by lightning as he sheltered under a tree during a storm. He was badly burned but survived; however, his close friend and relative who was sheltering next to him did not.

St Barbara is the patron saint of artillery soldiers, firefighters, architects, miners, firework makers, mathematicians, chemical engineers and anyone who faces sudden or violent death at work.

When something was lost, we'd say a prayer to St Anthony to help us find it: 'Anthony, Anthony, come around, something's lost and must be found.'

If you've been brought up Italian Catholic, you know saints play a big part in our lives – not because of the Catholic Church dogma about saint days and their official day of observance (FYI, many Catholics don't go to church at all), but because of the folk magic rituals associated with them that blend the pagan with Christianity (syncretism). Think special foods, rituals and all those protection amulets!

Practising folk magic creates a less formal relationship with the saints, who are more like ancient pagan deities. People will venerate particular saints when they need a specific favour, whereas Jesus and Mary are always considered sacred and treated with much more reverence.

Today, those who work with saints, not just the *benedetti* (the blessed) who practise *benedicaria*, usually have a strong connection to the saint because of the issues they face in their daily lives. St Expedite, the patron saint of procrastination, has recently become more popular – procrastination is a common problem in our fast-paced world. There is no special way to work with saints who are meaningful to you, or who are patrons of causes dear to you. And you don't need to be a practising Catholic!

In Italian folk magic, we use invocations and blessings to call upon the assistance and guidance of spiritual forces, deities, saints, ancestors or other beings of power. We often recite these invocations and blessings during rituals, spellwork or sacred ceremonies. Here are some common examples of invocations and blessings, with regional variations:

Invocation to the divine

O Divina Forza, presenza sacra,
Ti invochiamo in questa ora magica.
Concedi la tua luce e protezione,
Guidaci nel cammino della benedizione.

O Divine Force, sacred presence,
We invoke you in this magical hour.
Grant us your light and protection,
Guide us on the path of blessing.

Blessing for prosperity

Con questa preghiera, chiedo la prosperità,
Che abbondanza e ricchezza vengano da me.
Che la generosità del cielo sia mia alleata,
E la prosperità cresca e fiorisca ogni giorno.

With this prayer, I ask for prosperity,
May abundance and wealth come to me.
May the generosity of the heavens be my ally,
And may prosperity grow and flourish every day.

Tools

The tools for working with saints are used both for sacramentals by the *benedetti* and folk magic healing. While these objects are used for Catholic rituals and blessings, they can also be used for magical work. The list is quite extensive, and it's not essential to have or use all these items – only those that resonate with your beliefs and practices.

ASHES	These are from leaves burned on Palm Sunday and blessed by the priest at mass. But you can use olive leaves or any replacement of palm leaves.
BELLS	Used traditionally in mass to punctuate different parts of the prayer rituals. It may be used to begin and finish a petition to a saint.
CANDLES	Each saint has their preferred colour of candle, but white is the standard.
CROSS	To ward off evil or as a protection talisman
CRUCIFIX (CROSS WITH BODY OF CHRIST)	For protection spells, talismans
EX-VOTO	An offering to a saint or deity to thank them for a miracle granted (symbol of gratitude for answered prayers). Traditionally, ex-votos were gold and silver jewellery pinned on the saint's dress or, more often, the Madonna's dress as part of the processione (street procession).
FLOWERS	Special flowers are attributed to saints on saint days, such as white lilies for St Joseph, or roses for the Madonna or St Teresa.
FOOD	Offerings of cakes or bread. In the case of perishable foods or water/drink, the offering is replenished daily while the candle burns each day.
HOLY OIL	Oil blessed by a priest that's usually applied to the sick, but it can be oil infused with protective herbs (see page 90).
ICONS	Statues, portraits and saints' cards
INCENSE	Traditionally, this was frankincense and myrrh.

MARY GARDENS	A garden feature (many homes have a Mary statue or grotto in the front yard), consisting of a statue of the Blessed Virgin surrounded by a flower garden. It usually resembles a grotto.
NOVENA	A series of prayers said over nine consecutive days to petition a saint for help with a specific need, serious problem or miracle. Lighting candles may be an alternative for those uncomfortable with praying the novena.
PATRONAGE ITEMS	Items or tokens representing what the saint is patron of (such as keys for St Peter, candle for St Lucy).
ROSARY BEADS	The beads of a rosary help you count the prayers as you recite them out loud or in your mind.
SAINT MEDALLION	Flat, round or oval piece of metal impressed with the image of a saint. These small medallions are worn as necklaces or carried in the pocket with the saint's image on one side. Often, the inscription 'pray for us' or 'protect us' is written on the back.
SCAPULAR	A small square cloth sewn on two sides with an image of Jesus on one side and Mary on the other. These cloth squares are connected by two strings and joined like a necklace. The scapular is placed over your head so that one small square rests on the back and the other on the breast (near the heart).
TRADITIONAL CATHOLIC PRAYERS	Reading prayer cards, for praying while burning candles, or morning, afternoon and evening prayers.
WATER	This is spring water, holy water blessed by the church or a shrine (such as Lourdes), or special saints' water such as Mary Water or St John's Water (*Acqua di San Giovanni*).

Non-traditional tools

- ▶ Anything made from iron (for good luck)
- ▶ Crystals
- ▶ Feathers
- ▶ Herbs and branches of trees, such as olive
- ▶ Oracle or tarot cards
- ▶ Salt
- ▶ Small stones
- ▶ Vaporiser or oil burner with essential oils

How to work with saints

If you're interested in establishing a relationship with a saint or saints you have a heart connection with, you don't need to be Christian or Catholic to venerate them. However, you should work with saints with respect and integrity, regardless of your personal beliefs or practices. You may wish to adapt your rituals to add to existing traditional Christian ones. In folk magic, working with saints is an eclectic mix of Catholic beliefs and ancient pagan customs.

Some saints feel more demanding to work with than others. It all depends on your experience with them, but normally, they will come to your aid when they consider the request or petition is appropriate or acceptable.

How to ask for a saint's help in the traditional way

Find some quiet time and go to a space in your home that feels comfortable.

1. Take a deep breath and ground yourself.
2. Approach your saint altar or the item you associate with that saint.

3. Light a candle and say: 'This is for you [saint's name].'

4. Imagine your request in your mind (if you want money, then imagine a holiday). Then make your request clear. Say it out loud.

5. Promise a votive (devotional gift) or series of prayers dedicated to the saint.

6. If you want to make it simple, just ask for help from the saint with an open heart in any way you choose – via meditation or prayer.

Find your patron saint

Before petitioning and working with any saint, research their history, story and patronages to learn about their personality and preferences.

For those with ancestral connections to Italy, you could find out who the patron saint of your family's town(s) is. You'll have a family connection to this patron saint even if you live in the Italian diaspora, whether through your relatives' names (normally some family members are named after the saint), and recipes connected to the saint's feast day when the special foods were enjoyed.

If you share a name with the saint, you could find out more characteristics and details about that saint. Different professions – such as butchers, sailors, doctors and midwives – have their own patron saint. Perhaps this is where you'll find a connection. Some of these patronages are based on their stories and others have been adapted to our modern needs to reflect that saint's legacy.

Prayers and votive offerings

The main way to work with saints is through prayers and votive offerings. Praying to a saint means you are using the saint as an intermediary to intercede on your behalf to God or a higher power. Votive offerings are things you dedicate to God or a saint to request their help or thank them for their help.

Also known as an *ex-voto*, it could be any 'gift' or 'offering' that reflects your gratitude. Those who don't wish to use folk Catholic rituals and prayers may adapt them to their own spiritual belief systems. It's important to give an offering before/during the petition, thank them afterwards and also thank them when you receive what you asked for.

Creating an altar

Where you create your altar depends on whether you're comfortable with displaying a saint altar for everyone to see. If you feel the altar reflects a private relationship you want to develop with the saints of your choice, then make your sacred space more secluded.

You can use anything for an altar, depending on your space limitations. It may be a shelf, table or several surfaces, and may be dedicated to as many saints or deities as you wish. I have an antique dresser I picked up at a second-hand (goodwill) store with two drawers in which I keep all my votives and altar items. The surface has my nonna's hand-embroidered linen hand towel that acts as a table runner. I rotate some of my altar items, depending on what I am in need of at the time. Usually, I have one or two saints or deities for whatever my current need is. You are only limited by your imagination.

Be creative with your altar – a lovely colourful scarf for a tablecloth, statues and rosary beads, candles, small painted ceramic dishes, and framed pictures of your saint – even if you print one on your own printer and reuse an old photo frame. Make what you can and be natural, using flowers from your garden, rocks or pebbles from nature, or feathers from a favourite bird found as you walk in the park. Think what you would have brought home as a child. Once I found a beautiful bird's nest, perfectly formed, that had fallen out of a tree – I used it on my altar. I was offering nature's handiwork as a symbol of gratitude and admiration.

Some like to keep their altars separate – for saints and deities or nature spirits. Others prefer to have the spiritual and magical together to bring in all the energies meaningful to them or that are part of their cultural heritage. I combine both *benedicaria* and *stregoneria* in my work. On my altar is a ceramic statue of Mary, my favourite crystals, an oil burner with essential oils, dried lavender from my garden, a Tibetan singing bowl, candles, a sage bundle, my oracle card for the day, saint prayer cards, incense, a plant, rosary beads and a bracelet with a saint medal.

HOW TO SET UP YOUR ALTAR

Before you set up your altar, have a clear intention of its purpose in your home.

1. Declutter the room and clean it thoroughly. Do a smoke cleansing with bay leaves or similar herb for protection and blessing.

2. Use a new damp cloth (preferably using bottled water) to gently wipe down the items you will be placing on the altar.

3. Wipe the surface of your altar. If you wish, cover it with a tablecloth, cloth or scarf to protect your altar from scratches or candlewax.

4. Place all your items on your altar.

5. Place your votive offerings to your saint or deity. Light a new candle of any colour. When you have finished your devotion, blow out the candle with a candle snuffer.

La Madonna – Our Lady, the Virgin Mary, Holy Mother

The most common girl name in Italy has always been Maria and Mario for a boy – named after the Madonna. Other names for Maria include Concetta (Immaculate 'conception'), Assunta (the Assumption), Immacolata (Immaculate), Regina (queen 'of heaven'), Addolorata (Our Lady of Sorrows), Stella (star 'of the sea'), Rosaria/Rosario (rosary). I'm sure I've missed some, but you can see the popularity and level of adoration Our Lady receives. Unlike the saints, Mary is on a much higher standing when it comes to veneration and spiritual influence.

The feast of the Madonna (Our Lady) – Virgin Mary and Holy Mother – is celebrated all over Italy. It's not a singular event either. There are numerous feasts of the Madonna depending on the locations and individual Madonnas being celebrated. The events range from colourful pageants and processions to more subdued worship, depending on regional cultural traditions.

As a Catholic saint, the Madonna is Mary, the Virgin and Holy Mother of Jesus. She was born without sin and assumed bodily into Heaven after death. Although a saint and deity in her own right, the spiritual face of the Great Goddess was syncretised to Holy Mother Mary with Christianity. Her influence is reflected in the traditional Italian family structure, in which the mother nurtures the family unit to thrive. Mary's help is invoked when healing and protecting the family and home.

Images of Mary

The Madonna is the ultimate spiritual mother. It's surprising to see the sheer number of *madonelle* (small Madonnas) and shrines to her – in churches, grottos, city streets or hillside towns. Many sites now dedicated to the Madonna were originally pre-pagan sacred sites. Natural sacred sites on hills and mountains, in grottos, or by the water all had special landscape features and had been places of worship in much earlier times. Ancient Italian peoples worshipped mother goddesses long before the Romans introduced their pagan gods, which themselves were syncretised from other cultures. In early Christianity, Mary was not 'worshipped' as a sacred deity, but people were used to having a mother goddess whom they could venerate and ask for assistance in their time of need. Eventually, the Madonna became the personification of all other ancient mother goddesses and in her own right, as mother of Jesus. You will notice several animistic and pagan symbols in her images – such as the snake, moon, stars, colours and flowers – these all remained part of the Catholic tradition of Mary veneration.

The Virgin Mary is often depicted with a snake under her feet, symbolising her power over evil, and with a crescent moon above her, representing her cosmic rule over the world. She is also represented with stars and crowns and, as Our Lady of Sorrows, wearing black clothing with a heart pierced by swords, representing her grief. The rosary is dedicated to her life with each bead representing important life events. 'Rosary' derives from 'rose'; Mary is known as Mystical Rose.

Mary's feast days

Quite a few Marian (meaning dedicated to Mary) feast days appear in the Catholic calendar. May is the month of Mary, and the month of the rosary is October. But the ones that are special to our family are Our Lady's birthday on 8 September and her Assumption on 15 August. The Assumption commemorates the belief that when Mary died, rather than going through the natural process of physical decay, her soul and body were both taken to heaven.

The Black Madonna

The original feminine spirituality that connected women to the spirit world is represented by the Black Madonna. She was the colour of earthiness – of blackness. The Black Madonna of Montevergine is an example of primal mother goddess and earth mother devotion. She is considered a patron saint of the LGBTQ+ community because she once saved two boys in love, who were condemned to death in 1256. This then allowed gay men (*femminielli)* to be accepted by the community, which remains today. The Black Madonna is believed to have emerged from the cult worship of the goddess *Iside* (Isis), then the variants of the other Madonnas followed from there. She is revered in many other places in Europe and is known for her healing powers and protection of those who are marginalised or discriminated against.

Altar/votive offers

Here are votives I've used for Mary's altar. It's important to create your individual altar using items that are sacred to you.

A CANDLE	To keep her in our memory
FEATHERS	Collected on walks, feathers represent the wings of angels, the birds and doves that are goddess companions and our symbol of freedom. Some of my favourites include ebony raven, white cockatoo, the humble wood duck, colourful parrots and bronze wild dove feathers.
FLOWERS	Mary's namesake as the sacred rose
HOLY IMAGES OF MARY	To pray to her many roles
LEAVES, SEEDS, PODS	A reminder to be aware of the cycles of nature and of life
PEBBLES AND ROCKS	From brooks and clear mountain streams, a favourite landmark of Mary where she has appeared. Water is a conduit for healing.
PERFUMED OILS AND INCENSE	To send prayers and requests to her
ROSARY BEADS	Made of glass, crystals or wood – all for saying the rosary or novenas
SHELLS FROM THE SEA	A tribute to Mary's title of Star of the Sea and the majesty of the ocean

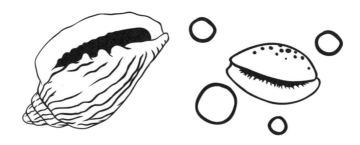

How to make Mary's flower water

Mary's water has protective and sacred qualities.

YOU WILL NEED

Rose petals

Mint leaves

Bowl

Water

METHOD

1. On the night of Mary's ascension – the Feast of the Assumption on 15 August – place fresh rose petals and mint leaves in a bowl of water (Mary's flower is the rose).

2. Pray that the Madonna will bless the water then leave the bowl with the water and flowers overnight. In the morning, wash your face with the water.

3. The belief is that the Madonna has come down overnight to bless the water. This is similar to *acqua di San Giovanni,* in which holy water with flowers is blessed by a saint on the eve of their feast day.

Saints

The saints are often associated with specific attributes, symbols and domains of influence. For example, St Anthony is the patron saint of lost items, St Agatha is invoked for protection against fire and volcanic eruptions, and St Lucy is associated with eyesight. These attributes make certain saints particularly relevant for specific magical intentions.

San Giuseppe (St Joseph – 19 March)

St Joseph is a popular saint throughout Italy. He is the patron saint of Sicily, after saving the people from drought by bringing in spring rains. His feast day, known as the *Festa di San Giuseppe*, is celebrated on 19 March (in Italian spring) on the same day as Father's Day. On 1 May, he is celebrated in honour of workers' rights.

A carpenter by trade, St Joseph is the foster father of Jesus and husband of the Virgin Mary. As a loving and devoted father figure, he played a vital role in nurturing and raising Jesus. He is the patron saint of the church, families, fathers, expectant mothers, travellers, immigrants, house sellers and buyers, craftsmen, engineers, workers, and for granting a peaceful death.

Many saints are associated with seasonal foods. Because 19 March falls within Lent, when Catholics traditionally abstain from meat during the purificatory process leading up to Easter, St Joseph's traditional foods are vegetarian, or delicacies like snails and sardines. St Joseph's Day is renowned for two foods – bread and fava beans. On the feast day, it's traditional to bake *pane di San Giuseppe* (St Joseph's bread), a type of bread shaped like a staff or cross. I remember going to mass on his feast day and everyone got a bread roll to take home and eat after being blessed – called *la pagnotta di San Giuseppe*.

This bread is a symbol of blessing and abundance – a tribute to St Joseph as the breadwinner of the family. A special pastry called *zeppole*, made from a doughnut base, fried in oil and filled with custard, is eaten in the home in his honour. (For more, see zeppole recipe, page 264.)

It's amazing to see elaborate altars and tables filled with all types of bread dedicated to St Joseph, especially in Sicily where they have a special veneration for the saint. St Joseph's altars typically have three levels, representing the Holy Trinity or Holy Family, depending on who you ask. The large breads in the centre are dedicated to the Madonna, baby Jesus and Saint Joseph. This temporary shrine to St Joseph may be in parishes or at home, with other decorations and foods such as breads, zeppole, fruit, baked goods, wine, candles and fava bean dishes. Fava soups and recipes are part of the St Joseph's dinner table – this bean is lucky because it commemorates the time when it was the only crop that survived the drought.

According to the legend, during a severe drought and famine in Sicily, the crops were failing, leaving the people hungry and desperate. The farmers prayed to St Joseph for relief from the famine and for rain to water their crops. When the rains came, the only plant salvaged was the fava beans. The famine was averted so Sicilians have honoured St Joseph ever since.

The fava bean has become a symbol of St Joseph's protection and the harvest's abundance. On the Feast of St Joseph, many Sicilian households will prepare a special dish called *macco di fave*, or *maccu di San Giuseppe* – a fava bean soup.

Other symbols of San Giuseppe include carpenter tools and the *bastone di San Giuseppe*, or St Joseph's staff, flowering with a white lily, which is believed to invoke healing miracles.

HOW TO WORK WITH ST JOSEPH

When selling your home, St Joseph is who you need to turn to for help. You can purchase a St Joseph Home Seller Kit with details of how to create this ritual.

- ▶ Bury a statue of St Joseph in your yard, maybe wrapped in a cloth. But it must be upside down, near the 'For Sale' sign, facing the house. If you have an apartment, you can use a flowerpot in the same way.
- ▶ Once your house is sold, dig up the statue – make sure you remember where you've buried it. Clean it and put the statue in your new home, maybe on your altar or a prominent place of honour.
- ▶ St Joseph Real Estate kits are available online or in Catholic supply stores. Do an internet search and find one that delivers to your area. The instructions are the same and all kits come with a statue of St Joseph, a holy card with image and prayer, and instructions. If you need visual details, search for YouTube videos.

It may seem strange that St Joseph has to 'work' for or 'earn' his place of honour in your home, but essentially that's what he does. He is the patron saint of workers, after all. Once he makes sure your house is sold for the best price, only then will you take him out of his undignified upside-down position underground. Saints in Italian folk magic have this type of relationship with people – they have to deliver on their invocations, or they will suffer consequences. That could mean disloyalty, with a new saint established as the family's favourite patron saint.

ALTAR/VOTIVE GIFTS

Recite prayers and novenas to St Joseph, expressing gratitude and asking for his protection and blessings:

O St Joseph, whose protection is so great, so strong, so prompt before the throne of God, I place in you all my interest and desires.

Votive offerings: bread and breadcrumbs to symbolise sawdust, carpenter tools, white lilies, dried fava beans or pulses such as lentils

What to ask for: protection of your home and family, buying and selling real estate, looking for work, or if you are a single mother and need financial help

St Joseph Prayer suggestion

O, St Joseph, hear my earnest plea. I wish to sell this [house/property] quickly, easily and profitably, and I implore you to grant my wish by bringing me a good buyer, and by letting nothing hinder the closure of the sale. Amen.

Traditional prayer to St Joseph

O St Joseph, whose protection is so great, so strong, so prompt before the throne of God, I place in you all my interests and desires.
O St Joseph, do assist me by your powerful intercession and obtain from your Divine Son all spiritual blessings through Jesus Christ, our Lord, so that having engaged here below your heavenly power I may offer my thanksgiving and homage to the most loving of fathers.
O St Joseph, I never weary of contemplating you and Jesus asleep in your arms. I dare not approach while He reposes near your heart.
Press Him in my name and kiss His fine head for me, and ask Him to return the kiss when I draw my dying breath. St Joseph, patron of departing souls, pray for us. Amen.

How to make basic zeppole

Zeppole, frittelle or *sfinge* are variations of the same recipe to honour
St Joseph – fried doughnut balls with icing sugar on top. Some fancier
zeppole have custard in them and a different type of dough. This is an old
basic recipe passed on to me by a Sicilian friend.

YOU WILL NEED

2 cups self-raising flour

2 eggs

Water (about ½ cup)

Sultanas or raisins (to taste)

Fennel seeds (to taste)

Vegetable oil (not olive oil) for frying

METHOD

1. Mix the ingredients together to make into a cake consistency.

2. Add a spoonful of mixture about the size of a small ball in hot oil.
    Fry the spoonfuls of the mixture until golden. You may only fit four
    or five at a time.

3. Remove the cooked *zeppole* and place on some paper towel.

4. Dust with icing sugar and serve.

Santa Lucia (St Lucy – 13 December)

Saint Lucy's feast day falls on 13 December. The name Lucia comes from the Latin word *lux,* meaning 'light'. St Lucy is venerated for her association with light, vision and protection against eye ailments. St Lucy was born in Siracusa (Syracuse), Sicily in 283 CE and is the city's patron saint.

According to tradition, Lucy vowed to remain a virgin and consecrated herself to God, which led her to refuse to marry a pagan suitor. Lucy's decision angered her suitor, who reported her Christian beliefs to the Roman authorities. Lucy was arrested and tortured. Legend tells that her eyes were gouged out as punishment for her unwavering faith. Despite her ordeal, she miraculously regained her sight. But alas, she still met her martyrdom; she is one of the early Christian martyrs. All martyrs have a palm frond in their image, indicating that they died horrible deaths as martyrs. St Lucy is historically important to Sicily as the saint who fed the city of Siracusa during a famine by delivering a ship full of wheat.

My mother had a special devotion to Santa Lucia. She collected saint cards of her with an image on one side and a prayer on the other. I morbidly couldn't take my eyes off the image of the young woman holding a dish with her eyeballs on it. In some regional ceremonies, people have their eyes blessed in honour of St Lucy, seeking her protection and healing for their vision. St Lucy is the patron saint of the blind. People may wear or carry protective charms or amulets bearing her image or name to safeguard their eyes and vision.

On the evening of 13 December, people place candles in their windows to symbolise the light brought by the saint and ward off darkness and evil. Her feast day coincides with the shortest day of the year (winter solstice) in the old Julian calendar. Her festival is one of light as people await the sun to return and the birth of Jesus at Christmas, who is also known as 'the light of the world' in Christian terms.

HOW TO WORK WITH ST LUCY

Colours and symbols associated with St Lucy:

- ▶ Red – martyr
- ▶ White – purity
- ▶ Yellow/orange light (vision)

Votive offerings:

- ▶ Oil lamp/salt lamp/candle with battery for ongoing light
- ▶ Cake or bread
- ▶ Palm branch (martyr's victory over evil)
- ▶ Candle (white)

What to ask for: protecting your eyesight, being able to see your situations clearly, having courage for standing up for your beliefs, helping to bring your light to the world, and not hiding your truth or talents.

How to make cuccia

Cuccia con ricotta is a Sicilian dessert prepared on 13 December (St Lucy's Day). The name *cuccia* comes from the Sicilian word *cocciu* (meaning 'grain' of wheat). Wheat is symbolic for its 'eye' like shape once it opens, which honours St Lucy and her feast day.

There are two versions – one sweet with ricotta and the other savoury with chickpeas. For grain, use farro, orzo (ancient grain barley), spelt or wheatberries. If using wheatberries, you must soak them for at least 24 hours to soften. Wheatberries are whole wheat kernels. They look like thick, short grains – similar to brown rice.

Here is a simple recipe for cuccia – each ingredient is used as an offering to St Lucy. Some add chickpeas to represent St Lucy's eyes. The basic cuccia recipe includes cooked wheat and ricotta. After that, you can season it to your liking with chocolate shavings, cocoa, honey, cinnamon and vanilla.

If you use pearled farro, this is much quicker to cook. It will cook in about an hour without needing soaking.

Sweet cuccia with ricotta

YOU WILL NEED

1 cup dried wheatberries or farro

Pinch of salt

1½ cups fresh whole-milk ricotta

1 tablespoon caster sugar

Honey, to taste

Toppings: cinnamon, shaved chocolate, orange zest

METHOD

1. Put the wheatberries or farro in a pot and cover with enough water so it's submerged. Add a pinch of salt. Bring to the boil and reduce to simmer for 30–50 minutes or until tender.

2. Turn off the heat and leave in the pot to slowly cool, or use a fine mesh strainer and drain thoroughly under cool water.

3. Combine the ricotta and sugar with some honey to taste and stir until smooth. Use the best possible ricotta.

4. Fold the cooled wheatberries into the ricotta mixture. Add honey for a sweeter taste. Dust with a pinch of cinnamon and top with shaved chocolate or orange zest.

5. Serve at room temperature in individual bowls.

Savoury cuccia with chickpeas

This recipe was given to me by Giovanna. It is part of the
cucina povera and, as per Italian custom, it has no measurements. Each
recipe is created to a specific taste according to individual family tradition.
This is a soup, but the consistency is more of a porridge drizzled with
olive oil. It's a perfect dish for a winter's day.

YOU WILL NEED

Barley (¾ of total amount)

Dried chickpeas (¼ of total amount)

Water

¼ teaspoon bicarbonate of soda

Salt

Olive oil

METHOD

1. Wash the barley and chickpeas separately. Let them soak overnight separately, adding ¼ teaspoon bicarbonate of soda to the chickpeas.

2. The next day, rinse, drain and place both the chickpeas and barley in a pot of water. Bring to the boil and cook. This will take a few hours.

3. Once it's a porridge consistency, remove from heat. Add salt and olive oil to serve.

San Giovanni Battista
(St John the Baptist - 24 June)

St John is associated with purification, baptism and spiritual rebirth, symbolising the transition from darkness to light. While the patronage for St John the Baptist is not consistent, it commonly includes nurses, printers, tailors, religious converts, bird dealers and firefighters.

Feasts of saints are normally celebrated on the anniversary of their earthly deaths, but we celebrate St John the Baptist's birthday. The feast of the Nativity of St John the Baptist is celebrated on 24 June.

St John is the patron saint of my family's *paese* (town). My nonna was born in a small village on the outskirts called, you guessed it, San Giovanni. Our house was filled with images of the saint, wearing his animal skins instead of fine clothes like Jesus, holding a cross with a lamb beside him against a wild landscape backdrop. I loved that his feast day fell in the middle of summer (around the summer solstice). In our *paese*, the day was filled with processions and holy rituals, and the night was lit up with torches, lights, music, dancing and revelry.

Australia is in the southern hemisphere, so 24 June is wintertime (around the winter solstice). Growing up, we didn't gather on St John's feast day, and we had no revelry to speak of – our poor San Giovanni was lucky if we even remembered his birthday. But when we did, we celebrated with a glass of home-made red wine and home-made sausages.

Who was St John? He was a preacher who spent time living in the desert, proclaiming for people to be baptised and repent. St John wore clothes made from camel's hair, a leather belt around his waist, and survived on eating locusts and wild honey.

His purpose was to prepare the way for Jesus in the world. After baptising him, he continued to preach that Jesus was the saviour people had been waiting for. St John was imprisoned, sentenced to death and beheaded in about 30 AD by King Herod Antipas. Herod gave St John the Baptist's head to his stepdaughter, Salome, as he had promised.

The day of the feast and birth of St John the Baptist takes place just after the summer solstice, the longest day of the year – midsummer. The summer solstice is a powerful time when the energies of the sun and earth converge. The veil between the physical world and the spiritual realm is believed to be thinner during this time, making it ideal for performing magical rituals, divination and connecting with spiritual forces. It's also a time of abundance, fertility and the height of the sun's power.

It's no surprise then that St John shares his celebration with witches – the night of 23–24 June is known as the night of the witches *(la notte delle streghe)* – a powerful night for magic. In Rome, the streets are lit by torches and coloured lights. The fires symbolise the power of the sun, cleansing negative energies and protecting against malevolent spirits. Loud noises made by instruments such as drums or trumpets and even firecrackers are encouraged to scare the witches away and prevent them from picking magical herbs.

Love ritual

St John's Eve was traditionally a time for lovers to find out who they would marry by contacting the spirit world through divination. One of these methods was melting lead and dropping it into cold water. It would freeze into various shapes that could then be interpreted by people familiar with the symbolism.

The ritual took place after a novena, which lasted from the evening of 15 June until the eve of the feast. This ritual can also be done with the egg in water divination method.

METHOD

1. Fill a large clear glass with water.

2. Crack an egg, separating the whites from the yolk. Drop the whites only into the glass of water. Leave out overnight on the windowsill (this is another version of the egg and water *malocchio* removal method).

3. The next day, if the water is covered in bubbles, it means you'll find a mate who is perfect for you; the shape of a church or building means potential marriage. If no shapes can be recognised, it means try again next year.

Prayer to San Giovanni

San Giovanni benedetto,
pe' un infame maledetto,
foste a morte condannato,
con sto' piombo coagulato,
conoscere mi fai,
la fortuna che mi dai,
San Giovanni della vita.

Blessed St John,
cursed by an infamous one,
you were condemned to death,
with this coagulated lead,
let me know,
the fortune that you give me,
St John of life.

ACQUA DI SAN GIOVANNI (ST JOHN'S WATER)

St John is associated strongly with water as his name implies. At midsummer, many herbs and plants are at their peak potency, making it an opportune moment for gathering and using herbs and flowers in magical practices. The dew collected overnight, combined with herbs and flowers between 23 June and 24 June, is believed to be magically potent. The *acqua di San Giovanni* can protect against the evil eye, envy and curses, while also attracting love in your life.

- 273 -

TRADITIONAL FLOWERS USED IN *ACQUA DI SAN GIOVANNI*

I have made *acqua di San Giovanni* on his feast day, which falls near the winter solstice in Australia, to honour my town's saint. It's not the same as the summer solstice flower gathering. I had to use whatever flowers were available to me in winter. Traditionally, you should use wildflowers, but it was impossible to find them at this dormant time. I managed to find these varieties in our neighbourhood – banksia, rosemary, camellia, hellebore, daphne, salvia, French lavender and a mixture of herbs.

As I was writing this list of flowers, I've just realised why St John's wort is regarded an essential flower for the water. St John's wort, or *iperico* (hypericum), is a plant with yellow flowers that has been used in traditional European medicine since ancient times. The name St John's wort refers to John the Baptist, because the plant blooms around the time of his feast day.

How to make acqua di San Giovanni

YOU WILL NEED

A mix of flowers: basil, broom, chamomile, fennel, garlic, gentian, honeysuckle, iris, lavender, mallow, mandrake, marjoram, mint, mugwort, rose, rosemary, rue, sage, St John's wort, thyme, verbena and walnut leaves are traditional. Some, like mandrake, might not be easily available. Trust your instinct and use what you feel best resonates with creating a love and protection elixir that brings harmony and protection into your home.

Bowl

Water

Glass bottle

METHOD

1. Gather flowers and leaves of plants on the Eve of St John. Find any of those listed above or create your own mix. In some regions, you're supposed to pick 24 different flowers and plant leaves in honour of the feast date (24 June).

2. Add the flowers to a bowl of water. Make sure they are immersed in water first so each petal or leaf is absorbed. Leave the bowl outside in the moonlight overnight.

3. The next morning, strain and place the water in a glass bottle to be used for blessings, or as holy water.

4. Traditionally, only the dew from the flowers was collected. This was known as *guazza* (dew) – *la guazza di San Giovanni*. I use the water 'immersion' method, which honours St John who immersed those he baptised.

5. I keep the water in a cool, dry place and use it for washing down my front doorstep and front door to protect against negative energy and in my vaporiser with added essential oils to cleanse the space.

Other popular Italian saints and patronages

Saints' attributes and patronages vary from region to region and even in Catholicism itself. Here are some of my favourite saints and their patronages.

SAINT ANNE (SANT' ANNA)	Unmarried women, housewives, women in labour or who want to get pregnant, grandparents, mothers, educators, equestrians, miners, cabinet makers
SAINT ANTHONY (SANT' ANTONIO)	Finding lost items, people and stolen articles, older people, poor people, sailors and fishermen, travellers. He is known as the wonder worker of miracles. He's the go-to saint for just about anything.
SAINT CECILIA (SANTA CECILIA)	Music and musicians, composers, musical instrument makers, poets, singers, blind people
SAINT FRANCIS OF ASSISI (SAN FRANCESCO)	Ecology, animals
SAINT GERTRUDE (SANTA GERTRUDE)	Cats mostly, but also rats and mice, travellers, gardeners, mental illness
SAINT PADRE PIO (SAN PADRE PIO)	Winter blues (seasonal affective disorder), civil defence volunteers, teenagers, stress relief. Padre Pio is a popular folk saint due to his humble but mystical nature. A mystic, he suffered from stigmata (Christ's wounds appeared on his hands and body) and was known for his prophetic ability and healing power. Padre Pio has huge devotional support in Italy and the diaspora.
SAINT ROCCO (SAN ROCCO)	Dogs and their owners, pestilence and contagious diseases, knee problems, invalids, bachelors, surgeons
TWIN SAINTS – ST COSMAS AND ST DAMIAN (SANTI COSMA E DAMIANO)	Doctors, surgeons, pharmacists, twins

Gli angeli (the archangels – 29 September)

Angels may be approached similarly to saints, but given that anyone can enjoy angel spirituality, you can work with your angels in a more intuitive and modern way. The church recognises three archangels – St Michael (San Michele), St Gabriel (San Gabriele) and St Raphael (San Raffaele). The feast day of all three is on 29 September, although their feasts used to be celebrated separately (Gabriel on 24 March, Raphael on 24 October). If you have an Angelo or Angela in your family, they are named after these angels.

Archangels are messengers of God/Source and can intervene on our behalf to help us with our problems, providing protection, healing and assistance when we need it. If you work with angels outside of the Catholic folk tradition, you'll recognise more than the three listed here, so feel free to add others of your choice. Angels and archangels have filtered beyond religion and folk magic into the realm of metaphysics and have modern affiliations.

Each angel has colours associated with them, but they vary according to personal faith beliefs. If you decide to work with the angels, you will feel intuitively what colours best represent them. Wear a particular colour, make a votive offering in this colour and surround your home altar with the colour so you can connect with the best angel to help you at the time.

HOW TO WORK WITH ARCHANGELS

- ▶ Close your eyes and breathe deeply and slowly, emptying your mind.
- ▶ Focus on your intention and hold it closely to your heart, imagining the outcome.
- ▶ Invoke the archangel(s). You may say their name out loud.

- ▶ Close your eyes and visualise them – what they look like, their colours, qualities or anything else that will make them feel real to you.
- ▶ Feel the presence of divine energy in you as they grant your request.
- ▶ Thank the archangel for granting your request.

ARCHANGEL MICHAEL – HEAD OF THE HEAVENLY ARMY

NAME MEANING	Who is like God
MISSION	To protect
COLOUR	Red or blue
QUALITIES	Truth, honesty, justice
VOTIVES/ OFFERINGS	Red items, white feather, candle (blue), medallion
HELPS WITH	Protection from negative energies and obstacles needing to be overcome, especially our inner and outer battles and with issues of self-esteem, justice
PATRON SAINT OF	Grocers, police officers/first responders, radiologists, soldiers

The most widely venerated archangel whose help is most requested is Archangel Michael – Arcangelo Michele or San Michele Arcangelo.

Countless images and statues of Archangel Michael depict him with his shield up and sword drawn, aiming at Lucifer. As such, he is considered the principal archangel, protector of the church and against evil in general. His feast day, known as the *Festa di San Michele Arcangelo*, is celebrated on 29 September.

Archangel Michael holds a special place in Italian folk magic as a powerful and benevolent protector. Invoking his name can help to ward off evil and bring about divine assistance. He is often invoked in rituals to protect homes, crops and animals from harm. Such is Michael's power against dark forces that, in certain regions, it's customary to seek blessings and exorcisms from priests invoking Archangel Michael's name to purify spaces or individuals from negative influences.

Protection talismans and amulets featuring Archangel Michael's image or name are common. These objects may serve as guardians against negative energies and malevolent forces. Rituals may include specific prayers, incense and blessed water.

Archangel Michael's colour is different from traditional angel work. In Italian folk magic, red is Michael's special colour because he is invoked for protection against the evil eye, and as you've gathered already, red works best against the *malocchio*. He is also fiery, assertive and powerful, and fights for you against injustice – as a warrior angel, red suits Michael's image. Personally, I prefer the colour blue, which he is traditionally known for in angelology. Blue represents the power of his spirit and his spiritual nature as protector of mankind.

Asking for help: if asking for Michael's help for yourself, imagine a blue light around you or a shield in front of you. In your mind's eye, visualise Michael's sword cutting away ties and releasing cords, giving you the courage you need at this time. Any protective invocation or prayer is suitable, but using the attributes of Archangel Michael to help you in your time of need will aid your cause. An example would be:

Archangel Michael, I ask you to guide and protect me, to give me strength and courage to fight for my beliefs. Protect me with your love and your sword of justice. For this I give thanks to you. Amen.

ARCHANGEL GABRIEL – THE HEAVENLY MESSENGER

NAME MEANING	God is my strength
MISSION	To communicate
COLOURS	Blue, white, gold
QUALITIES	Strength, persistence, commitment
VOTIVES/ OFFERINGS	White candle (purification), spring water, book or artwork, any symbol of communication (even your journal), angel medallion
HELPS WITH	Communicating our thoughts and ideas, clearing our mind, accomplishing our goals through persistence
PATRON SAINT OF	Broadcasters and communicators, messengers, postal workers, creative arts and creative expression, childbirth, diplomats, stamp collectors

Archangel Gabriel appeared to Mary, the Virgin Mother, announcing she would have a baby, Jesus. He appears in other places in the Bible as a messenger angel to help interpret dreams. Gabriel is commonly regarded as the archangel of dreams, premonitions and clairvoyance because he will offer his wisdom and spiritual advice in the form of dreams and visions.

As a communicator, it's not surprising he is the patron saint of those who work in the communication and artistic fields. Gabriel will come to us when we need help with communicating effectively or when we need to clear away confusion to make important decisions. We recognise him in artwork by his symbols – holding or blowing a trumpet, and carrying a lily and sceptre.

Asking for help: ask Gabriel for help with how to express yourself most effectively with people, and to help release stress when you're working with deadlines or are juggling too many jobs. You may say:

Archangel Gabriel, I ask that you give me wisdom and guidance to cope with my current situation. For this I am grateful.

ARCHANGEL RAPHAEL – THE HEALING ANGEL	
NAME MEANING	God has healed
MISSION	To guide and heal
COLOUR	Green (related to health and healing) or yellow
QUALITIES	Wholeness, acceptance, healing
VOTIVES/ OFFERINGS	Green candle, flowers, green foliage from nature, angelica (herb of healing), angel medallion, bowl of water left under the full moon or on the eve of his feast day (29 September)
HELPS WITH	Healing of all kinds – emotional, physical and mental, recovery from illness
PATRON SAINT OF	Travellers, blind people and those with eye problems, bodily ills, counsellors, healers, health technicians, lovers, nurses, doctors, pharmacists, young people leaving home, protects against sickness

Raphael is described in the Bible as a wonderful healer, fellow traveller and teacher. He is responsible for healing the body, mind, soul and spirit. He is often depicted with a wooden staff, a symbol of helping travellers, and the caduceus for his healing work (a more modern look). A caduceus is a staff with two snakes coiled around it. It is a symbol of medicine and the medical profession, honouring the Greek god of medicine, Asclepius. Raphael can also be seen with a fish – this was a miracle healing Raphael had performed to cure blindness – he wears a gourd of water or wallet attached to his travelling belt.

Asking for help: Raphael helps with all kinds of healing and unhealed wounds, such as trauma. You may call on him and say a simple prayer: 'Archangel Raphael, I invoke you to help me be well. May your healing love make me whole. I give thanks and gratitude. Amen.'

Spirituality in Italian folk magic is not just about religious saints and angels. It is a deeper reverence for what is not seen but felt to be part of life's wheel of fortune – fate and destiny. The more fervent your belief in a saintly being, the better chance you had of them granting a request or looking favourably on you. In earlier times, people shared their home and land with other 'spirits' and pagan deities. You needed to keep on good terms with them all.

Chapter 12

Working with deities, fairies and nature spirits

Y ou are likely to be familiar with the ancient Greek and Roman pagan gods and deities; nature spirits such as imps, elves, nymphs and fairies; and other supernatural spirits. Younger generations today can make these connections easily, but my parents' and grandparents' generation didn't use names of deities – and regional name differences meant no commonality. I never grew up knowing Diana or Venus – the only pagan god was the one I heard my father say occasionally: *'Perbacco!'* I wasn't aware this referred to the Roman god Bacchus (Dionysus), the god of wine and good times. The phrase is an expression of surprise (Gee! Good gracious!). When I shared this with my Italian friends, they all agreed that their knowledge of Roman gods was quite thin.

Gods and goddesses

In the spirit of Italian folk magic tradition, these Greco-Roman deities are the ones usually historically familiar and normal to work with – Ecate (Hecate), Diana (Artemis), Venus (Aphrodite), Ceres (Demeter), Proserpina (Persephone); Juno (Hera), Apollo, Bacchus (Dionysus), Mars (Ares), Cupid (Eros) and other more ancient ones – Cibele (Cybele) and Iside (Isis). Adopting foreign deities was a common religious practice as the Romans integrated them with their own gods and goddesses. These deities had an impact on Italian spiritual and cultural beliefs because Christianity adopted and assimilated many of the roles and feast days of these pagan gods and goddesses.

ROMAN GODDESSES AND GODS	
APOLLO	God of light, the arts, music, medicine, archery
BACCHUS	God of wine and revelry
CERES	Goddess of the harvest
CIBELE	Great mother goddess, originally from Anatolia; the original Black Madonna figure
CUPID	God of romantic love
DIANA	Goddess of the hunt, the moon
ECATE	Goddess of sky, earth and sea; magic and spells
ISIDE	Egyptian mother goddess; goddess of healing and magic, also believed to be an ancient representation of the Black Madonna
JUNO	Goddess of marriage
MARS	God of war

ROMAN GODDESSES AND GODS

PROSERPINA	Goddess of spring and the underworld
VENUS	Goddess of beauty and love

Goddess Fortuna

If you wanted a good marriage, children, wealth, success or abundance, then Fortuna was the goddess to call on. Fortuna was the ancient Roman goddess of luck, chance and fate. She was associated with all fortunate events in the lives of gods and humans – especially abundance, fertility, motherhood and wealth. Fortuna's ancient Greek counterpart, Tyche, was more associated with chance or luck in daily life.

For many Romans, Fortuna could grant them security, high productivity and prosperity through a bountiful harvest. Her symbol, the cornucopia, or horn of plenty, is still recognised and used as a good luck charm today. She was also invoked at marriage ceremonies for fertility and a happy marriage.

Fortuna was 'Lady Luck' – part of all aspects of Roman life with the wealth, health, life and death of everyone in her power. But she had two sides. Her image is blindfolded (like the Justice card in the tarot), symbolising the randomness of chance. She dished out good and bad luck at her whim. She had the power to give luck and take it away.

Fortuna's major symbols include:

▶ Wheel of fortune – she spins it to bless whoever she pleases.
▶ Ship's wheel – she steers our destinies and provides guidance for the best way ahead.
▶ Ears of wheat – these represent wealth and prosperity.

- ▶ Rotating globe – this represents unpredictability; that things can change quickly when your world turns upside down.
- ▶ Cornucopia – she has an endless supply of abundance and growth.
- ▶ Wreath – this is a reward for a victory or win.

Fortuna was worshipped through public and private votives, prayer and invocations; people hoped that, in spreading her cult she would likely grant them more favours. Many Italians who enjoy gambling still call out to Fortuna to bring them luck and make them win more. But as we know, Fortuna doesn't distribute her gifts to those who really deserve them, but totally by chance. We know we're at the whims of Fortuna – she's both fickle and unpredictable, just like chance and luck.

HOW TO WORK WITH FORTUNA

- ▶ Set up an abundance altar.
- ▶ Give offerings to Fortuna – a cornucopia of harvested apples, grapes, rosemary, berries and flowers as well as coins.
- ▶ Burn incense that symbolises good luck – nutmeg, cinnamon, vanilla and especially frankincense.
- ▶ Wear an amulet in her honour to attract luck – a cornucopia filled with fruit, amulet of the Wheel of Fortune tarot card, ship's wheel, coins as part of jewellery – I have some ancient Roman coin charms I wear on my bracelet with saint medallions.
- ▶ Light a fruit-scented candle.

Magical folk

Several magical beings and entities play significant roles in Italian folklore and traditional beliefs, which have been passed down through generations. They are intermediaries between the human world and spirit realm and are believed to influence different aspects of daily life, from luck and fortune to protection and guidance. People, especially in rural Italy, would seek to work with or appease these entities through rituals, offerings and charms to gain their favour and blessings.

Le ninfe (nymphs)

In rural communities, streams and fountains were meeting points for women. They did the laundry in the streams, and filled their urns with fresh water from the public fountains if they didn't have their own wells.

My nonna used to do her laundry in the local *fiume* (stream), as did so many women in pre-World War II Italy. She used to leave offerings of flowers or small pebbles to thank the nymphs (she would call them '*le fate*' because *ninfe* was not a common word in her region) for the use of the water and ask for protection against snake bites.

Nymphs were female nature spirits, considered the guardians and protectors of the natural elements – rivers, springs, forests and mountains. They were believed to embody the spirit of these places and were revered for their connection to the land and its energies.

They dwelled in places that eventually became sacred sites, especially caves with water sources, springs, mystical wells and rivers. People would respectfully ask for the nymphs' blessings and protection when embarking on journeys or facing difficult times. They held rituals and festivals to honour the nymphs and seek their favour, especially during the changing of the seasons or during agricultural events.

You can work with these pagan nature spirits simply by being respectful of sacred sites and landscapes near water.

Le anguane (female water spirits)

The Dolomite regions – Veneto, Trentino-Alto Adige and Friuli-Venezia Giulia – have a legend about the *anguane*. They are mythical female-like figures with nails instead of hair, who inhabited waterways and underground places such as rivers, streams, caves and grottos. They were keepers of these openings to the underworld. They were considered to be supernatural and minor deities, like the ancient Greek nymphs.

Work with the *anguane* like you would with nymphs, leaving offerings near caves and respecting the waterways by cleaning them up where needed or taking care of aquatic wildlife if injured.

La Commare ('fairy' godmother)

Commare is a term used to refer to a female spirit, often associated with maternal figures or midwives. The *commari* hold knowledge of herbal medicine, childbirth and protective rituals. People may seek their guidance for matters related to fertility, health and protection. They are practical magical women who appeared in times when most needed for advice. The word *commari* is used in various ways today – it could mean godmothers, good female friends, ladies or even wives.

To work with a *commare* energy, show gratitude and politeness when meeting with a friendly, mature-looking woman.

La fata (fairy)

A fairy in Italian folklore is called *la fata*. These magical beings are known for their beauty and otherworldly nature. When a baby is born, a *fata* will take an interest in the welfare if the child needs special protection.

Fate are often associated with enchantment, granting wishes and bestowing blessings on those they favour. They can also be capricious, however, and may take offence if treated disrespectfully.

They were described as beautiful young women, sometimes small and fairy-like (think Tinkerbell) and other times they had human features. We were told never to touch any food found under a tree — this was for the fairies and if you stole it, they would take their revenge. As nature spirits, one had to greet them politely and request permission to sit under a tree and eat your lunch. The Fairies' Hill (*colle delle fate*) in Roccacasale in Abruzzo is believed to be the place where fairies used to once meet.

Working with both the *commari* and *fate* is best when you need advice about your life's direction or family. You may wish to leave them offerings on a table you've prepared in your yard — fill it with small posies of flowers, a small flowering plant, a shallow bowl of water with pebbles or coloured marbles, a sealed container with a biscuit or sweet — and a note asking for help. Leave the offerings out for three nights.

Le janas/gianas (fairies of Sardinia)

The *janas* are tiny female fairies of Sardinia, who were said to be so beautiful that even today we say someone is attractive like a *jana* (*bella come una jana/giana*). Unlike traditional fairies, the *janas* lived in the *Domus de Janas* (houses of the fairies), holes built into the rock. Their skin was white and delicate, and they avoided the sun's rays during daylight, only coming out after sunset. On moonless nights, when they'd pray near the Nuragic temples, they had to walk on steep paths covered with brambles and thorns. *Janas* became luminous to avoid the thorns, which signalled their presence.

They hand-weaved fine clothes on golden looms and baked bread lighter than a wafer using silver sieves. The legend says that filigree jewellery was 'woven' by the *janas* during the nights of the full moon. Their role was to guard long-forgotten treasures, and they sang their melodious songs on dark and silent nights, while comforting lonely travellers.

Work with the *janas* as you would with the fairies (*fate*).

I folletti (elves)

The *folletti* are small mythical creatures often associated with the fairy folk or nature spirits. They are mischievous and can either bring good fortune or cause mischief, depending on how they are treated. In some regions, they are seen as household spirits who protect the home and its inhabitants. In others, they are shape-shifters who live in wild places in the landscape. You might be lucky to see one, because they often wear red or brown hoods, but make sure you keep on their good side and don't offend them.

Elves are similar to the *lares* of ancient Rome. The *lares* were guardians of the home, the fields, boundaries and crossroads. They were believed to be spirits of a place – rivers and springs, valleys, and homes and their inhabitants – whose role was to guard and protect.

To connect with the *folletti*, leave them food offerings, such as milk, bread and fruit. As spirits of the forest, these fairy-like creatures will appreciate the effort and will be more likely to help you be protected and safe from imps, who are likely to cause much more chaos in your home and garden.

If you have a household spirit, acknowledge, feed and care for them, so they will watch over you and help in your magical workings when asked. Your house has a spirit too – even though it's a physical structure, it's also your refuge. It shelters you from outside forces and is your family's sanctuary. It is a physical extension of who you are – it houses your energies. Show gratitude by saying thank you; keeping it clean; decorating it with plants, fresh flowers, and new cushions and throws yearly; and asking permission to make renovations. Show it love and it will love you back.

Il mazzamauriello (imp)

In southern Italy, sleep paralysis is usually explained by a troll or sprite (*mazzamauriello*) or *scazzamauriello* sitting on the dreamer's chest. Due to its weight, the victim becomes aware of its presence but cannot move. The *mazzamauriello* can paralyse and no amount of crying out for help will do any good. He can also be invisible.

If the person manages to catch the sprite or steal his hat, they have room for negotiating. While not as scary as the *strega*, the *mazzamauriello* enjoys scaring people and creating havoc, and can be vengeful if not treated well.

This mischievous Italian goblin is known by different names in different regions. For instance, he is called ma*zzamauriell'* in Molise, Abruzzo and Campania; *mazzamureddo* in Sicily; and *scazzamauriello* in Puglia. My family in Italy, when recalling the mischief they'd experienced at the hands of the *mazzamuriell'*, first remember the noise it made to signal its presence. Strange knocking noises from an invisible entity frightened the children and worried the adults. They believed the *mazzamauriello* always carries a stick, which he bangs against the walls or trees to make a loud knocking sound.

The name *mazzamauriello* comes from the words *mazza*, meaning 'stick', and *muro*, meaning wall. Nobody knows when or where the noises came from

– maybe it was when the *mazzamauriello* or even the family was in danger, with the knocking on the wall being a warning. Many believed they were passing on a message from a deceased loved one, who was trying to communicate with the living family. They also may have been a spirit, shadow or ghost (*ombra*); locals referred to it as evil or a devil, who created chaos and disturbed the peace. If a domestic animal (such as a donkey or horse) was unwell, the farmer would check for bite marks because they believed the *mazzamauriello* could suck blood.

In our *paese*, the *mazzamauriello* was known for plaiting horses' tails and manes. They would take great delight in sneaking into barns and riding the horses during the night. In the morning, the farmer would find his horse sweaty from the night's ride, with its mane and tail in plaits and knots. In pre-war Italy, rural families lived above their stables, so they could see or hear anyone entering the barn. Besides, the barn was bolted from the inside.

My father told how he found his mare in a distressed state when he went to check on her one morning. Her white mane and tail were covered in knots; her back was sweaty and nostrils flaring.

'What did you do to stop it from happening again?' I asked my father.

'Well, we had this woman, you know, a woman who knew things …' he began.

'You mean a type of *strega*?'

'She was more of a wise woman and herbalist, but knew a lot about magic and *mazzamauriell*,' he said. 'So I went to her for help and brought my mare with me. She took one look and said, "*È ru' mazzamauriell.*" ("It's the *mazzamauriello*.")

'She gave me a pouch with some herbs. "Hang these in the barn. They don't like them. It'll keep them away."'

The magic knots on the mare no longer appeared and the horse became calm once again.

Imps are spiteful pranksters, who you can recognise by their red pointy hats. But if you treat them well, they'll look after the home and family and maybe even bring good luck.

Il monaciello (little monk sprite)

The *monaciello* (little monk) as he is known in Campania is closely related to the *mazzamauriello*. A small, hooded being resembling a small monk, he is mostly harmless. According to legend, when workers were building a new aqueduct under Naples, they used to wear long, dark cloaks and helmets to stay dry. When they came up for a break, residents saw underground beings emerging with their cloaks, looking very much like short monks.

Another legend from Basilicata talks of the *monacielli* as the spirits of children who had died without being baptised. These regions share borders so it's interesting how they both have this magical creature as part of their folklore.

Il mazaròl (imp/gnome)

The *mazaròl* is the name given to a playful imp or gnome dressed in red with a cap, who is said to take great pleasure in leading people astray, causing them to lose their way especially at dusk. The people living near the Dolomites in northern Italy see the *mazaròl* as a stocky old man dressed in red with a turquoise jacket, a hat and black cloak. He can be bad tempered if bothered by people and beware if you betray him. If you put a foot over his footprint, you'll have to follow his footprints until you come to the cave where he dwells. And after that, the victim loses their memory and remains with the *mazaròl* until he releases them.

Il laùro (puck)

In northern Puglia, close to Molise border, lies the Gargano Peninsula, a limestone mountain range by the sea. According to legend, the limestone caves housed pagan gods, while the deep forests sheltered witches. Local lore also warns of werewolves. The Gargano region is the birthplace of San Padre Pio, Puglia's patron saint.

In this landscape, the *laùro,* a puck, roams the area sometimes helping farmers and playing tricks on people, much like the neighbouring *mazzamauriello.*

Il lupo mannaro (werewolf)

My biggest fear as a child was hearing a wolf's howl in the mountains – not only because of the danger in the 'Little Red Riding Hood' fairy-tale, but because of the werewolf, the *lup menar'* (*lupo mannaro*). According to local lore, people born on Christmas night are cursed because they dishonour the birth of Jesus, God's son. Once they reach 20 years old, they may become werewolves. Hearing three knocks on the door indicated that a man who had turned into a werewolf during the full moon or other magical nights was now back home as a man. The unfortunate young man could only be saved by being hit hard from above, spilling some blood.

Each region and locality has its unique creatures and entities. These magical beings reflect the rich and diverse cultural heritage and contribute to the vibrancy of Italian folk magic. It may seem nonsensical to believe in imps, vampires and fairy folk today, but when I speak with the elders, they are convinced these creature once existed, and that they had witnessed them (perhaps as a manifestation of their fears, who knows?). I believe our elders.

Chapter 13

Divination

Nothing is set in stone – your future can change in an unforeseen event or change of heart. Whether it's the tarot, pendulum, palm reading, scrying or something else, divination has been used to predict the events that shape people's lives. Today it's no different – whether it's a partner, house, job, children or health – we humans live in a world of uncertainty we have little control over. But perhaps with a little warning, or guidance, we could avoid the worst-case scenario. Or, if luck or success is just around the corner, it inspires us to keep going.

Divination is a practice that involves seeking insight, guidance or predictions about the future. It's an integral part of Italian folk beliefs and traditions, with practitioners using different techniques to gain spiritual knowledge or answers to questions, which have been passed down through the generations.

Egg divination

The egg divination method, also known as 'ovomancy' or 'egg reading', is a traditional practice used for fortune-telling and gaining insights into a person's life, health and future. It is a form of scrying, in which diviners interpret patterns and shapes formed by the whites and yolks of cracked eggs when dropped into water.

Practitioners can use the egg divination method to detect the presence of the evil eye and identify any negative energies or spiritual disturbances affecting an individual. The egg is believed to absorb and capture negative energies, allowing the diviner to read the patterns formed to diagnose the presence of psychic fright or spiritual imbalance. (For method, see Chapter 7.)

Babies and birth

To find out an unborn baby's due date, health and gender, rub a raw chicken egg on the pregnant mother's belly. Crack the egg into a bowl. If the broken egg contains one yolk, then the mother will give birth to one child. If the egg contains two, three or more yolks, the mother will give birth to twins or even triplets. If the yolk has spots of blood in it, this may suggest a miscarriage or complication during childbirth.

Malocchio (evil eye)

When performing this ritual, the egg is passed over the person's body or rolled upon their skin, so it can absorb the negative energy thrown at them. They then place the egg beneath their bed. After a day, the egg is cracked into a glass or bowl half-full of water, which is interpreted to see if they had evil eye and if it has left the body. (For more information, see Chapter 7.)

Pendulum with wedding ring and string (traditional)

Traditionally, the pendulum was used to diagnose illness, find missing people, and locate gems and minerals under the earth. Before the pendulum, people used divining rods (dowsing) to find water, oil and minerals. Today, we use the pendulum mainly for getting a 'yes' or 'no' confirmation to questions.

A pendulum is a symmetrical weighted object (usually a crystal) hung from a single chain or cord, which is swung. The pendulum acts as a receiver of information and moves in different ways in response to your questions.

It is used for:

▶ healing purposes
▶ cleansing bad energies in a room
▶ helping you find lost objects
▶ finding water, ley lines or metals.

The pendulum was often a wedding ring strung on a ribbon; the wedding ring was a blessed item and thus held strong powers against evil.

To find out a baby's gender, the pendulum was placed over the pregnant woman's belly and asked whether the child was male or female. The male was indicated with a side-to-side movement, whereas the female was in circles. I've also used the pendulum to decide in which area I should buy a house. I held it over a map and asked the question: 'Is this where I will live?' It was a big help in confirming where I was definitely *not* going to be living.

HOW THE PENDULUM WORKS

Some say the pendulum creates a bridge between the logical and subconscious (intuitive) mind. It connects us to a higher power (divining) – which is where the information is believed to be coming from. Science tells us that the pendulum responds to electromagnetic energy radiating from everything on our planet. Whatever your personal belief is, by learning to work with this energy, you can find immediate answers to your questions.

HOW TO USE THE PENDULUM

You could use your own wedding ring but most people use a commercially made pendulum.

- ▶ First, cleanse your pendulum by leaving it on the windowsill for a day to be charged by the sun.
- ▶ Then charge it with your energy by holding it in your hands for 15 minutes and imprinting your energy onto it.
- ▶ Sit holding your pendulum between the thumb and forefinger of one hand, and run your other hand down the length of the pendulum chain or cord. Hold the chain steady. Rest the bottom tip above your open palm.
- ▶ The pendulum should now be completely still. Move your hand away from the bottom of the pendulum. As you move it away, the pendulum may begin to move.
- ▶ Relax. Take a few deep breaths. Watch the pendulum while it moves.
- ▶ Ask your pendulum out loud or in your mind: 'Please show me a "yes" response.' Pause then ask the pendulum to show you a 'no' response. Usually you'll see circular movements for 'yes' and backwards and forwards for 'no', but this can be different for everyone. Do this exercise for a few times so you know what these answers look like.

QUESTIONS TO ASK THE PENDULUM

It's best to ask questions with 'yes' or 'no' answers. To determine what works for you, first ask some obvious questions: 'Is today Monday?' or 'Is my name Mary?' The more you use the pendulum, the more it will respond. As you become more experienced, you'll be able to ask bigger life-decision questions and get some guidance from your intuition, which communicates to you from the pendulum.

Fava beans

The tradition of fava beans divination, also known as favomancy or bean divination, originated in southern Italy and Sicily. During this divination practice, you use a group of fava beans, with each bean representing a specific individual participating in the divination. The beans are typically uncooked and left in their natural form, but may be placed in a bag or container. The participants, usually family members or friends, gather around the beans and take turns selecting one bean from the bag without looking at it. The colour and shape of the fava beans are then used to interpret the outcome.

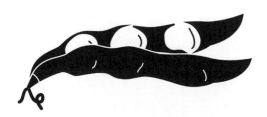

MEANING OF THE COLOUR AND SHAPE OF FAVA BEANS

STRAIGHT AND SMOOTH	A straight and smooth bean is a positive sign, indicating good luck, blessings and favourable events ahead for the person who selected it.
CURVED OR MISSHAPEN	A curved or misshapen bean is less fortunate, suggesting potential challenges or obstacles in the future.
DARK OR DISCOLOURED	A dark or discoloured bean may symbolise negativity, illness or a difficult period.
DOUBLE OR TWIN BEANS	If two beans are stuck together, this is an auspicious sign of a close bond or union with another person.
EMPTY-POD BEAN	An empty fava bean pod is regarded as a neutral sign, implying no significant changes or events.

Fava bean divination is viewed as a fun and light-hearted tradition in many families, especially during the festive atmosphere of St Joseph's Day. The interpretations are often taken with a grain of salt. It is a way to gather, enjoy each other's company and celebrate the holiday while taking part in an old folk custom.

You can do this divination with any type of dry bean or legume, and at any time – some use black-eyed peas. Have the confidence to take a risk and see what 'fate' holds for you, and not be too attached to the outcome. It encourages you to get out of a fixed mindset or comfort zone and perhaps get the impetus to start new things.

Cartomancy

Italians enjoy playing cards – I grew up around card nights with my parents, their friends and family. It was the only time I really saw my parents let their hair down. Drinking, smoking, gossiping and eating were all part of the evening's entertainment. By the time I was two, I knew the words *scopa* and *briscola*, and loved to carry the cards over to my dad when it was our turn to host. That was in the homeland. In Australia, the women – my aunts and *paesane* (Italian women from our town), would gather on a Saturday or Sunday evening to play cards and *tombola* (bingo). They caught up on news and talked about women's business without the men around.

Cards fascinated me because of the effect they had on the grown-ups. So much drama and heightened emotions – the sound of laughter and banter; a card hand slammed down hard on the table in frustration, causing it to wobble and scrape the floor; the free-flowing curses; and the quiet sulking when a game was lost. When my siblings and I would play a round of cards with Dad, we inevitably ended up losing badly. He used to tell us to stand up and lift our arm. He'd place the card deck under our armpit and tell us to bring our arm down, holding the cards. Then he would pat us on the shoulder and say the same words: 'Go back to school.' We were such amateurs!

Cards hold our imagination because of their possibilities and the unpredictable hand of fortune. Cartomancy involves using standard playing cards for divination. Each card has its own interpretation, and the reader uses the combinations and positions to provide guidance or predictions.

I tarocchi (tarot)

Reading Italian *tarocchi* follows similar principles to reading other tarot decks, but the design is quite different from the modern Rider-Waite Tarot. In fact, the Rider-Waite was inspired by the Italian *tarocchi*. The history of Italian *tarocchi* dates back to the 15th century; it is one of the earliest known tarot systems.

The earliest surviving complete deck is the Visconti-Sforza Tarot, created in about 1450 for the Duke of Milan. Similar to the modern tarot, this deck consisted of 78 cards, including 22 major arcana and four suits of 14 cards each. The major arcana was made up of 21 cards known as trumps (*trionfi*) with the fool added to make it 22. The minor arcana was the standard Italian four suits: *Bastoni* (Wands), *Coppe* (Cups), *Spade* (Swords) and *Denari* (Pentacles).

As the tarot gained popularity in Italy and other European countries, people began to use the cards for divination and fortune-telling. Over time, different regions in Italy developed their own variations, leading to *tarocchi* decks with unique artwork and interpretations. Some well-known Italian *tarocchi* decks include the Tarocco Siciliano, Tarocco Piemontese and Tarocco Bolognese.

MAJOR ARCANA

The major arcana has 22 cards, each with a unique symbolism and imagery. These cards represent significant life events, major themes and spiritual lessons. They are often seen as powerful forces that guide us through life's journey and provide insights into deeper aspects of our experiences. Each major arcana card has a specific name and number, which often depicts prominent figures, divine beings or symbolic imagery. It's the 'big' life decisions and guidance section of the tarot. I find it interesting seeing the card names written in Italian, because I've always read the tarot in English. When I say each card out loud in Italian, the meaning takes on a new perspective.

0. *Il Matto*: The Fool
1. *Il Bagatto*: The Magician
2. *La Papessa*: The High Priestess
3. *L'Imperatrice*: The Empress
4. *L'Imperatore*: The Emperor
5. *Il Papa*: The Hierophant/Pope
6. *Gli Amanti*: The Lovers
7. *Il Carro*: The Chariot
8. *La Forza*: Strength
9. *L'Eremita*: The Hermit
10. *La Ruota*: Wheel of Fortune
11. *La Giustizia*: Justice
12. *L'Appeso*: The Hanged Man
13. *La Morte*: Death
14: *La Temperanza*: Temperance
15: *Il Diavolo*: Devil
16. *La Torre*: The Tower
17. *La Stella*: The Star
18. *La Luna*: The Moon
19: *Il Sole*: The Sun
20: *Il Giudizio*: Judgement
21. *Il Mondo*: The World

THE FOOL

MINOR ARCANA

The minor arcana contains 56 cards, divided into four suits of 14 cards each. This varies from the regular playing cards with 13 cards in each suit.

Suits: *Bastoni* (Wands), *Coppe* (Cups), *Spade* (Swords), *Denari* (Pentacles)

Court Cards: *Re* (King), *Regina* (Queen), *Cavallo*, (Knight/Horseman), *Fante* (Page)

The minor arcana cards provide insight into everyday situations, events and influences that shape our experiences. They offer practical advice, guidance and detailed information about specific areas of life or day-to-day decisions.

Each suit represents a different aspect of life with its own set of meanings and interpretations.

BASTONI (WANDS)	Related to action, creativity and passion. *I Bastoni* cards represent ambition, growth and the pursuit of goals.
COPPE (CUPS)	Linked to emotions, love and relationships. *Le Coppe* cards reflect matters of the heart, emotional connections and the fulfilment of feelings.
SPADE (SWORDS)	Associated with thoughts, intellect and communication. *Le Spade* cards often deal with challenges, conflicts and mental struggles.
DENARI (PENTACLES)	Concerned with material aspects, finances and practical matters. *I Denari* cards focus on work, finances and material well-being.

If you want to work with *tarocchi*, familiarise yourself with the different Italian regional designs and feel which images and symbols best suit your intuitive nature. You can use any spread you'd normally use for tarot: Celtic cross, three-card spread or five-card spread.

Tarot reading requires practice, patience and an open mind. As you become familiar with the deck and its symbolism, you'll develop a deeper connection to the cards and their meanings.

Carte da gioco (Italian playing cards)

Card readings using playing cards is similar to traditional tarot card reading, but it uses a standard deck of playing cards, which have their own meanings and associations.

The cards used in each region, and part of each region, vary greatly. My family and *paesani* used Spanish-style playing cards, which are used in central and southern Italy. My deceased father's card decks are the Napoletane version – as I shuffle and run my fingers through them, I feel his ancestral energy there.

The northern Italian decks came from the original *tarocchi* design and may have sayings on the aces such as *Non ti fidar di me se il cuor ti manca* (Don't trust me if you don't have courage) on the Ace of Swords. The images on the Triestine and Trevigiane cards are fascinating with their geometric art-deco style and prominent blue colour.

Suits: *Denari* (Coins/Diamonds), *Spade* (Swords), *Bastoni* (Clubs), *Coppe* (Cups/Hearts)

Court cards: *Asso* (Ace), *Fante* (Knave/Jack), *Cavallo* (Horseman/Knight), *Regina/Donna* (Queen)

French-style cards are mainly used in these regions: Liguria, Aosta Valley, Piedmont, Tuscany, parts of Sardinia. The suits in these cards use *Cuori* (Hearts), *Quadri* (Diamonds), *Fiori* (Flowers/Clubs), *Picche* (Spades) and other differences in value. The court cards include a *Re/Regio* (King), *Donna* (Queen) and *Fante* (Knave/Jack).

German-style cards are mainly used in the province of Bolzano. The suits are different: Acorns, Bells, Hearts and Leaves.

Interpretation of the card deck (*mazzo di carte*)

This is a basic guide to using *le carte da gioco*. There is no 'right' or 'wrong' way to read playing cards, each family would have their own traditions handed down. Like the tarot, you can use any of the spreads you are comfortable with. If you don't have Italian playing cards, use a standard playing deck or the tarot minor arcana.

Each suit (*semi*, meaning 'seeds') corresponds to specific areas of life.

***DENARI* (COINS/ PENTACLES)**	Money, material matters, communication
***SPADE* (SWORDS)**	Challenges, conflicts, problems, tears, intellectual matters
***BASTONI* (CLUBS/ WANDS)**	Creativity, work, friends, projects, business, career, contracts
***COPPE* (CUPS/ HEARTS)**	Emotions, love, relationships, family
***NUMERI* (NUMBERS)**	The card numbers have their own significance and may indicate timing or levels of influence. For example, aces represent new beginnings, and 3s signify growth and expansion.
***LE FIGURE* (COURT CARDS)**	The court cards represent individuals or personality traits, as well as aspects of the querent's personality or people involved in the situation.

Trust your intuition and personal experience when interpreting the cards. The meanings may vary depending on the context and specific question. As you become more experienced with cartomancy, you may develop your own personal connections and understandings of the cards.

HOW TO READ THE CARDS IN THE OLD-FASHIONED WAY

If you don't have the Italian cards, use normal playing cards and remove the cards not mentioned here.

- ▶ Clear your space and mind so you can focus on the cards' messages.
- ▶ Substitute the Jack for the Queen. Some Italian decks have the *Donna* (Lady/Queen) card, but most haven't − they only have the *Re* (King), *Cavallo* (Knight) and *Fante* (Page/Jack) cards.
- ▶ Shuffle the cards and cut the deck into three sections while you focus on the question you need answered.
- ▶ Any spread you normally use in tarot works for this set of cards too.

SUIT	COPPE/CUPS (HEARTS IN NORMAL PLAYING CARDS)	BASTONI/CLUBS (CLUBS IN NORMAL PLAYING CARDS)
MEANING	*Represents family, love affairs, pleasure*	*Represents work, friends, projects, business contracts*
RE/KING	Man with brown hair who is honest and loving	A dark-haired man who is hard working
DONNA/ LADY	Woman with brown or fair hair who is social and good potential for marriage	A dark-haired woman who is clever and faithful
CAVALLO/ KNIGHT	Young attractive man who has social connections	Young man who is ambitious
ASSO/ACE	House and anything associated with it such as family and relationships	A letter that is an invitation to create new life
2	Love, kisses in an early relationship	A disappointment or disagreement
3	Longer term relationship, joy	Good partnership with a timing of 3 months
4	Social invitation but beware of temptation	Long journey or illness
5	Marriage or pregnancy, money is coming	News coming from far away, business concerns especially related to a will or settlement
6	Love affairs, jealousy, insecurity	Bad business proposition, complications
7	Celebration with family or to do with new relationship	Business deal completed, a new investment coming

SPADE/SWORDS (SPADES IN NORMAL PLAYING CARDS)	DENARI/COINS (DIAMONDS IN NORMAL PLAYING CARDS)
Represents challenges, conflicts, problems, grief	*Represents money, material matters, communication, success*
An older man who can be difficult to love	Man with fair hair or light eyes who is good with his money
A mature woman who can be spiteful and vengeful	Woman with fair hair who is fond of pursuing pleasure
A determined young man who enjoys a challenge but can take it too far (harassment)	Younger man who takes a gamble, can be irresponsible
Vindictiveness, anxiety, worry, heartbreak and news	Change of fortune and luck. A ring.
Tears – a break-up or loss	A meeting to discuss future agreement or money matters
A short trip, argument	Good business proposition, overspending
Illness, accident, conflict	Financial loss, short trip
Anger, regret, quarrels	Good news on all fronts – wealth, happiness and health.
Influence of someone of bad character, blockage, pain	Sorrow, loneliness, a financial offer to help with a bad business decision
Distraction, loss of familiar life, a holiday	Letter, money, potential scandal

HOW TO READ A CARD SPREAD

If using a three-, five- or seven-card spread in one line, read the cards from left to right. I prefer to use a three-card spread, but if I don't get clarity I keep going until I do.

Shuffle the cards in your familiar way. Concentrate on the question and focus your intention on what you want from the answer. I asked the cards: 'Will my new project be successful?'

I pulled out these three cards:

- ▶ 2 *di Coppa* (2 of Cups/Hearts)
- ▶ 7 *di Bastoni* (7 of Wands/Clubs)
- ▶ 4 *di Denari* (4 of Coins/Diamonds)

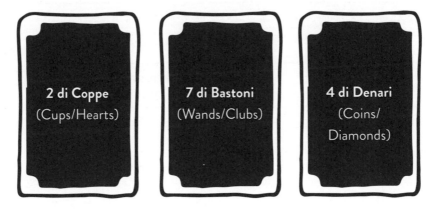

First card: the 2 of Cups/Hearts came up because I'm working with someone else on my current project. This confirmed that I asked the question correctly.

Second card: the 7 of Wands/Clubs confirmed that the project would be completed.

Third card: the 4 of Coins/Diamonds advised me that there would be little financial profit in the short term, but the project would eventually make (some) money. It was risky but I would not fail too badly.

Reading the cards can give you a deeper insight or point out what your subconscious might have been trying to tell you all along. This is the same with dreams. There is no right or wrong answer, but deep down we know what it is we're wanting to know.

● ● ●

Divination has survived for many generations in Italian folk magic. We all seek to be reassured and prepared for what unpredictable fate will hand us. Using divination methods can help us feel more in control of the world around us, whether it's through nature (birds in flight, animal encounters or herbal allies) or a game of chance such as cartomancy or the pendulum. Using these divination practices enhances our lives and keeps us from getting overwhelmed in a world filled with too much information.

Chapter 14

Dreams and their meanings

Dreaming was significant to our ancestors. Ancient Romans encouraged people to report their dreams in case they carried messages of potential danger to the empire. The ancients created shrines and built temples where dreams were incubated for healing purposes. The fascination with dreams is seen no more vividly than with the Neapolitans and their *Smorfia Napoletana* – playing the lottery with dream symbols.

La smorfia

La Smorfia refers to a traditional system of dream interpretation that assigns specific numbers to dream symbols. The word *smorfia* is associated with the ancient Greek god of dreams, Morpheus. People believed their dreams could hold hidden numbers that may be used as lucky or significant numbers, particularly in games of chance like the lottery. This system has been linked to the Bible, particularly by followers of the Kabbalah (mystical Judaism). Many believe the imagery from the Old Testament can also be decoded.

The meaning of each number was transferred orally from one generation to the next, before it was noted in illustrations and finally in a book of words. The *smorfia* is mostly used in Naples and has been a part of their local culture for centuries.

How *smorfia* works

In the *smorfia*, dream symbols are associated with numbers from one to 90; these numbers are then used for betting or playing the lottery. The *smorfia* system is not a statistically proven method for winning the lottery or predicting outcomes in games of chance. It's more a fun cultural practice that adds an element of excitement and folklore to dream interpretation and lottery playing. Although, some people take it very seriously.

This free online book maps out the original dream symbols and their numbers: *Nuova Smorfia del Giuoco del Lotto* (1866), by Giustino Rumeo.

This *smorfia* website can assist you with your dream symbols and numbers: https://www.lasmorfianapoletana.com

I keyed *cavallo* (horse) into this website for a simple meaning and number combination – the horse is not part of the 90 symbols, so I was interested to see what number would be attributed to it. There were 19 combinations for a dream about a 'horse', depending on the context.

Here are two examples:

90. *Cavallo di marmo* (a marble horse); *relazioni pericolose* (dangerous relationships/dealings)

9. *Cavallo che mangia* (a horse that is eating); *situazione tranquilla* (a peaceful situation)

Dream images and meanings

I inherited the ability to understand and interpret dream symbols intuitively. Over the years, I've adapted the meanings to suit my life. In the context of Italian folk magic, dreams are often a means of communication between the dreamer and the spiritual world, offering insights and guidance for daily life. Every dream is connected to our own reality. Whatever we suppress in our conscious life will be revisited in our dreams. If you interpret them wisely, the answer you are looking for will be revealed.

Before I go to sleep, I 'ask' for a dream to give me clarity or an answer to a question. So I set the intention, which then rests in my subconscious mind while I sleep. The trick is to remember your dreams. You can use various methods to help you remember your dreams, but the main tip is to write down the smallest dream fragments as soon as you wake up. If you want a quick reference to a dream symbol, here is a basic list incorporating traditional Italian folk magic meanings.

WHEN YOU DREAM OF ...

ANTS	Hard work/earning and spending
BIRDS	News – can be good or bad
BLOOD	Heart health (take care)
BOAT	Safety, feeling of support
BREAD	Money/wealth
BRIDGE	Change of life plan
CANDLES	Death, sorrow

WHEN YOU DREAM OF ...

CAR	A speedy trip somewhere not local
CAT	Lucky but only until your nine lives run out
CELEBRITY	Disappointment
CHILD	Waiting for a situation to unfold
COOKING	Dream fulfilled
COW	Satisfaction
CROW	Messenger of bad news or from a dead relative
DEAD OR DEATH	A long life lived. Dreaming of a person being dead will add 10 years to their life (traditional Italian folk magic meaning). A new beginning will soon start.
DOG	Loyalty
FABRICS/SEWING	Deception hidden in plain sight
FIRE	Urgency, passion, gossip
FISH	Prosperity
FLOWERS	Celebration
FRUIT	New friendship
GARDEN (FLOWER)	Good times won't last
GHOST	Burdens disappearing, closure
GOAT	Fertility and wealth
HORSE (BLACK)	Lack of control

WHEN YOU DREAM OF ...

HORSE (WHITE)	Moving quickly in the right direction
HOTEL	Visitors
INSECTS	Hurtful and annoying petty gossip
KISS (FRIEND)	Good fortune coming
KISS (IN A CHEATING SITUATION)	Betrayal and instability
KISS (LOVERS/SPOUSE/ PARTNER)	Stability, love
LAKE	Grief
LOTTERY	A risky venture (loss of winnings)
MAN/WOMAN (OLD)	Using time wisely, ancestral wisdom
MONEY	Loss of fortune, losing valuables
MOON	Good omen for future plans
MOUNTAIN	Obstacles
PLANE	Freedom ahead
PREGNANCY	New event happening within the year
PRIEST	Bad sign, warning
RAT	Treachery or disloyalty
RIVER	Life passing by, loss
ROAD/CROSSROAD	Opportunities, separation, choices
ROOSTER	Warning

WHEN YOU DREAM OF ...

ROSES	Pink – appreciation, white – purity, red – passion, yellow – joy (or envy)
ROYALTY (KING OR QUEEN)	Honour restored
SCORPION	Painful or toxic situation
SEA (ROUGH WAVES)	Emotional turmoil, lack of control in something about to come
SEA (SMOOTH WAVES)	Happy and tranquil times ahead
SEWING NEEDLES	A curse (such as *malocchio*)
SHADOW	Loss of previous lifestyle
SNAKE	Potential danger
SUN	Good times await
TEETH	Loss of control, death of someone you know or a situation ending
TRAIN	New life direction
TREE(S) (HEALTHY)	Vitality, opportunity
TREE(S) (WITHERED OR CUT DOWN)	Stagnation, loss of prosperity, sorrow
WATER	Tearful situation
WEDDING	Possible news of death
WINDOWS (OPEN)	Good luck, new opportunities
WOLF	Bad company in disguise
WOMAN (ALLURING AND USUALLY BLONDE)	Avoidance or distraction

Chapter 15

Ancestor worship

This chapter honours our ancestors – those who have gone before us, extending back to the beginning of time. We honour their memories and invite them to guide us in our lives. Honouring our ancestors helps us feel grounded in our own histories by making us feel connected to them and the web of life too.

In my family, we remember our more immediate relatives who have died. By remembering their stories, courage, deeds and those things that made them memorable, they are a constant presence living in our memories. By connecting with their stories, retelling them at family gatherings, on their anniversary or at other occasions, we create a bridge where we can receive assistance and guidance from them in our time of need.

Our house had walls lined with photos of generations of family members. All special occasions were recorded – weddings, baptisms, confirmations, holy communions, graduations – they were our family's visual stories we could reference at any time.

Ancestral altars

My mother kept an altar to all those who had passed with photos, candles, saint statues, rosary beads, a vase of fresh flowers and crucifix. She would have said Mass regularly for her parents and close relatives. I've continued the tradition of honouring my dead relatives and adding my own rituals, such as including items on my altar that represent their stories. For my dad, it's a small vial of olive oil, because he loved pruning our olive trees; for my nonna, it's a drop spindle she once used for weaving; and for my nonno, it's a river stone, because he used to be a stonemason. Their spirit of who they were can live on by making our memories of them tangible in some way.

You can create your altar in a way that's meaningful to you, so you can keep the memory of your loved ones alive. It doesn't have to be a special space in your home – it could be using your nonna's old pasta machine or recipes, maybe those she wrote down. It could be a photo on your phone that you bring up around their death anniversary or birthday. Maybe you play their favourite song on that day too. All these rituals are part of venerating the ancestors so we remember them and pass down their memory to the next generation.

How to create an ancestral altar

Creating an ancestral altar is a meaningful way to honour and connect with your ancestors in the Italian folk magic tradition. The altar serves as a sacred space to pay respect to your ancestors, seek guidance from them and strengthen your ancestral ties.

1. CHOOSE A LOCATION

Select a suitable location for your ancestral altar. It could be in the corner of a room, or on a table or shelf. Choose a place that feels peaceful and undisturbed, because it will become a sacred space for connecting with your ancestors.

2. GATHER ITEMS

Gather significant items that represent your ancestors, including photographs of deceased family members, small heirlooms, sentimental objects or other mementos.

3. ADD SYMBOLS OF CONNECTION

Consider adding symbols that represent your ancestral lineage or cultural heritage, such as an Italian flag, images of Italian saints or spiritual figures, or traditional arts and crafts.

4. INCLUDE CANDLES

Place candles on your altar to represent the element of fire, symbolising spiritual connection. White candles are commonly used, because they represent purity and can serve as a connection between the physical and spiritual realms.

5. OFFERINGS AND EX-VOTOS

Offerings are a way to show gratitude and respect to your ancestors. Place small dishes of food or drinks that your ancestors enjoyed during their lifetime as offerings: their favourite fruit, bread, wine, or any other symbolic food or drink.

6. FAMILY TREE OR GENEALOGY

If you have information about your family tree or genealogy, you can include a representation of it on your altar. This can help you visualise your ancestral lineage and honour your heritage.

7. CREATE A SACRED SPACE

Cleanse and consecrate the space where you'll place the altar. This could be a simple smoke cleansing ritual, using herbs like sage or rosemary, or by sprinkling blessed water around the area.

8. PERSONALISE THE ALTAR

Arrange items on the altar in a way that feels authentic to you. Take your time to set up the space with intention and love.

9. REGULARLY MAINTAIN THE ALTAR

Keep the altar clean and fresh. Change your offerings regularly and keep the space well tended. Regularly spend time at the altar, meditating, praying, or simply connecting with your ancestors and their wisdom. Remember, an ancestral altar is a deeply personal and spiritual space. The most important aspect is your sincere intention and connection with your ancestors. As you work with your ancestral altar, you may feel a deeper sense of connection with and guidance from your ancestors, enriching your spiritual practice.

Communicating with your ancestors

In your meditations or quiet moments, ask your ancestors for their guidance and wisdom. Listen for any insights or messages they may offer, and be open to receiving guidance through dreams, signs or intuition. Take some time to rest and slow down so you can hear them. Here are some ways you may experience your ancestors' messages.

Repetitive thoughts

If you keep thinking about them regularly, there is a good chance they want your attention. Maybe you're going through a hard time and they want you to talk to them so they can give you guidance or offer support.

Daydreams

If your thoughts are interrupted by something your ancestor said, or might have said, it's a sign they're around you and are interested in what you're doing. If this is followed by synchronicities, such as meeting up with an old neighbour who used to live next door to them, or seeing someone on social media visit their home town in Italy, these indicate your loved one is trying to connect with you and give you a message about returning to your ancestral roots.

Dreams

One major way ancestors try to contact us is through dreams. We need to pay attention to the contents of our dreams. These dreams are known as visitation dreams. Our loved ones come to us in dreams to let us know that they are fine and they love us, to give us news or warn us about something.

How to connect with your ancestors

Language

Speak Italian and take opportunities to teach the young ones their ancestral language or even simple expressions. Many families continue to speak Italian at home and use dialect with older family members, keeping the ancestral links activated.

Celebrations and festivals

Get involved or attend festivals and events that celebrate all things Italian to honour your heritage and connect with your ancestral roots. During annual Italian street and community festivals, we share our cultural practices with others. I enjoy attending Italian film festivals – not only to connect with my heritage and language as it's spoken by contemporary native speakers, but to experience people's Italian-ness – their emotions, appearance and lifestyles, which I'm so far away from.

Family traditions and stories

Ancestral links are best preserved through family traditions, stories and oral histories. Find out more about your family history and your ancestral connection by talking to older family members and recording the lives of your parents or grandparents. If you want to delve deeper, you may wish to do some ancestry work. When I went to the records in my nonno's home town in Italy, I discovered he had served in several wars and had medal of honours. If you have visited your nonni's *paese*, you'll know the one place you can be guaranteed to be shown is the cemetery where all the family members are resting. This is a great place to learn and show respect to ancestors you never knew but whose bloodline you carry.

Visit ancestral lands

To physically connect with your ancestors, visit the lands where they lived. Spend time in nature, walk the paths they might have walked and immerse yourself in the local landscape. This can deepen your connection to your ancestral landscape. If you don't know your ancestors, you can assume the land is an ancestor. You can come from a family or from a region. You belong to those who have gone before you who lived in that part of Italy.

Volcanoes, mountains, seas and valleys – the land of your ancestry lives within your DNA from the ancestors who lived before you. Walk in their footsteps and experience the warm breeze from the dry but rich volcanic landscape, smell the salt air of the vast seas, and experience the fertile valleys from the dizzying mountain ranges that run the spine of Italy. I visit Italy whenever I can. While I always go to see my family in my home town, I make a point to visit each region with its unique tapestry of experiences. I treasure, absorb and bring these back with me to Australia and share them with my family, keeping our ancestral link alive: swimming in the Mediterranean, taking volcanic mud baths on the Aeolian islands, walking through wildflowers in the valleys and climbing the steep terraces of Cinque Terre or the Amalfi coast lined with lemon trees.

Plant a heritage garden

Create a garden with plants significant to your ancestral culture. Choose herbs, flowers and trees traditionally used or celebrated in your family's *paese*. Caring for and nurturing these plants can be a profound way to

connect with your roots. Having an ancestral connection with plants can help honour your heritage, culture and the wisdom of your ancestors.

Land has always been vitally important to the immigrant. As soon as they could re-create their version of the land they left behind, they would do so. It was about creating a space where they could feel at 'home', and be at 'one' with. Whenever I move house, I always plant my heritage plants and trees, which include some olive, citrus, fig, apple, pear, chestnut, oak and birch trees; Italian herbs, tomatoes and vegetables; berries; and geraniums, roses and lilies. These were the plants and trees I grew up with.

Discover herbal traditions

Learn about your ancestors' traditional herbal practices and folk medicine. Investigate the plants they used for healing, spiritual purposes or magical rituals. This research will help you understand the significance of specific plants in your ancestral heritage.

Our ancestors had protection allies – the most powerful ones could be found in every household: salt, olive oil, sage, basil, rosemary, rue and chamomile. Salt is part of our ancestor story. It has powers to clean, heal and protect, and it can be used in so many ways: sprinkle it on your doorstep to keep out negative energy, add warm water and use it as a mouthwash for ulcers, bathe in it, and carry some in your pocket. Olive oil is liquid gold; it both shields and blesses you. Smoke cleansing uses burning plants whose smoke rises to the heavens in prayer and clears negative energies in your home and sacred space. Teas support, fortify and allow your body to heal.

Trust your intuition and let yourself be open to the subtle ways in which plants and your ancestors may communicate with you. Embrace this journey as a way to honour your heritage, connect with nature, and gain a deeper understanding of your place in the world.

Celebrating feast days and cooking family recipes

Religious beliefs and practices are significant in maintaining connections to Italian ancestry. For every religious festival, a special dish is made in celebration. Preparing and enjoying these dishes creates a sensory connection to our heritage and ancestors. Religion has not only influenced the types of dishes prepared in different regions but also how food is consumed and enjoyed – around the table with family.

Easter is the most important event in the Catholic calendar; it's when our family made most of our special foods, especially the sweets. We did no baking on Good Friday – this was a day for going to church. Any form of work was considered *un peccato* (a sin). Instead, we would eat fish of some sort – most likely *baccalà* (salted codfish) – which was cooked in sauce and used on pasta or polenta. We couldn't wait to break Lent. For us, this happened on Easter Saturday when it was time to bake the *dolci* (sweets). As kids, we'd sneak some warm *crostoli*, biscotti or *pizzelle* (waffles) when our mum wasn't looking. The *dolci* served reminded us of our religious connection. Family recipes were passed down from mother to daughter, including symbolic foods associated with Easter, such as breads shaped into crosses and doves.

Easter in Italy is very different than in a secular country like Australia. In Australia, Easter falls in autumn and is a time for holidays before winter comes. When I travelled to Italy during Easter time, the streets were filled with people celebrating and religious processions. Shops were closed and lights were lit in every home in the evening. It was impossible not to feel the spiritual nature of the place; the sense of cultural traditions blending with religious beliefs; and the ancestral connection to the sights, smells and tastes of these feasts.

Christmas without sharing panettone is not a real Italian Christmas. It's a strange custom we have – giving panettone to family and friends and receiving them in return – you could simply buy your own. But where's the element of surprise in that?

Every region has its special festive foods. One of my favourite sweets is the *mostacciolo* – a spicy, fragrant, chocolate-coated, rhombus-shaped sweet. Celebrating special feasts with ancestral recipes is a way to honour your ancestral cuisine and all those who've enjoyed it.

In typical nonna fashion, family recipes don't have exact measurements for the ingredients, but you would learn by observing and practising each time you re-created the dish. This repetition and personal touches to a traditional recipe create a strong generational connection, such as where we come from, who we are and the feel-good vibes associated with making a favourite food from childhood.

The following *crostoli* recipe is suitable for all occasions, festive and non-festive, and we could never eat enough of them as kids. My *cugina* (cousin) Maria teaches regional Italian cooking at a community centre and *crostoli* are always a hit with her students.

How to make crostoli from cugina Maria

You'll find mounds of these delicious, crispy fried pastries piled high on platters at family occasions, dusted with icing sugar, ready to be devoured by all – accompanied by an espresso or glass of prosecco. Everyone makes *crostoli* differently – every region, town, family and even within a family has its own variation.

YOU WILL NEED

For the dough

2 eggs

2 tablespoons vegetable oil

2 tablespoons marsala or brandy

2 tablespoons sugar

1 cup plain (all-purpose) flour

1 cup self-raising flour (optional). If you want a very crunchy taste, just use plain flour.

Extra vegetable oil, for frying

Icing sugar, for dusting

Equipment

Pasta machine (optional)

Rolling pin

Sperone (spur-shaped fluted pastry wheel/cutter)

Electric frying pan or deep-sided frying pan

Paper towel

Sieve

METHOD

1. Mix the eggs, oil, marsala and sugar together, then add 1 cup flour and slowly combine. Add the remaining flour until you have a stiff but malleable dough. It should be soft, but not sticky.

2. Flatten the dough so it will go into the pasta machine, if using. Start the machine at its widest section, then as you work the dough, stop when you reach a thin consistency, as you would when making lasagne.

3. If you are not using a pasta machine, the old-fashioned traditional way is to use a rolling pin. Roll the dough into a wide circle about the same thickness as for pasta. The thinner the pastry, the crunchier the texture.

4. Cut the rolled-out dough with the *sperone*. The shape of *crostoli* resembles a bow. In our dialect, we call them *nocc'tell'* (little bows). You shape them by cutting a slit into the strips of dough and folding one end through the slit. If you want it to look more like a bow tie, pinch the strips of the dough in the centre. You'll find plenty of examples online.

5. If using an electric frying pan, add 1 cm vegetable oil. Dial it to the highest temperature then test the oil is hot enough by dropping in a small piece of the dough. If it quickly bubbles up, the oil is ready. The oil should be hot, about 180°C (350°F). If using a frying pan, make sure it's deep enough so the oil won't splatter.

6. Add the bow-shaped dough and leave it until it's a nice pale-golden colour. Turn it over.

7. When the *crostoli* is ready, remove with tongs and place on paper towel to absorb any excess oil.

8. Using the sieve, dust with icing sugar. Allow to cool and serve. *Buon appetito!*

Seasonal cooking and eating

As well as traditional feasts and foods, we can follow our ancestors' seasonal approach to eating, cooking and preserving. Making passata in summer, home-made wine in autumn, and dried sausage or prosciutto in winter are just some of the ways we gather as a family to re-create rural traditions of the past. Eating seasonally with home-grown vegetables, home baked bread, and preserves – roasted peppers, olives and artichokes, which are usually kept in recycled glass containers in the 'second' kitchen in the garage.

The vegetable garden was composted with chickens running around the backyard, which offered their eggs for yummy omelettes in our school sandwiches. Other than the oil from the omelette that dripped in our school bags, the taste was amazing. The secret to healthy vegetables and fruits wasn't just the chickens, but how our ancestors planted in the homeland – by the moon.

While the wise women would create magic with herbs and cooking in the kitchen, the men made their magic by planting crops and providing nourishment for the family. Their nature-based methods created magical results. Our ancestors who practised folk magic aligned their planting and gardening activities with the moon's phases to harness its energy for successful growth.

PLANTING BY THE MOON

NEW MOON	The period when the moon is not visible from earth. This phase is ideal for planting root crops and perennials, which benefit from strong root development. Plants to sow during the new moon include garlic, onions, potatoes and rhubarb.
WAXING MOON	The period between the new moon and full moon, when it appears to be increasing in size. Plant leafy greens, fast-growing herbs and annual crops during the waxing moon phase. Plants to sow during this time include lettuce, spinach, parsley and basil.
FULL MOON	This is when the moon is fully illuminated. It's associated with abundance, fertility and heightened energy. The full moon phase is favourable for planting fruit-bearing plants and crops that produce above-ground fruits. Examples of plants to sow during the full moon include tomatoes, peppers, beans and berries.
WANING MOON	The period between the full moon and new moon, when the moon appears to be decreasing in size. It's best for activities that involve pruning, harvesting and focusing on root development. It's a suitable time to plant bulbs and transplant seedlings. Examples of plants to sow during the waning moon include carrots, beetroot and radishes.

Remember, lunar gardening is a traditional belief and practice; its effectiveness relies on the practitioner's connection to nature, intention and belief in the moon's influence on plant growth. Whether or not you follow lunar gardening, nurturing plants with care, attention and love will always benefit your gardening endeavours.

Companion planting

This is the careful placement of plants that have beneficial effects on one another. The benefits of companion planting are impressive, and yet

I remember scoffing at my dad when he explained why it was such a good practice. All I could see were plants and herbs all leaning on each other at different times – a mish mash of colours and textures – and I kept away because the bees loved to be there.

What I didn't know then, but know now, is that companion planting repels pests, encourages pollination (hence the bees), increases production, reduces the need for chemical garden pest sprays and helps to keep the soil healthy. And it's the natural way of gardening.

Here is some of my dad's advice on companion planting:

▶ Grow basil near tomatoes, peppers and eggplants – it makes them grow, improves the taste of the tomatoes and the basil scent keeps away mosquitoes and bugs.
▶ Plant parsley near tomatoes and asparagus.
▶ Lavender goes everywhere in the garden – this fragrant plant repels flies and beetles, but attracts bees and pollinating insects. Plant it near cauliflower, cabbage, kale and broccoli.
▶ Rosemary is good with broccoli, cauliflower and cabbage because its strong scent confuses the cabbage butterfly and repels beetles. Keep rue, strawberries, tomatoes and garlic away from the cabbage family.
▶ Dill attracts predatory wasps, so plant them next to kale and broccoli, but don't grow it near fennel or they will cross pollinate, ruining their taste. Don't grow carrots near dill.

My father owned an apple orchard in Molise, so he knew a thing or two about growing things. Like so many men of his generation, however, he would take to pruning trees with great vigour – not realising ornamental trees didn't need such a heavy pruning. When I saw him cut back the magnolia tree I watched grow over the years, his reply was inevitably: 'Don't worry, it will grow back in a few years.' In the meantime, our eyes had to readjust to the spindly magnolia tree.

Italians integrated into the diaspora, using all the traditional agricultural skills they'd grown up with. Entering their space was like stepping back into the past – copious amounts of greens, bean tendrils climbing over preloved trellis, grapevine winding around the back patio, tomato plants planted in even rows and tied with bits of twine, and home-made watering systems with the ubiquitous scarecrow near the olive or plum tree.

Live a greener life – recycle and upcycle

Our ancestors worked closely with the natural world and protected their environment. They gently cared for the world around them, which sustained and kept them healthy. Living a greener life is one way to honour our family's past ways of living – by slowing down and being mindful of the things we do and the impact they have.

Could you imagine our nonni eating in a hurry, or eating while walking and crossing the road, or while sitting in the car? Food was to be savoured and enjoyed, and time was allocated for the day's main meals where everyone had to sit around the table.

We can honour their gentleness with the environment by following their example:

- ▶ Walk as much as you can whenever you can.
- ▶ Take public transport if possible.
- ▶ Grow your own food.
- ▶ Eat good food and eat it mindfully, sitting down (but not at your desk or in front of a screen).
- ▶ East less meat – Italian cuisine does not include the daily consumption of meat. The main staples are legumes, vegetables, corn and grains, and we know we should eat more of these.
- ▶ Pass on what you no longer need – donate, rather than discard.
- ▶ Compost your food scraps and coffee grounds – the one thing all Italians have at home.

Avoid using plastic bags and plastic/paper products in general. Do you remember the old string bags that expanded? Recyclable and convenient for grocery shopping. Other clever ways they avoided paper and plastic like clingwrap was to cover dishes with another dish or saucepan lid. Everything was stored in reusable ceramic or glass. It's time to go back to this green habit.

Most importantly – recycle. I remember opening my nonna's refrigerator and finding what I thought were tubs of yoghurt, ice cream, butter or jam, only to open the lids and be amazed by the contents: frozen green beans, roasted red pepper strips in oil, leftover bolognaise sauce, fried zucchini flowers, fresh fava beans … the surprises were endless. One thing we were sure about, it was *never* the item shown on the container. At the heart of it all was the beginning of recycling as we know it today.

Women's circles

When women gathered, they did so in the community or with family and it involved some type of productive activity, such as kneading dough, weaving, knitting, saying the rosary, shelling peas, plaiting garlic garlands, cooking or picking fruit. My zia lived next door. She would come over to our house weekly and sit in the warm kitchen where we had a wood-fired stove, knitting with my mother and nonna. We had hand-knitted jumpers and scarves throughout childhood. Eventually, my mum moved on to crochet … then the doilies never stopped coming.

As life evolved, this activity became modernised. Women would come together to dye their hair, do their nails, play bingo – and all the time, they would be teaching the younger women all about life and what they needed to learn. The older women passed on their wisdom through their lived experience, leaving an imprint on each generation.

Although they came together for practical reasons, they were creating a link between each generation. We can honour our ancestors by continuing to gather in circles, and share our experiences and wisdom down the family line.

Doing it our way

Just because our ancestors used to do things a certain way, doesn't necessarily mean we have to do it the same way. They came from mostly rural and agricultural roots. They were torn from the countryside to be parcelled out into urban factory jobs in a foreign land where the old ways weren't known nor accepted. To survive, they had to assimilate. And so, they did their best to keep their cultural memories alive through their family and community rituals.

Despite the physical distance from Italy, the Italian diaspora community has shown a remarkable commitment to preserving and cherishing their ancestral links. Their efforts to maintain and pass down Italian traditions, language and culture have contributed to the enduring global legacy of Italian heritage, and the sense of unity among people of Italian descent, no matter where in the world they live.

We can create our own traditions based on the original ones and honour our ancestors by never forgetting where we come from. Most importantly, we have to adapt because life changes rapidly in our time.

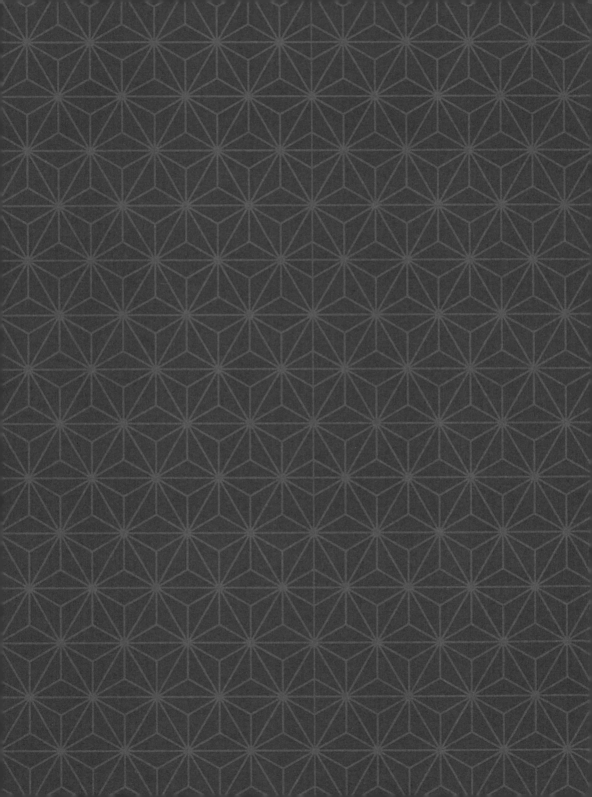

Conclusion

When you travel to regional Italy, the parades with the saints and Madonnas – with their magnificent show of music, dance, procession of honour, elaborate adornments and *ex-votos* on the statue – are heady reminders of ancestral spirituality. You can be living in a modern city yet can go back in time through the ancient and medieval hilltop towns that still embrace and celebrate the old practices as *feste* (feast days). They are a form of entertainment with a good dose of respect for tradition.

In the Italian diaspora, where there is no such display of worship, the ancestral memories fade with assimilation. This makes us feel less connected to the spiritual life of our parents, grandparents and all those who lived in the motherland for millennia. We need to find ways to recapture the essence of these traditions and distil it in a way that is modern but respectful.

It comes down to a change in our identity – we're no longer struggling for physical survival and at the mercy of the *malocchio* – but integrating past beliefs into our modern culture to revive the old ways of living sustainably. As culture changes, so do traditions. We are becoming citizens of the world rather than a nationhood.

For those of you with a different cultural heritage, which you may feel disconnected from, I hope these chapters inspire you to reacquaint yourselves with your ancestry. What is unique about folk magic is that it's the foundation of living sensibly with nature and magic; anyone can easily practise this way of life. It's an invitation and opportunity to approach living from another culture's perspective. Terms such as Anglophile, Francophile or Italophile describe an admirer of a country and its language, culture and people. I've travelled to places and met people with whom I felt totally at home who were not of my heritage.

As a society, we should question whether we can be considered thriving. We are devolving at a fast rate, and I believe returning to the old ways could be regarded as a form of survival – a way of reminding us how to live as one with nature before we lose the ability entirely.

The ancient Italian traditions have thousands of years of mingling with other nationalities and cultures – Italy consisted of city states until its unification in 1861. There is a bit of everyone in Italian folk magic. Its revival for this new generation is vital to continue the magic of the wise women of Italy.

The healers, midwives, wise women and *streghe* all played important roles in connecting us to our natural and intuitive aspects. Foraging is not new. Recycling is not new. Protection and blessing practices are not new. Herbal and natural medicines are not new. Magic-making and dreams are not new.

The old Italian folk magic hasn't died with cultural assimilation or modern life. It's there every time you plant basil by your front door, cook with love, smoke cleanse your home with bay laurel, hang garlands of garlic for protection, create an altar and tend to your garden. I hope this book becomes a touchstone – a way to reconnect to tradition – and that you find yourself enriched by reading it.

Every household is a magical one. Using this book as a guide, I sincerely hope it brings you knowledge and confidence as you begin or continue your journey into Italian folk magic practices.

Until next time, *arrivederci e buona fortuna,*

Rosa
(my original birth name)

Glossary

Abitino/i: charm bag(s); herb pouch

Amaro: bitter/bitters (alcohol)

Antenato/i: ancestor (s)

Befana: old woman who brings presents to children on 6 January (Epiphany)

Benandanti: 'good walkers' or do-gooders, who fight witches in astral battles

Benedicaria: 'way of the blessing', which uses Catholic prayers and practices as a healing method

Benevento: city in the region of Campania where witches were said to gather for their sabbath

Breve/i: another word for *abitino*

Briscola: a popular Italian card game

Carte da gioco: playing cards

Cimaruta: a protective charm in the shape of a rue branch

Coccinella: a ladybird protective charm

Commare/i: godmother(s); also women with magical knowledge

Compare/i: godfather (s), friend(s), comrade(s)

Corallo: coral

Cornicello: a protective charm against the *malocchio* in the shape of a small horn

Corno: a bigger version of the *cornicello*

Cucina: kitchen

Ex-voto: an item used as a special offering to a saint

Fascino: a *malocchio* spell

Fattucchiera/e: a woman who casts a spell or removes a spell or curse

Fattura: spell, curse or hex; something that requires undoing

Festa/e: feast day, holiday, celebration, party

Gobbo: a protective charm against the evil eye in the shape of a hunchbacked man

Guaritore/guaritrice: male healer/female healer

Janara/e: witch (Campania)

Legatura/e: binding spell(s)

Levatrice/i: midwife

Magara/e: witch (southern Italy)

Majara/e: witch (Sicily)

Majarza/e: witch (Sardinia)

Maledizione/i: curse(s)

Maleficio: a spell to harm

Malocchio: the evil eye, a curse believed to be cast either intentionally or unintentionally by someone who is jealous of you

Mano cornuta: protective charm of a horned hand

Mano fica: protective charm of a fisted hand

Nonna: grandmother

Nonno/nonni: grandfather/grandparents

Paesano/i: countryman/countrywoman (from the same town)

Paese: a town, mostly describes a home town

Puppia: poppet

Scongiuro/i: spell(s), incantation, exorcism

Scopa: broom, Italian card game

Segnature: hand signs or gestures, referring to symbols drawn on someone's body for healing with special words

Smorfia: Neapolitan dream interpretation with symbols associated with lottery numbers

Strega: witch

Stregone: male witch, sorcerer

Stregoneria: witchcraft, witchery, folk magic

Suffumigi: fumigation (literally), smoking of leaves/herbs/resin for smoke cleansing a room

Tarantella: a lively Italian folk dance

Tarocchi: tarot

Vermi: worms – physical and metaphysical

Votives: offerings given or done to honour or thank a deity or ancestor; devotional gifts

Zia/zio: aunt/uncle

Acknowledgements

I wish to thank:

My aunt, Zia Maria, who was so generous with her time in passing on valuable ancestral traditions and stories from Molise.

All my wonderful kinswomen, who contributed recipes and folk magic information – Maria, Joanna, Mary Joan, Gina, Domenica, Linda, Giovanna, Flora, Lucy, Silvana, Giuliana and Zia Rosa.

My editing helpers – Rebecca, Helen, Angeleah and Kerrie – thank you for your assistance. A special thank you to Jessica Cox, who did a brilliant job in editing this book.

My husband, Peter, for your unwavering support, patience and encouragement at all stages of this long writing process.

References

Most of the practical information collected in this book comes from people of Italian ancestry who I interviewed.

Other sources

Abruzzissimo Magazine, no. 13, June 2021.

Belloni, Alessandra, *Healing Journeys with the Black Madonna*, Bear & Company, Rochester, 2019.

Brannen, Cyndi, *Entering Hekate's Garden*, Weiser Books, Newbury Port MA, 2020.

Bruce, Marie, *Green Witchcraft*, Arcturus, London, 2022.

Crisis, Karyn, *Italian Magic, Secret Lives of Women*, Golden Bough Books, 2020.

De Martino, Ernesto, *Magic, a Theory from the South*, Hau Books, Chicago 2015.

Fahrun, Mary-Grace, *Italian Folk Magic: Rue's Kitchen Witchery*, Weiser Books, Newbury Port MA, 2018.

Inserra, Rose, *Dreams: What Your Subconscious Wants to Tell You*, Rockpool Publishing, Sydney, 2020.

Jalal, B, Romanelli, A, and Hinton, DE, 'Sleep Paralysis in Italy: Frequency, Hallucinatory Experiences, and Other Features', *Transcultural Psychiatry*, vol. 58, no. 3, pp. 47–66, 1985. https://journals.sagepub.com/doi/full/10.1177/1363461520909609

Krippner, S, Budden, A, Gallante, R, and Bova M, 'The Indigenous Healing Tradition in Calabria, Italy', *International Journal of Transpersonal Studies*, vol. 30, no. 1, pp. 48–62, 2011.

Magliocco, Sabina, 'Spells, Saints and Streghe: Witchcraft, Folk Magic, and Healing in Italy', *International Journal of Pagan Studies*, vol. 13, no. 13, pp. 4–22, 2000.

Michael, Coby, *The Poison Path Herbal*, Park Street Press, Rochester, 2021.

Murphy-Hiscock, Arin, *The Green Witch*, Simon & Schuster, Stroughton, 2017.

Pagliarulo, Antonio, *The Evil Eye*, Weiser Books, Newbury Port MA, 2023.

Parente, Anthony, *Italians R Us* [website], https://www.italiansrus.com

Puca, Angela, 'The Tradition of Segnature. Underground Indigenous Practices in Italy', *Journal of the Irish Society for the Academic Study of Religions*, vol. 7, pp. 104–124, 2019.

Vaudoise, Mallorie, *Italian Folk Magic* [website], https://www.italianfolkmagic.com

About Rose Inserra

Rose Inserra was born Rosa Diamente in Spinete, Italy. She arrived in Australia with her family when she was nine years old. Italian folk magic has always been a big part of her life and identity. Her love of nature, foods, herbs and traditions stems from growing up in rural Italy then in regional Victoria. Until recently, Rose produced cold-pressed extra-virgin olive oil on her farm. She is currently studying herbalism, combining ancestral traditions with health-centred practices.

As a former teacher, she has a passion for history and passing on knowledge of traditions; esoteric, herbal and folk lore; and all manner of subjects essential to our human evolution on this planet.

Rose Inserra has been published locally and internationally by leading trade and educational publishers, and is a well-known author in the Mind Body Spirit genre. She presents at seminars and workshops, and delivers courses both in Australia and overseas, with frequent appearances on radio, television, podcasts and in magazine articles.

Her books with Rockpool Publishing include *Dream Reading Cards*, *Dreams: What Your Subconscious Wants To Tell You*, *Sweet Dreams* mini cards, *The Gift of Dreams*, *Mists of Avalon Oracle* cards and *Avalon Magic* mini cards. For more information, go to: roseinserra.com and rockpoolpublishing.com

Index

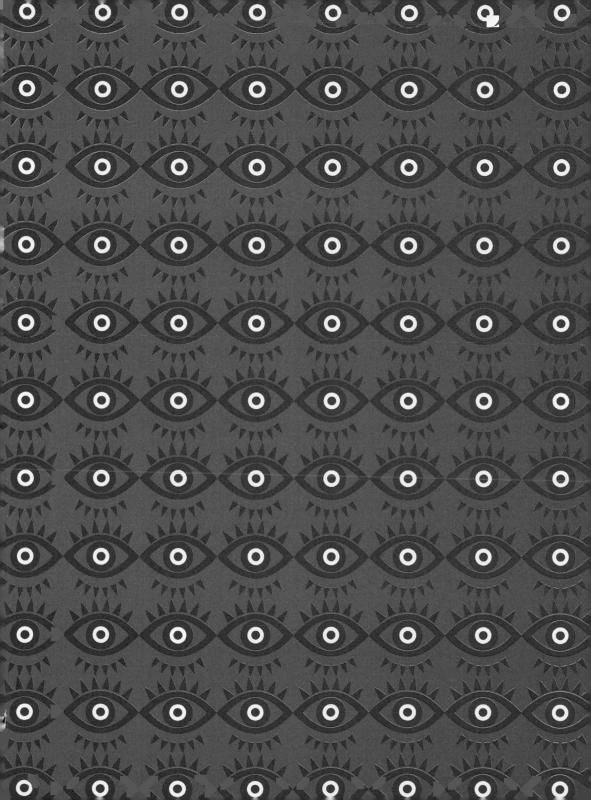